D1084078

DISCARD

Date Due

ROMANCE MONOGRAPHS, INC.

Number 20

THEMATIC ANALYSIS OF FRANÇOIS MAURIAC'S *GÉNITRIX*, *LE DÉSERT DE L'AMOUR*, AND *LE NŒUD DE VIPÈRES*

ROMANCE MONOGRAPHS, INC.

Number 20

THEMATIC ANALYSIS OF FRANÇOIS MAURIAC'S *GÉNITRIX*, *LE DÉSERT DE L'AMOUR*, AND *LE NŒUD DE VIPÈRES*

BY

RUTH BENSON PAINE

UNIVERSITY, MISSISSIPPI

ROMANCE MONOGRAPHS, INC.

1 9 7 6

Library of Congress Cataloging in Publication Data

Paine, Ruth Benson, 1927-
    Thematic analysis of François Mauriac's Génitrix, Le désert de l'amour,
and Le nœud de vipères.

    (Romance monographs; no. 20)

    1. Mauriac, François, 1885-1970 — Criticism and interpretation. I.
Title: Thematic analysis of François Mauriac's Génitrix...

PQ2625.A93Z689   843'.9'12   76-8024

To

GEORGE PORTER PAINE

*source of unending
encouragement and counsel.*

CONTENTS

CHAPTER I

THE AUTHOR OR THE WORK?

THE INTEREST AROUSED by the personal lives of many authors is acknowledged to be, often, at least as great as that which the reader finds in the man's works. The particular experiences of a writer, his religious formation, and his shaping of philosophy or point of view, frequently hold a fascination which is justified as an enrichment of insight into the works he has written. The case of François Mauriac is no exception to the temptation to add the dimensions of an author's own characteristics, tendencies and background to a work which is being read. Indicating his own awareness of this preoccupation on the part of the reading public, Mauriac goes even further and suggests that it is the author himself who is always the more interesting subject matter. He cites the broad public attraction over the years to Rousseau's *Confessions* (especially Book I), rather than to *Emile*. With few exceptions, he points out, it is to the correspondence of Voltaire, among the great number of his works, that readers turn to seek what remains of the once-living literary giant. Mauriac's *Journal* accepts that posterity often rejects the greater part of a man's works, preferring to concentrate on those elements of a literary production which illuminate no other subject than the author himself:

> Le roman qu'ils [les écrivains] ont vécu nous retient davantage que tous ceux qu'ils ont pu écrire, et nous écartons la foule importune de leurs héros inventés....[1]

---

[1] François Mauriac, *Journal*, III (Paris: Grasset, 1940), 203.

Mauriac has reiterated his belief that there is a "disproportion" between the attention focused on the author and on the literature he creates. "C'est précisément l'écrivain lui-même que la plupart des lecteurs d'aujourd'hui cherchent dans son œuvre." [2] The fact that in Racine's case the imbalance persists, but always in favor of his works, is for Mauriac a final confirmation of the merit deserved by the playwright.

Disappointment lies ahead for the reader who tries to lose himself in a biographical study of Mauriac. In view of his recent death, on September 1, 1970, the definitive account of his life has yet to be published. However, interest in him and his works has been sufficiently great to provide over 6,000 references in a single bibliographical source, which includes works and articles about or by Mauriac. [3] Mauriac had advised his readers that they avoid taking the letter of any biographical matter too seriously, and learn to know the author by reading, in effect, between the lines, where may be found the true sense of the man, "malgré lui." [4] He is quick to assert, however, that the world will come to know an author best through his novels.

The novelist whose output is substantial makes his reader's task of acquaintance easier as the importance of memories and influences becomes obvious in their recurrence throughout his works. Mauriac employed such an explanation of his dissatisfaction with efforts to write down his *souvenirs*.

> La vraie raison de ma paresse n'est-elle pas que nos romans expriment l'essentiel de nous-mêmes? Seule, la fiction ne ment pas; elle entr'ouvre sur la vie d'un homme une porte dérobée par où se glisse, en dehors de tout contrôle, son âme inconnue. [5]

And in such a way Mauriac's viewpoints will truly become vivid in the reader's mind. A description in *Génitrix* of heavily-laden peasant women walking like beasts of burden behind empty-

---

[2] François Mauriac, *Dieu et Mammon*, in *Œuvres complètes*, VII (Paris: Grasset, 1952), 279.

[3] Keith Goesch, François Mauriac, *Essai de bibliographie chronologique, 1908-1960* (Paris: Nizet, 1965).

[4] Mauriac, *Commencements d'une vie*, in *Œuvres complètes*, IV, 128.

[5] *Ibid.*, p. 129.

handed, overbearing husbands does not need the documentary echo, nearly verbatim, which appears ten years later in the author's personal observations on "l'éducation des filles," in *Le Romancier et ses personnages*. Yet its repetition suggests ideas of male-female relationships, social hierarchy, pride and submission, which were impressed early on Mauriac, and which are representative of his frequent references to such thematic possibilities. Innumerable similar examples are to be found in the author's continual infusion of powerful impressions into his works of fiction, which also appear independently, and often identically, as scattered reminiscences in his non-fiction writing. The closeness of his fiction to his own life serves to tell us *en profondeur* not only what he believed and learned, but also what shaped so immutably the imagery which burned in his inspiration through a half-century.

These *rapports* between the life and the work of Mauriac (or of any other writer) serve only as distractions from a detached evaluation and analysis of a work itself. The more of an author's writings which are read, and the more frequently the same images evoke particular events or observations, the greater this diversion of reader interest can become. Mauriac, too, had known a similar problem in divorcing study of any single work of art from others by the same man, or from the life of the artist himself. It was following a visit to a showing of paintings by Cézanne that a ground-rule for criticism and creation was noted by Mauriac in his *Journal,* a viewpoint which conforms well to twentieth-century separation of author and his works for purposes of criticism.

He wrote of the importance of detachment on the part of the artist. "...La vocation de l'artiste tient dans une recherche désintéressée."[6] This must be, he insists, matched by a similar willingness on the part of the reader, or viewer, to remove from his consideration, information which is extraneous to the work itself. The responsibility of the reader lies in his being objective. Mauriac, as a mature writer, will declare in 1940: "Mais que nous importe le mobile qui pousse un homme à faire son œuvre? L'œuvre seule, et non le mobile, relève de notre jugement."[7]

---

[6] Mauriac, *Journal*, III, 46.
[7] *Ibid.*, p. 48.

Reading Mauriac's writings on his own literary offerings, and surely reading the works themselves, reveals that for him, more often than not, the man and his work are inseparable. Even accepting his description of the novel as "une transposition du réel, et non une réproduction du réel,"[8] it is on the reality of his own past that he must draw for his inspiration. The years he spent as "un enfant espion, un traître, inconscient de sa traîtrise,"[9] absorbing details of persons, places and things, produced a reservoir of *minutiæ* regarding specific physical characteristics and surroundings, which would reappear in the familiar settings of his novels over a lifetime.

A younger, more vulnerable Mauriac had spoken intensely, in 1929, of the intimate participation of the author in his works. He refuted then Jacques Maritain's naturalistic view of the novelist as a kind of scientist who regards his work as coolly as a scientist might lean detachedly over the subject of his experiments:

> ... le romancier, le vrai n'est pas un expérimenteur. ...
> Il n'observe pas la vie, il crée de la vie ... il cède à la
> tentation de se confondre et en quelque sorte de s'anéan-
> tir dans sa créature, pousser la connivence jusqu'à de-
> venir elle-même.[10]

An inherent contradiction persists in Mauriac's views. The work of an artist is so much a part of its creator that the most secret and intimate details of his being are exposed in the "union mystérieuse" of the artist and reality. It is in a figurative self-immolation that the author lives again through the characters he has created. Yet, Mauriac insists, "Ce qui importe, ce n'est pas nous-mêmes; c'est l'œuvre dont nous contenons les éléments. L'œuvre. Notre œuvre."[11]

A more serious accusation of intrusion on Mauriac's part goes beyond the biographical or philosophical identifications which are so often subject to notice. His repeated personal interpolations, which accelerate impatiently the reader's grasp of a situation, or

---

[8] Mauriac, *Le Romancier et ses personnages,* in *Œuvres complètes,* VIII, page 306.

[9] *Ibid.,* p. 289.

[10] Mauriac, *Dieu et Mammon,* p. 314.

[11] *Ibid.,* p. 304.

more importantly, of a character, do much to destroy his intention to remain aloof and let his personages develop freely and naturally. The complexity of Mauriac's own attitude toward the creatures of his invention suggests that criticism of his treatment of them may be justified. In *Le Romancier et ses personnages,* Mauriac writes of how much he values the vitality of those characters which resist his manipulative power: "il y a, pour le romancier, qui crée des êtres de cette sorte, un merveilleux plaisir à lutter contre eux."

In the next sentence, while still applauding their resistance, Mauriac exults in the finality of his power over them.

> Comme ces personnages ont, en général, de la résistance et qu'ils se défendent âprement, le romancier sans risque de les déformer ni de les rendre moins vivants, peut arriver à les transformer, il peut leur insuffler une âme, il peut les sauver.... [12]

The lot of his characters is anticipated, in each of the novels discussed in succeeding chapters, by the author's comments on what their outcome will be. Sartre's essay on the lack of liberty in Mauriac's novels is a keenly perceptive view into this basic problem. [13] Mauriac's difficulty on the technical plane is the same one which he proposes on the theological level. How can the freedom of the individual (or character) to exercise his will in search of maximum fulfillment be reconciled with the irresistible forces which mete out a predetermined fate? It is the discrepancy between the liberty of the human soul and the freedom of the Creator which prompts Mauriac to speak of the writer as "le singe de dieu." [14]

In dissociating oneself as a reader from the motivations which prompt the author to write, the possibility remains of considering his purposes in offering his work to the world. If it is asked, not, "why did he write this book?" but for what purpose the text is intended, we are coming closer to a more restricted view of attention focused on the contents of the work itself.

---

[12] Mauriac, *Le Romancier et ses personnages,* p. 299.

[13] Jean-Paul Sartre, "M. François Mauriac et la liberté," *Nouvelle revue française,* No. 52 (1939), pp. 212-232.

[14] Mauriac, *Le Roman,* in *Œuvres complètes,* VIII, 278.

Mauriac had to reply defensively to his critics, as will be discussed more fully in a later chapter, who saw his novels as damaging influences to Christian morality. His response indicated that he had had a purpose in choosing the grotesque, the deviant or the repulsive to illustrate his ideas.

Nelly Cormeau is the author of a volume which received exceptional approval from the novelist.[15] "Voilà l'étude qui répond le mieux à ce que j'ai souhaité qu'on pensât de moi. Voilà les sentiments que j'ai rêvé d'éveiller dans les êtres."[16] Cormeau is one of those accepting Mauriac's emphasis on the use of the distasteful to illustrate the desirability of human effort to overcome the forces hostile to man's spiritual endeavors. Cormeau's text approves Mauriac's reiterated belief in the proselytizing value of literature. "Une seule chose compte en ce monde: c'est le perfectionnement intérieur. Introduire dans une jeune âme cette idée que cela seul importe...."[17] The same critic applauds, for example, the moral lessons provided by Mauriac's examples. Cormeau sees readers, regardless of their faiths, burned by "une sorte de splendeur terrible...."[18] She accepts Mauriac's underscoring of the effort to overcome sin as the most important single human undertaking.

Cecil Jenkins' book[19] touches upon Mauriac's profound conviction that the prevalent use of "grievous images" of sexuality and love is a means to dramatize the most basic religious conflicts. The intricate and delicate link between love and passion, between passion and religion, and (in a hasty syllogism) between the search for love and the quest for God, is cited as the underlying basis for their use as moral examples. It is interesting to note that, in an interview mentioned by Jenkins, which was granted by Mauriac on May 23, 1923 to Frédéric Lefèvre, the novelist still had such a purpose but proposed some other means of achieving it.

Dans mes prochains romans, le catholicisme touchera de moins en moins mes héros, et ce sera cependant faire

---

[15] Nelly Cormeau, *L'art de François Mauriac* (Paris: Grasset, 1951).
[16] Mauriac, *Préface* to *L'art de François Mauriac*, p. 3.
[17] Mauriac, *Le Romancier et ses personnages*, p. 324.
[18] Cormeau, *op. cit.*, p. 171.
[19] Cecil Jenkins, *Mauriac* (New York: Barnes and Noble, 1965), p. 73.

œuvre catholique que de montrer l'absence du catholicisme et les conséquences lamentables que cela entraîne. [20]

Six years later, in 1929, Mauriac will write in *Dieu et mammon* that he agrees with Gide that "aucune œuvre d'art ne se crée sans la collaboration du démon." [21] He felt that a moral responsibility did lie on the artist, although at the same time he professed to believe that the novelist should avoid trying to prove something by his novels. Further discussion in Chapter V of this presentation will speak of the abrupt change in purpose evinced by Mauriac in this regard.

Yet another view of what Mauriac was aiming toward is touched upon in a critical analysis of Mauriac, "l'homme et l'œuvre." The purpose, in this case, is seen as correlative to the spiritual objective of illuminating an exemplary path to salvation. The secondary objective is cited as the humanist attempt to diffuse the belief that the proper study of mankind is man. The self-knowledge thereby acquired will render more desirable the love of man, as it must ultimately that of God. Romantic, ideological literature has given way, Mauriac wrote in *Le Roman,* to the probing of the individual inner self: "...nous ne concevons plus une littérature romanesque détournée de sa fin propre qui est la connaissance de l'homme." [22]

He seems to recognize, with reserved approval, the giant steps taken by Proust in exploring the secret life of man which does exist, and he accepts as valuable Proust's awareness of "ces mystères de la sensibilité, dont Maritain nous adjure de détourner notre regard." [23] Mauriac reaffirms that it is from the interior world of every individual, which lies concealed beneath the façade imposed by his work, family and social situation, that the complete man will be found: "...c'est souvent au fond de cette boue cachée à tous les yeux, que gît la clef qui nous le [l'homme] livre enfin tout entier." [24]

---

[20] Frédéric Lefèvre, *Une heure avec* ... (Paris: NRF, 1924), 1re série, p. 220.

[21] Mauriac, *Dieu et Mammon,* p. 312.

[22] Mauriac, *Le Roman,* p. 271.

[23] *Ibid.,* p. 273.

[24] *Ibid.*

The somber, negative emphasis found in Mauriac's works is reflective of what was generally recognized in the 1920's to be the purpose of the novel. He cites the objective of such works as "une tentative pour aller toujours plus avant dans la connaissance des passions." [25] Mauriac neatly makes the transition from knowledge of self, to knowledge of sin, and then to pride in the Christian humanistic patrimony. "Qu'est-ce d'abord un Chrétien? C'est un homme qui existe en tant qu'individu, un homme qui prend conscience de lui-même." [26]

The man who, like Mauriac, writes novels with a seemingly "Christian" purpose becomes thereby a "Catholic" author with responsibilities to avoid offering "occasions of sin" to his readers. Mauriac's reply is that one cannot depict life by portraying only saints. The goal should be rather, "tout oser dire, mais tout oser dire chastement...." [27] His reply to criticism which suggests an unwholesome effect on his readers, to their spiritual detriment, is to admit that a work which will, as he hopes, help some toward salvation is likely to lose others. But the road to Christ, he says he is sure, will be found by a journey through a world of sin. Mauriac closes the text of *Le Roman* with what amounts to a statement of spiritual progress, taken from the writings of Jean Balde. " 'J'ai poursuivi la vie dans sa réalité, non dans les rêves de l'imagination, et je suis arrivé ainsi à Celui qui est la source de la Vie.' " [28]

The "recherche désintéressée" which Mauriac advocated in 1940 had been anticipated in *Dieu et mammon* when the neutral spiritual state of an author, as such, was declared: "Un auteur n'est pas en soi moral ou immoral..." [29] His greatest service is to make his prose and its meaning as clear as possible. When Mauriac writes, "Je suis persuadé maintenant que la sainteté est, avant tout, lucidité," he is speaking only partly of a novelist's style. To present a virtuous person as though he had attained saintly perfection is to deny credibility of the creation to the reader. The author rather must seek to create beings with all

---

[25] *Ibid.*, p. 282.
[26] *Ibid.*
[27] *Ibid.*, p. 277.
[28] *Ibid.*, p. 284.
[29] Mauriac, *Dieu et Mammon*, p. 290.

"l'illogisme ... l'indétermination ... la complexité des êtres vivants," while continually clarifying and constructing a comprehensible creature which will be worthy "des écrivains d'ordre et de clarté." [30]

In the same general period as appeared *Le Roman* and *Dieu et mammon,* E. M. Forster's *Aspects of the Novel* was published. Completely devoid of the personal conflicts which are so evident in Mauriac's works, Forster's book nevertheless touches immediately on areas of common agreement with Mauriac. Forster accepts as natural the "mysterious union" of the author and reality which results in an affinity between the creator and his personages. These inventions are, after all, merely reality as seen in refraction by the writer. When Mauriac describes himself, in spite of hope for cool objectivity, as an "intuitive" writer, he is not very different from Forster's description of any author in relation to his characters: "They [the characters] do not come coldly to his mind, they may be created in delirious excitement, still their nature is conditioned by what he guesses about other people and about himself...." [31]

In reply to a question in Frédéric Lefèvre's interview, which asked Mauriac if his work were an involuntary or conscious effort, the author replied: "Entièrement subconscient. Je ne travaille que d'enthousiasme." He objected that in straining toward edification in a work, "... on trahit son art en travestissant la nature." [32] It is the novelist's role to explore ever further "la zone des terres inconnues" of the human psyche. Forster shares Mauriac's view of the obligation which the novelist has to his public: to transform into literature the two planes of human existence, the one overt and the other arcane. The hidden life, he says, is by definition, hidden: "And it is the function of the novelist to reveal the hidden life at its source...." [33]

The inner, turbulent world of man is seen by Mauriac as one which blurs the identification of his emotional and spiritual drives. When Mauriac is described by critics as "the least cerebral of

[30] Mauriac, *Le Roman,* p. 276.
[31] E. M. Forster, *Aspects of the Novel* (New York: Harcourt, Brace, 1927), p. 72.
[32] Lefèvre, *op. cit.,* p. 223.
[33] Forster, *op. cit.,* p. 72.

writers," [34] or as a man of "hyperesthésie sensuelle," [35] it is in part
a confirmation of Mauriac's assimilation of a particular brand of
religion into his rational and emotional processes. "The touch-
stone of truth for Mauriac comes to life in intensity of feeling." [36]
The ardent responses in worship inspired by the Marian fathers
who trained Mauriac, were stimulated not by religious instruction
which was "à peu près nulle," but by constant submersion of the
young in an "atmosphère céleste." The pupils of the Marian priests
were formed not as "intelligences catholiques mais des sensibilités
catholiques." [37] It is not difficult to see the emotional alienation,
experienced by the Mauriac personages to be encountered, trans-
formed into spiritual alienation. The human quest to love is
readily metamorphosed into a larger search for divine love and
redemption.

Returning briefly to Forster's treatment of the role of love and
sex in the novel, he cleverly differentiates their demands from
those of other major forces of human existence. Being born and
dying, sleeping and eating, can be identified with actions or events
which are measurable, and which can be pinpointed in the narra-
tion of a novel. Love (like Grace) is invisible, and nondimensional.
Its beginnings, endurance and endings are verifiable only by some
exterior signs so varied in possibility that they must be more as-
sumptions than observations. Love, and its similar or contrasting
emotions, are what make up the secret life which it is the duty
of the novelist (as both Mauriac and Forster agree) to explore.

Yet the very attempt to dissect so scrupulously the human
make-up, so that every nuance of its natural complexity is understood and isolated, is self-defeating. Dealing with the nondimensional elements within the limitations of the novel, where all
events, attitudes and actions must be presented as though on a
flat surface, results in distortion. To analyze "completely" Félicité's extraordinary passion for Fernand results not in an expansion of our total understanding of her, as is meant in the
phrase, "connaissance de l'homme," but rather terminates in a

---

[34] Conor Cruise O'Brien, *Maria Cross* (Fresno, California, 1962), p. 34.
[35] René Vincent, "Mauriac et l'amour tragique," *La revue du siècle*,
No. 4 (1933), p. 105.
[36] Jenkins, *Mauriac*, p. 26.
[37] Mauriac, *Dieu et Mammon*, p. 288.

curious immobility. Her personality is so focused in the examination of one single characteristic trait that, while understanding of that facet may be more profound, she is seen only in caricature. The detachment of the artist which encourages such clinical dissection of a personality, fails in providing an overall appreciation either of the individual or of his relationships with life in its larger sense. We know the individuals, not "in all their complexities," but in a single perspective of aberration.

A critic may be concerned, not with what happens in a novel, but how the novel was structured, and may call upon the reader to abandon his sentimental response to a work's content, and instead concentrate on how the artist employed the material at his disposal. To call on the reader in this way asks of him that he actively participate in making a judgment of the work, and that he end his passive role as a receptacle for facts handed to him in chronological order. Jacques Maritain, cited so often in Mauriac's own writings, rejects the passive response to art, which produces docility and receptivity. "Il est bien vrai que l'art a pour *effet* de provoquer en nous des états affectifs, mais ce n'est pas là sa *fin* ou son *objet*" [38] (italics in text). He repeatedly, on a somewhat philosophical plane, discusses every art form in terms of the "intellectual virtue of construction." The artist has been able to produce something "intellectually, to manufacture an object rationally constructed...." In an essay, "L'art est une vertu intellectuelle," he attempts to identify the nature of art:

> L'art est avant tout d'ordre intellectuel, son action consiste à imprimer une idée dans une matière: c'est donc dans l'intelligence... qu'il réside, ou, comme on dit, qu'il est subjecté. Il est une certaine qualité de cette intelligence. [39]

It is without such a philosophical orientation that Forster urges readers to abandon the simple formula, "What happens next?" which is what he calls a primitive emotional reaction of curiosity. He urges the use of the question "Why?" to enable the reader to move beyond the visible world of actions, events, and environment into the intangible world of motivations and emotions. The reader

---

[38] Jacques Maritain, *Art et scolastique* (Paris: Rouart et fils, 1927), p. 308.
[39] *Ibid.*, p. 12.

can frequently determine more about a character in a novel he is reading than he can about any human being among his acquaintances. The author can give insights into the secret world of one of his characters. In life we would have to observe and guess what is happening in the inner existence of the person. But a novelist can tell as much or as little as he chooses of interior information which would not be revealed either in the story-line of the novel. Once a character, however indirectly, reveals what he is experiencing within himself, that revelation is no longer part of his secret world, and instead becomes merely another of his overt actions, even if an insignificant one.

This brief discussion leads to the consideration of a specific means for studying works of art from a detached and analytical viewpoint. Here will be presented an approach to novels, in particular, which will provide for the reader a consistent method of application of criteria, and which is reliable in the congruence of the results it produces. The reader may well be seeking a means whereby he can apply a uniform standard of examination to works of literature, so that with comparable results, he can reasonably evaluate the works he has studied.

It would seem desirable to avoid the "fragmented" approach of much of the literary criticism, in which various related, and sometimes unrelated, elements are touched upon briefly in a single undertaking, often with little documentation. Major studies on Mauriac and his works, such as those of Cormeau, Flower, Jenkins, Majault, [40] Moloney, O'Brien and Turnell [41] are often rich in insights and provocative in their imaginative interpretations. Yet when the fact that Mauriac produced more than one hundred key works is appreciated, of which at least twenty-three are novels, these slender critical observations must perforce be restricted to a review of only a very small part of the total material. The effect of any attempt at detailed analysis of individual works is usually diluted further by the critic's attraction to the often identical material to be found in Mauriac's autobiographical or literary comments.

---

[40] Joseph Majault, *Mauriac et l'art du roman* (Paris: Robert Laffont, 1946).
[41] Martin Turnell, *The Art of French Fiction* (New York: New Directions, 1959).

In the works of the few authors cited above, their analyses begin invariably with a *reprise* of either the life of Mauriac or important literary influences (especially Pascal) on him. Continuing the *mélange* of creator and his creations, each commentator selects for discussion such general topics as "Le caractère," "Les personnages," "Les grands thèmes," "L'expression" (in Cormeau); while *Intention and Achievement* of J. E. Flower focuses on "Catholicism and the novel," "The first steps," "Mauriac's bourgeois world," and "Mauriac's enchanted family." Yet another series of topics is offered by Michael J. Moloney in a book whose title reveals the basic dichotomy, *François Mauriac: a Critical Study*. Of course, it is the works and not the man which will be studied critically, but the critic's problem is thereby indicated. These few comments represent the general similarity and necessarily superficial viewpoint of studies which try to encompass the whole of "the man and his works."

In making the ultimate fusion of the identities between artist and his work, the critic falls victim to the same paradox which condemned the novelist in his desire to know "the whole man." In an effort to know "all of Mauriac," in "all his complexity," they succeed only in fragmenting him, and thereby probably impede possible deeper understanding, not of the man, but of his works.

An ideal basis for the study of literature would be the undertaking of intensive, rather than extensive, probing into the text itself. The exclusion of the author from such an examination, in terms of biographical or literary influences, leaves the reader face to face with a work which awaits penetration in an ever-richer detailed study.

An alternative to generalized study is available in a theory of thematism. The word theme is sufficiently varied in its meanings that the critical studies mentioned promise a discussion of "themes," but usually in the sense of a topic or subject. It is not as a series of topics or subjects that Eugene H. Falk proposes their study in his book, *Types of Thematic Structure*. [42] The title is suggestive that "theme" may be employed with yet another mean-

---

[42] Eugene H. Falk, *Types of Thematic Structure* (Chicago: University of Chicago Press, 1967).

ing in mind. The uses of themes, as they are related to each other, form patterns which make up the structural framework of the novel.

The theme is one which emerges in concentration on a single work at a time, and as a result of observation of component elements in that text. The most basic element, the motif, will carry an idea. The manner in which the idea is linked to another idea, either in repetition or recurrence, in growth or development, in similarity or in contrast, is what makes up the intellectual and aesthetic substance of the novel. The point must be reiterated, however, that in reading the text, themes are not general topics or subject matters which have been predetermined, and for which the reader tries to find supporting data. The themes may be said, rather, to reveal themselves literally, if the reader will accept the work as independent and viable at the outset. If he will, as well, keep in mind an organized basis for observing motifs, the themes will become readily apparent and will have been classified according to the plan of analysis.

The novels to be discussed in the succeeding chapters, *Génitrix, Le Désert de l'amour,* and *Le Nœud de vipères,* have been read with the understanding that themes in three different coherences could be anticipated. The Themes of the Story would arise from what Forster called the "what happened next" elements; from the actions, events, environments and attitudes. The Themes of the Plot would arise from the "why" elements, as actions are examined to see what was their motivation and whether their purposes were the ones given. In the behavior of fictional characters, as with human beings, there is often a discrepancy between what are said or even believed to be the motivations, and purposes, of actions. The difference, if any, is also a possible source of additional themes. The relationship between the themes of the story and those of the plot obviously contributes to creating the multi-dimensional aspect of the work's structure.

Ideas which the author wants to stress may appear in themes not solely identifiable as either those of story or plot. Such themes are related only by their similarity or contrast, and may appear anywhere in the text, once their identities are established. These themes are said to be generically coherent.

It will be noted that the novels which are discussed in the following sections are ones which have strong story lines with many themes to be derived therefrom. Mauriac's reputation for psychological probing is apparent in the number of themes which are abstracted from consideration of his characters' motivations and purposes. His concentration on particular themes, and his rich imagery are important reasons why so many generically coherent thematic units can also be determined. Yet the fact that the three-dimensional approach is rewarding in its findings should not imply that all novels will produce similar thematic structures.

Types of Thematic Structure reveals that themes may be so manipulated by the author that any of three basic divisions of themes may be given the emphasis to the exclusion of the other kinds. Falk's analysis shows that Albert Camus' short novel, *L'Étranger,* for example—an account of an apparently unmotivated man—derives its important themes from the novel's actions and events, and not from a study of the protagonist's motivations and purposes. A further illustration of a possible structural variation was seen in the analysis of Sartre's *La Nausée*. Since this novel lacks any clear linear progression of events, and therefore would lack motivational explanation for such incidents, the significant themes abstracted are found to be in their generic coherence to each other. There is a linear progression, and a perceptible thematic development, but it is not achieved in a chronological arrangement of the incidents.

It is paradoxical, perhaps, that in accepting the direction of a systematic approach, greater freedom can be achieved in interpreting the work under study. There is no strain imposed on the critic or reader to divine thematic or component standards which the author's thinking and his work must then be maneuvered to support. Analyses of several similar or differing works, which proceed from predetermined premises, are likely to reveal more of the preferences of the critic than of the intentions of the author. In noting and classifying motifs, the themes are found to be self-evident, and the critic is then free to interpret the significance and importance of their relationships. It is not the theme in itself which is the object of study. It is the manner in which the theme, or the thematic unit, fits into the tapestry of the work. There is both a design and structure to be considered. One is aesthetic, and subject to interpretation, while the other is rational and can be defined objectively. The manner in which design and structure are synthesized is what gives a work, and therefore its author, their individual and special qualities.

The clarity and order, for instance, on which François Mauriac set such a high value, are apparent in his works. His novels are careful confirmations of the order of the author's priorities. The very coherence of his thematic patterns, from one work to another (as well as within each work itself) would seem to leave open to question, statements made by some of his critics, such as that of Cormeau: "Rien dans François Mauriac ne paraît jamais tranquillement établi, froidement organisé, sereinement déduit selon les règles d'une logique inébranlable." [43]

Mauriac's ability to expand into ever-greater intensity the experiences of an individual, transforming, for example, "ardeur" into "ignition," or "souffrance" into "faim," is evidence rather of technical skill than one entirely of personal depth of feeling. The manipulation of emotional descriptions requires precisely a kind of "froideur" to achieve the degree of artistic detachment which Mauriac knew to be essential. His art is no less passionate for being controlled and disciplined. Spontaneity is not necessarily the most eloquent medium for the translation of passion into art. Lack of discipline can result in unclear expression, while control can result in more penetrating articulation. In the same sense, emotional reaction does not make the best criticism. Rational response is found only in the desired detachment on the reader's part to match the intellectual challenge proposed by the author in creating his work of art.

As for the author, we come to know him by inadvertence, in his involuntary self-revelation. "Car l'œuvre, si belle qu'elle soit par ailleurs, trahit toujours à la fin, avec une sournoiserie infaillible, les tares de l'ouvrier." [44]

---

[43] Cormeau, *op. cit.*, p. 189.
[44] Maritain, *op. cit.*, p. 182.

CHAPTER II

GÉNITRIX

THEMES OF THE STORY

IN DETERMINING the themes of the story to be found in *Génitrix,* the novel can be divided into three thematic units, each almost equally weighted, with the first two concluding in contingent incidents which will alter subsequent motivations, purposes, and therefore, events and relationships. With the occasional use of flashback technique, the story is related in a sequential manner, with memories and references to the past employed most often in elaboration of a character or trait, or in elucidation of attitudes and values which affect consequential situations. There is little difficulty in establishing the linear pattern with these reversions. It is the discrepancies which exist in terms of the novel's point-of-view which are awkward, although this particular technical aspect is only indirectly considered in this discussion.

Each of the three major divisions is a thematic entity in itself (and very nearly a dramatic entity as well, in its development, climax and *dénouement*). The cadence of the story accelerates within each of the segments, with a catastrophic event (the contingent incident) at the end of the section, which in turn sets the stage for the following segment. The momentum of this increased intensity is maintained by an *engrenage* of psychological manipulation among the characters and by ever-deepening concentration on those themes which develop from the component motifs.

The three principal thematic divisions of the story may be outlined briefly as follows:

(1) Mathilde Cazenave lies alone, dying of puerperal fever following a miscarriage at five months of pregnancy. Her life is allowed to flicker out by deliberate neglect on the part of her mother-in-law, Félicité, who refuses to have someone watch over the girl in her terminal fever, who dissuades her son from answering a call from the sick-room, and who abandons the girl after a final dawn visit when the patient was obviously *in extremis*. Mathilde dies alone hardly aware of the approaching end, thinking of early formative family relationships, and plotting another pregnancy to outwit her brutish, hostile mother-in-law. Fernand, to relieve his own anxieties, clips maxims from ancient writers to provide some tranquility, while awaiting the outcome of Mathilde's illness.

(2) Fernand, suffering from doubt and guilt, is repelled on realizing his mother's calculating cruelty to his wife. He accuses her openly of neglect, and withdraws in mind and body to a fantasy world with memories of Mathilde. He becomes unresponsive to Félicité and retires to a small memorial shrine he has created in his wife's room. In prolonged reveries, Fernand sees what love might have done to enrich his and Mathilde's life, and feels his loss the more deeply as his own senses awaken gradually. Félicité, torn by jealousy, anger and fear, loses her vitality and her ability to dominate her son, in the face of his indifference to her. Visions of a renewed erotic relationship between Fernand and his wife, now a spirit, torment Félicité. A vicious, shrill confrontation between Fernand, as accuser, and Félicité, as the accused, collapses into a scene of sensual submission, arousing in Félicité hopes for *une vie nouvelle*. Fernand returns, however, to Mathilde, mortally wounding his mother by remarking that his consideration of her must be attributed to Mathilde's wishes. A sense of peace invades Fernand which distracts him from Félicité's rapidly declining condition. A stroke leaves his mother paralyzed and speechless, living only for glimpses of her son, who awards them to her with condescension. Her death appears to leave Fernand virtually unmoved.

(3) In the absence of Félicité's overpowering presence, Fernand's life becomes further disoriented. Without her as goad or victim, his actions and thoughts lack direction. He turns to the

old servant, Marie, as a refuge, but she abandons any effort at care for his home or his health in her preoccupation with a beloved grandson, Raymond, who has come with his family to live in the house. Raymond's ignorant, rapacious parents abuse Marie's situation and Fernand's indifferent generosity. Fernand is eventually outraged by their aggressive excesses, and drives the child, his parents and even Marie, from his home. Alone in the inanimate house, Fernand regresses to a timorous, puerile state, unable to find comfort or consolation, or to reorient his energies to live. Marie, robbed of all by her children, returns alone by night, goes to his room, and on receiving from Fernand a signal to enter, approaches his bed and touches his face wordlessly.

Génitrix [1] is an account, not of creative power as the title might suggest, but of the degenerative force which can be unleashed in "...désir de possession, de domination spirituelle..." (p. 99). In the first segment outlined above, the relationships between the principal characters are laid out, and some motifs supporting themes of domination by physical intimidation and by spiritual or psychological manipulations are indicated. Each of the women is seen in her efforts to be the *conquérante* of Fernand. Félicité, in her lifelong determination to keep at her side this fruit of her womb, has succeeded in holding her son until the age of fifty in a state of adolescent subordination. She uses various masks to insure her control of Fernand, and she relies, as well, on sheer physical dynamism to keep him from normal emotional involvement. It will be seen that, for both Félicité and Fernand, the relationship of mother and son is considerably more complex than parental ties would require.

As she pretends to sleep between intermittent bouts of fever, Mathilde intuitively sees Fernand and his mother at her bedside as a single entity, "les deux ombres énormes et confondues" (p. 9). It will be noted that she is isolated in a wing of the house on the opposite side from the one, "...où la mère et le fils habitaient deux chambres contiguës" (p. 10). This couple, mother and son, leave the patient's bedside to adjourn, conspiratorially as they do

---

[1] François Mauriac, *Génitrix* (Paris: Grasset, 1923). Subsequent references are to this edition and are placed in the text in parentheses.

daily, to their little office, a private world to which only they
have a key. There is a heart carved fittingly on the door. Yet no
bower of Cupids is this haven from unwanted wives or daughters-
in-law. The table lamp within casts its glow on only utilitarian
objects: an open account book, some pens, a magnet, and sealing
wax. These tools of trade are, in fact, the religious objects of a
woman who "ne croyait qu'à ce qu'elle touchait" (p. 111). It is
therefore appropriate that the walls are decorated with "des cartes
en relief," providing further opportunity for tactile experience.

It had been in the same *bureau* that Mathilde was made aware
of her exclusion, early in her marriage. Seated side by side, Félicité's head on Fernand's shoulder, it was their custom to read the
daily paper together. When the door was opened by Mathilde,
"... en brusque recul ils se séparaient, affectaient de s'interrompre
au milieu d'un mot" (p. 96). This guilty start, at the entrance of
Fernand's wife, and their refusal to speak further, successfully
conveyed their alliance against her. It had been only two months
after their wedding that Fernand literally left Mathilde for
another woman: the other being, of course, Félicité, who received
with joy Fernand's command, "Tu referas mon lit dans mon an-
cienne chambre" (p. 116).

Fernand's union with Félicité had not always been so willingly
joined. In an angry insight into his mother's campaign to keep
him, her son, for herself, Fernand had cried: "Tu as organisé
ma solitude ...." Even the layout of the Cazenave property
favored supervision and containment. Motifs which carry the
theme of a *maison fortifiée* recur frequently, as the house is seen
surrounded by high walls, laid out like a fortress with *enceinte*
and *remparts*. Félicité can observe her son on each of the precisely arranged paths and when he makes "le tour du rond." The
extent of his subjection is revealed in his furtive efforts to smoke
a cigarette, "comme un collégien," hiding "le mégot dans un massif," and in the illicit enjoyment of a forbidden melon, eaten in
spite of warnings against "l'échauffement des entrailles." Félicité
has had built in each bedroom a platform at the window to make
her observations easier.

The nature of Fernand's mentality is established early in the
scene with the theme of his submission to authority. "Cet ancien
élève de Centrale" is the possessor of an intelligence "moins

exercée aux idées qu'aux chiffres." The need for an other-directed rule of life is seen in his modest searches among writers of wisdom (popular editions, to be sure) for that book which "... lui révèlerait mathématiquement le secret de la vie et de la mort" (p. 19). His obtuseness of perception occasionally proves a burden to his mother, as she tries to frighten him with the prospect of a child who might have been taught to hate him:

> Il fixa dans le vide ses yeux saillants et ronds comme s'il y cherchait le fantôme puéril, l'épouvantail frêle qu'inventait sa mère. Mais faute d'imagination, il ne le vit pas. (p. 27)

In contrast to the matriarchal mass that is Félicité, Mauriac presents the ambiguous character of Mathilde. The amorphous quality of her nature, behind its façade of mockery, is revealed only partially in her death-bed recollections of family relationships and experiences in her youth. Her relations with an honest, gentle father who was outwitted and abandoned by a conniving wife, and doomed to a pathetic life of genteel poverty, were devoted yet detached. So, too, was her indulgent but remote treatment of a spoiled, careless younger brother, Jean.

Mathilde's ineptitude at coming to grips with the reality of her situation is revealed in several important realizations as she lay dying. Although she had restrained her mockery of Fernand and his family during her engagement, she had dropped all effort at self-control in her marriage, and now in defeat plans to overcome "ses fous rires, émousser les points dont elle avait rendu furieux Fernand Cazenave" (p. 34). This final recapitulation also points up her misjudgment of the Fernand-Félicité relationship. She had not perceived until too late that she was only a temporary weapon, "une balle ... une arme dans le combat quotidien" between the son and mother. Although Fernand was always a force to be conquered by Félicité, the arrival of Mathilde introduced a new element into the struggle. The contestants had changed: Mathilde became the force to be met with force.

From Félicité's early, almost condescending use of terms like "l'idiote," "l'intruse," and "la coquine," her attack sharpens on news of Mathilde's pregnancy, and the battle is engaged in a continuum of motifs of combative terminology until Félicité's own death. Mathilde's room is "territoire ennemi." Even after Mathilde's death, Félicité will be in "la lutte contre la morte," in battle "contre un fantôme," and she will become helpless against "la tactique de la disparue ... tapie en Fernand, elle [Mathilde] l'occupait comme une forteresse" (p. 87).

The interiority of the scenes being played out in the Cazenave household is emphasized by the restless power and vitality of the passing trains. The ten o'clock night express, the last local, and the first train at dawn serve as a kind of clock marking off the passage of time and events within the house. In her agony, Mathilde "... jouait à suivre le plus longtemps possible ce grondement," with its implications of an "elsewhere," an escape. In contrast, the diminishing footsteps of Fernand and Félicité are listened to fearfully: only when they vanished, could she sigh with relief. The noise of the train and of her chattering teeth are assimilated as Mathilde tries to determine the source of the trembling. Is it within herself?

Mathilde's isolation is underscored by the play of memory and fantasy uninterrupted by human attentions. She is free to recall the past and anticipate a future since all avenues of physical communication are cut off. The servant, Marie, could not hear a call from this remote wing, while the ancient bell which Mathilde pulls in vain sounds nowhere. Even her fever helps to cut her off from contact with ordinary fears. No concern about an intruder can pass through this brazier of fever: "... personne au monde ne pouvait plus l'atteindre" (p. 16).

In this undisturbed revery, borne on the ebb and flow of fever, Mathilde touches on questions of potential and fulfillment. Her thoughts about the possibilities which exist in a human being are centered around the dead infant. Does God know what a human might have become had the promise of his life been fulfilled? Or, does one create his own character, and from that character, his destiny? As for herself, she does not know that she, too, has been deflected from her complete fulfillment: "... une existence misérable l'a ainsi façonnée ..." (p. 34). She, like her child, is no longer at liberty to become what love might have made of her. She believed she had seen (but not necessarily felt) love "sous les traits fraternels de l'ange aux plumes sales," her brother. But the faceless, rotted form of Jean is washed up on the shore in her dream, as she too is "rejetée sur la plage de la vie." Like her child and her brother, Mathilde comes to the end of life without ever knowing what her potential was. Never having been prepared by the ecstasy of love, she approaches the "dissolution éternelle" without being aware of its proximity.

Her isolation, once more and finally, spares her from pain. In "la mort douce de ceux qui ne sont pas aimés," Mathilde expires, leaving hoped-for immortality in that "paquet sanglant qu'avait emporté la matrone," and in that "... figure enfantine ... avec au coin gauche de la lèvre, ce signe que Mathilde avait aussi" (p. 20). Ironically, Félicité remains alive, "génitrix," "le type achevé d'une fondatrice de race," as Fernand obsequiously called his mother, whose principal fear is "... enfin l'ennemie aurait pu accoucher d'un garçon vivant..." (p. 25).

A distinct change of pace characterizes the second thematic unit of the story. The passive world of waiting, recollection and imagination becomes an active and powerfully charged universe of malignant forces. It is a vicious struggle for assertion by the three principal characters, even following Mathilde's death.

The principal theme is one of transition, in which Fernand's latent consciousness of his capacity for self-fulfillment becomes an awareness of his deliberate deprivation by Félicité. This had been climaxed by her elimination of Mathilde, which contingent event sharpens Fernand's realization of his loss. One of the themes correlative to this awareness is represented by Fernand's agressive, angry repudiation of Félicité as first, his mother, and the source and abuser of authority; and second, his rejection of her in the role of mother-seducer who has made him the object of a powerful passion since his youth. In spite of her denials and self-persuasion of innocence, that her responsibilities toward Mathilde were dutifully exercised, Fernand will relentlessly recall the event in a punitive manner.

He rejects not only his mother's word that the dead woman could not have been helped further; he refuses the assurances from a doctor whose word he had so characteristically accepted earlier that Fernand would "bury them all." His separation from Félicité is immediate and physical as these linking phrases indicate:

Fernand Cazenave dégagea le bras où s'était agrippé sa
mère.... (p. 64)
Il dégagea son bras sans même tourner la tête. (p. 66)
Il la repoussa. (p. 69)

Her customary efforts at control of his behavior by appeals
or warnings to his health are left unanswered:

"Si tu tombes malade, nous sommes bien avancés...."
Il parla enfin sans la regarder! (p. 66)
"Tu vas prendre mal."
...il ne répondait rien, ... (p. 94)

Fernand assumes a magisterial role, holding his astonished mother
accountable for her actions concerning Mathilde. She is "boule-
versée... elle a été interrogée comme par un juge..." (p. 67).
His attacks intensify from early bitter questioning to the deliberate, unexpected, wounding thrust.

"Si tu prends mal, qui sera obligée de te soigner? Ce
sera moi."
"Eh, bien, tu n'auras qu'à me laisser crever aussi."
(p. 94)
"Je ne veux pas que tu te laisses périr. Je ne te laisserai
pas mourir."
"Comme l'autre?" (p. 137)

It is only with her taunting challenge in a scene of violent
recrimination, "Frappe au ventre," urging physical retaliation on
behalf of Mathilde, that Fernand's new mastery weakens temporar-
ily and he cries out pitifully, "Maman." The consequences of this
draining experience, however, do not change the circumstances,
and Félicité must hear "ses pas décroître dans la maison morte,"
as he returns to Mathilde.

In contrast to these themes of rejection of maternal solicitude
is presented Fernand's alliance with the shade of Mathilde, in
which the sexual interest expressed only suggestively between
mother and son takes a new direction. Mathilde's passage from
this life, "...sa fuite glissante vers l'ombre" (p. 62), is followed
shortly by a linking phrase, when Fernand begins his journey
into the half-world of loving a spirit. "...[Fernand] se glissa dans

la colonne noire que formait l'entrebâillement de la porte [of Mathilde's room], ..." (p. 65).

Fernand's withdrawal from the essentially erotic relationship with Félicité is signalled gradually. He retires to the dead woman's room to pass his waking hours; he then makes of it a shrine in loving memory; and finally has Marie request bed-linen so that he can return to the nuptial couch. The irresistible attraction to the dead body is underscored in the motif of moths around the flame of the candle near the deceased, who now appears purified of all earthly disfigurements, "... de cette expression avide, dure, tendue d'une pauvre fille qui toujours calcule, méprise, et se moque ..." (p. 76).

He is bound by "un enchantement amer" to the flawless, touching figure of Mathilde. Félicité is literally locked out of this private world, as surely as in their conspiracies of old they had sought to exclude Mathilde. "Il poussa le verrou maintenant, comme si elle avait été Mathilde" (p. 97).

The same scissors used to assure maternal approval as a youth at his mother's knee, when Fernand clipped homilies and maxims, are used to cut Mathilde's face from a group photo which had shown Fernand and his mother as a happy couple with Mathilde, unsmiling, standing aside. Now it is Félicité whose image is in the wastebasket, while Mathilde's is lovingly framed on her altar. We can note the motif of the scissors to underscore the thematic change in Fernand's reactions—from attachment to severance from his mother. "Fernand ... s'était rassis près du guéridon où luisaient les ciseaux parmi les livres de sentences déchiquetés ..." (p. 23). "Elle [Félicité] regarda la table où luisaient les ciseaux dont Fernand se servait pour découper des sentences, — puis la corbeille à papiers" (p. 98).

Fernand's daily habits change as well, since he now sleeps late "... comme si l'autre serrait Fernand dans ses bras" (p. 112). He lies alone in Mathilde's bed: "... il se sentait filer entre deux eaux vers l'abîme à un repos sans fin. Elle était présente, non dans la chambre mais en lui, toute mêlée à sa chair ..." (p. 120).

The motif of water, carrying the theme of desire, is repeated when we learn in the same *rêverie* that Fernand is "ce vieil homme des eaux enfouies à quelles profondeurs." Their "route lente" and "source bourbeuse" have prevented Fernand, like Mathilde, from reaching the "anéantissement des caresses, la dissolution éternelle." The fusion of motifs of unplumbed depths and unslaked thirst supports the theme of unattained satisfactions. Aware that his life can only be seen as dry and barren, "désert morne," (p. 130), it is in this thirst, unknown through the years, that he "découvrait la torture." Fernand begrudges his deceased wife her death before realizing that her thirst had indeed been left unslaked. A sense of doomed destiny overhangs his prospects for assuaging his own desires.

Motifs of eating, carrying themes of pleasure and sensuality, appeared from early memories of Mathilde and her brother, Jean. His return from nightly excursions, smelling of musk and wine, nourished Mathilde, and she found in their *medianoches* "un délassement amer." Those bovinely slow-eating cousins, les La-chassaigne, were so perfectly attuned to the pleasures of the table that they had come to look alike, and to weigh the same, while "...la graisse leur mangeait les yeux."

The denial of this pleasure to Félicité's life, as Fernand avoids eating with his mother, is a source of infinite pain. When after some days he does resume coming to the table, it is without appetite. To Félicité, this is an indication of the end of life: "Qui a perdu l'appétit a perdu le goût de ce qu'il y a de meilleur au monde" (p. 95). The little *apéritif* of lifting the covers of steaming casseroles before they entered the dining room is part of the past. The same pleasures had been used as weapons when mother and son would sniff at Mathilde's offered dishes and by joint agreement disdain them. To encourage Fernand's appetite, Félicité forces herself to eat the red meats which are forbidden to her for reasons of health. She thus embarks on an ignominious martyr-dom, exposing herself to fatal damage, "...afin qu'il se fît du sang." Félicité's stroke follows the forbidden foods and the humiliation of knowing she is loved because, "...c'est elle [Ma-thilde] qui veut que je sois bon pour toi" (p. 166).

Félicité had undergone dramatic physical change as the object of her passion and life drifted from her. Frustration and fear wreak havoc on her massive constitution. It is due to internal stress that, "Elle ne savait pas si ce qu'elle entendait venait des grillons ou des mouches, ou de ses artères...." Just imagining her son perhaps lying in Mathilde's bed, "Félicité entendait son sang par saccades battre...." She stands in the burning heat, while "... dans une odeur de géranium battaient les gorges des lézardes" (p. 118). Fernand is aware suddenly that the powerful figure has become "affaissée, les joues pendantes et grises" (p. 106). Félicité is dying, "de ne posséder plus son fils." Fernand moves in a period of previously unknown peace and calm, as Félicité's tenacious grip on life weakens in her knowledge that his consolation comes from Mathilde. "Beaucoup [de vieilles femmes] meurent du désespoir de ne plus servir ... Félicité ne pouvait plus rien pour son fils" (p. 149).

Correlative is the theme of deterioration presented in motifs of the house, which as it gradually can no longer fulfill the needs of its occupant, Fernand, begins to die: "Comme dans un grand corps, près de sa fin, la vie se retira des extrémités de la maison et se concentra dans la cuisine" (p. 189). The repetitious labels, "grande maison muette," "maison morte," echo the moribund state of the family within.

Fernand's unsuccessful search with the scissors for the secret of life and death is enlightened by his discoveries, in effect, of life in death. As he rests on Mathilde's bed after her funeral, he feels his being invaded by the presence of his young wife, so much a part of his flesh that "sa chair vigilante ... se rappela les nuits nuptiales" (p. 121). He finds no comfort in the contemplation of her soul. "Ce qu'il voulait qu'on lui rendît vivant, c'était ce corps." His discovery is that pleasure is to be found not within oneself, but "... tout mêlé à la chair d'un autre corps que nous rendons heureux" (p. 81). He has found that, unlike the perversion of love which is his mother's consuming passion for him, destructive and distorting, unlike the chronicle of petty meanness that was "l'histoire de Fernand dans l'amour" (p. 91), it is the magnanimity of love in its maximum expression that brings man his greatest pleasure.

The contingent incident of Félicité's death, as noted, appears to touch Fernand only superficially. If neighbors were astonished at the vertiginous grief he displayed at her graveside, how could they know that he was leaning merely to glimpse the resting place of the dead Mathilde, now more vivid than ever?

Alone in the great house with Marie, Fernand rejects the
inherited mantle of his ancestors, "les amants jaloux des pins."
He intends to rid himself of estate details so that he can rediscover
the "hébétude douce" he enjoyed so with Mathilde's spirit

> Fernand Cazenave crut d'abord que seul un notaire
> importun le détournait de Mathilde. (p. 178)
> ...il se persuada que le seul fracas de ses rentes et de
> ses terres détruisait cette quiétude, cette hébétude divine
> où naguère il rejoignait Mathilde. (p. 179)

The talismans and charms that had so easily invoked the spell
of resuscitation—the "cadre en coquillage," the little shrine—fail
somehow to move Fernand. Curiously, now that the brazier of
his mother's love, so infuriating and inhibiting, has gone out, he
finds himself alone, shivering in the ashes. For further emphasis,
the motif of the "brasier" is strengthened to that of the sun:
"...le soleil maternel à peine éteint, le fils tournait dans le vide,
terre désorbitée" (p. 187). We are reminded that Félicité, *enfant
landaise,* had adored only "le soleil implacable," had known only
"cette toute-puissance de feu dévorateur" as the object of her
worship.

Fernand's "terre désorbitée" is underscored in the disorienta-
tion of his days. Part of the void is the absence of the fixed, gluttonous stare of Félicité. A walk in the garden, unwatched, has
lost its savor. He "...renifle un lilas, puis un autre ... sans que
la haie de troènes lui évoque aucun visage" (p. 185). *Nuits blanches*
follow as he tries first Mathilde's bed, then Félicité's, and finally
hopes "...retrouver le sommeil dans son lit d'enfant" (p. 189). A
transitory moment of well-being which encourages thoughts of a
visit to "l'habitude" results in no action, since the goad and reward of such a trip are lacking. Dust accumulates on the "cadre
en coquillage" on Mathilde's altar while Fernand, "à peine lavé,"
passes his days indolently in the chair where Félicité waited to die.

Fernand is aware only belatedly of the change in attitude in
his servant, Marie. She, like the donkey, Grisette, prodded into
life by Félicité, has spent her life on her feet, on the treadmill of
service to the Cazenaves. She has accepted their pain in her own
body, literally, since as a young woman carrying the children
about, it was she who was beaten if one of them cried. Now

purified by a life of selfless and unremitting toil, she, the vessel that contains the spirits of all that went before and were to come, is described as, "cette vierge en buis," or as one with "face de vierge noire" (p. 220).

Fernand, first seen through the privet hedge as "un dieu-terme moussu" by Mathilde, now is seen in familiar contempt by Marie as "la vieille idole déboulonnée, descendue de son socle." The call of her own blood, in fervent love for her grandson, Raymond, is stronger than Fernand's claim on her, whereby "... d'une voix pleurarde, la nuit, il la pût appeler."

It is not through his own strength that Fernand is able to reassert his rights of domain against the grasping, screeching overtures of Marie's daughter-in-law. It is the infusion of the spiritual vigor of Félicité that allows him to drive the aggrandizing relatives from his home. Félicité, like Mathilde, has rejoined Fernand at his meals, with each of the women in her original role. Félicité is enthroned, "majestueuse, dominatrice." She is the goddess-mother of "divin visage," who will arouse Fernand to magnificent fury. "Il rejetait sa tête, le cou gonflé comme une Junon—et l'on eût dit sa mère vivante" (p. 213). Correlative by contrast is the impression also given to Marie in Fernand's days of unkempt idleness in Félicité's armchair by the fire: "Qu'il aurait peur s'il avait su comme, dans cette demi-ténèbre d'un décembre ruisselant, tassé au fond de son fauteuil il rapellait sa mère au déclin..." (p. 206).

Mathilde has lost her primacy in the world of the spirits since Félicité has joined her there. Her place at the dinner table reverts to her customary degrading one, "loin du feu, dans le courant d'air..." (p. 199).

In sharp contrast to Félicité's first visit to Mathilde's shrine where she had sought her son, is Fernand's final tour to the little shrine of Marie in the glacial attic of the house. The mother had nearly been overcome by the sensual stifling atmosphere:

> Félicité dut cligner ses yeux: les deux fenêtres large ouvertes laissaient pénétrer les flammes de ce juin fauve. Des lis... saturaient la chambre. Un bourdon se cognait au plafond.... Alors son bourdonnement se perdit dans l'incendie du ciel. (p. 102)

Fernand seeking some haven in love, wanders among the empty, icy rooms on his way to the *soupente* where "Une lucarne ... re-cueillait comme de l'eau la clarté toute pure de la nuit, et l'épandait sur un coffre orné de tulipes peintes" (p. 217). Tripping over "les choses mortes," he reaches Marie's room where the light is further intensified, "... la lucarne concentrait la limpidité nocturne sur une vierge de plâtre, aux mains ouvertes, mais laissait dans l'ombre au-dessus du lit, un corps crucifié" (p. 218). Solitude and resignation are the closing themes for Fernand as he lies oppressed under "un poids infini." There is no suggestion of a future, or of hope for the man returned to a state of helpless dependence. Halted by an unnamed destiny, his life has reached a bitter stalemate. A suggestion of comfort, of some intercession in the unspoken prayer for help has materialized in the person of Marie de Lados, his final refuge, his "vierge noire."

THEMES OF THE PLOT

Unlike consideration of themes of the story, which was concerned with the sequential, probable development of the story's coherence, and which followed a linear pattern, determining the themes of the plot relies on an analysis of motivations and purposes. Because of this we identify salient traits of those principal characters who support these themes. It is their basic attitudes and predispositions which affect motivations and purposes, and which in turn underlie and generate the actions, events, moods and relationships revealed in the previous analysis. The causal nature of the relationship between the elements of motivation-purpose and actions-events allows us to interpret the interaction of forces and consequent developments without particular regard to sequential format.

Since *Génitrix* is a novel built principally around the interplay of three major characters, it might be useful to use each of these as separate sources of material in seeking motivations and purposes. Each plays a role at some time as aggressor and as victim in relation to the others, in a symmetrical and reciprocal balance of roles. It is a contingent incident, the catalytic event of the death of Mathilde's father which sets in motion the chain of events. This occurrence is outside the thematic framework of the novel, yet it is the means whereby Mathilde's presence is projected on the scene. It is Mathilde, as Félicité's neighbor and daughter-in-law, who poses a threat to the long-established relationship between mother and son.

In Mauriac's view of the family as a continuing chain of human links, there is emphasized the sense of legacy from one generation to the next. This is not to be interpreted only as the transfer of material possessions, a factor of great importance, to be sure, but the bequest as well of attitudes and values which necessarily color the philosophy and behavior of the legatees. These inherited approaches and responses to life are seen in conflict with the instinctive human drives which also affect activities and aspirations.

Félicité suspects Fernand of some divagation from the traditional family perspective of marital relationships when he asks about his father: "Est-ce que tu l'aimais autant que moi?" Her unsatisfactory response, "...ça n'avait aucun rapport," leaves unsaid the difference she acknowledges inwardly. There is no connection "entre le besoin insatiable de domination, de possession spirituelle" (p. 99) which Fernand inspires in her and "cet attachement d'habitude, ce compagnonnage" which was her marriage with Numa Cazenave. The conventional Landais view of matrimony as the perpetuator of family properties allows no room for passion or sentiment. The aim of conjugal relations is solely production of a male heir, and the motto, "Faites vite," of women on both sides of Fernand's family is empty of love.

Félicité represents "une tache de rouille," an exception on the unbroken family chain. It is she who hides a burning passion under "la tendresse jalouse" of motherhood and in this way binds her son fruitlessly to her. Interpolated is the observation, "Malheur à ceux qui viennent après." Félicité, in her role of loving mother, refused to leave her son's cure at a spa to be present at the death of her husband. Félicité never wanted to remember her satisfaction that she could fittingly avoid this distraction, although she found in the administration of his estate, "un agrément extrême." Neither does she think of "...ce honteux énivrement qu'elle éprouva à se sentir libre, seule avec l'unique objet de sa passion..." (p. 159).

Her stated purpose in life is to protect and sustain her son. This is emphasized by repeated admonitions regarding the state of his health. There had been little difficulty in restraining Fernand as a boy, when he felt only security and happiness in being near her. Even in moments which inspired fear in Fernand in his boyhood, "Il se souvient qu'il éprouva ... une sécurité bienheureuse parce que sa mère était là.... Un sécurité bienheureuse parce que sa mère était là" (p. 182). Up to the age of fifty, Fernand was dominated by implied threats to health. He does not answer a call he is sure he heard from Mathilde's sickroom because he would necessarily cross the icy vestibule and is warned, "Tu ne vas pas encore traverser le vestibule? Tu as toussé trois fois, ce soir" (p. 20).

Tenderness gives way to shrillness in the mother as any resistance appears in her son. Félicité had saved him from strain and overwork in denying him a small role in local political life and overrides his anger, "J'ai voulu que tu vives d'abord, entendstu? que tu vives!" (p. 49). It is indeed essential to Félicité's own life that Fernand live, to feed her passion. "Pour ne pas le perdre, elle l'avait voulu infirme; elle ne l'avait tenu que parce qu'elle l'avait démuni" (p. 123). Kept in a dependent state of arrested emotional development, Fernand will continue to find security in his childhood bed against the wall of his mother's room. Félicité on the other side, however, drank in the "musique délicieuse" of his heavy, sleeping breath. There, too, she slept, "les lèvres collées contre la cloison...." In the frightful days following Mathilde's death, when Fernand nearly strikes his mother in their quarrel, she collapses and in near-ecstasy is closely embraced by the momentarily remorseful Fernand. "Ah, qu'elle aurait voulu que la minute en fût éternelle" (p. 141).

There is, ever-present, the subtle bond of obligation created by the parent who "does everything" for her child. The many pains that are endured are infinitely pleasurable, and sweet, too, is the knowledge that a debt thereby is created. The "petit bourreau" who keeps her from her night's sleep so that he may rest comfortably is bound forever by his need as well for a willing victim of small tortures.

Félicité endures, even encourages, Fernand's periodic visits to "l'habitude" in Bordeaux. It is a kind of *péché utile*. No danger existed there to threaten the filial tie to Félicité. In fact, there were unspoken pleasures derived from the savage parting in which she made him the token gift of liberty. She rests secure in the knowledge that he left "avec une valise où manquait l'essentiel" and in the knowledge that until his certain return, they both died a little; "... jusqu'à son retour elle ne vivrait plus" (p. 186). Mathilde on her deathbed realizes what she had not known then, that "Félicité fondait sa sécurité" on these visits to Rue Huguerie.

A marriage represents to Félicité something to be avoided at all costs. Félicité saps Fernand's confidence in his belated desire to be a husband, "Toi, marié? mon pauvre drôle! Je voudrais t'y voir." Ashamed as she is of the Cazenave family background (she cannot tolerate recalling that her husband's grandmother "portait encore le foulard"), Fernand's pride at producing a male heir of this name is an affront to her. It is the loss of him, Fernand, as her child, however, and not the arrival of an infant grandchild, that prompts her scorn.

Félicité's problem is very nearly solved, and Mathilde removed from the scene, by the miscarriage of the baby. Félicité is innocent of blame for this unexpected event. "Elle a fait son devoir. Elle n'a rien à se reprocher." Her confidence, however, is short-lived in view of Mathilde's continued presence as a phantom. It had been a simple matter for Félicité to dismiss a maid who, in one of Fernand's childhood illnesses, claimed credit for his cure. Mathilde, so invisible, so easy to conquer in life, is invincible in the protection of the next world. "Femme positive [Félicité], ses armes accoutumées ne valaient pas contre un fantôme. Elle ne savait travailler que sur la chair vivante" (p. 86).

Her purpose following Mathilde's demise changes to that of recapturing a lost son. For the first time in their relationship, it is she who must consider altering her behavior to earn, or at least attract, Fernand's approval. And, she must do so against his wall of indifference. Yet it is an instinctive, last-resort reaction in the face of an irreplaceable loss, which changes her attitude: "... pour la première fois, [Félicité] ne songea pas à lui comme à son bien qu'une autre a ravi, et qu'il faut reconquérir avec violence" (p. 133). She would have called Mathilde "du rivage des morts," if that had been possible to make her son happy. "Tel est l'instinct de l'amour qui ne veut pas périr: lorsque se dérobe sous lui la terre, lorsqu'est détruit son ciel familier, il invente un autre ciel et une autre terre."

The instinct to love is suggested here as a fixed characteristic of the human make-up, a self-perpetuating, self-preserving pressure. This impetus of generous self-giving comes too late to Félicité who, greedily drinking in the pleasure of self-denial, is "ivre de sa défaite," and gluts her new-found sense of renunciation. Yet the old need to overpower is rekindled when Fernand remains unmoved by the change in his mother. She responds with an anger which "... passait en elle comme le feu, y consumait tous les désirs de renoncement à peine nés" (p. 134). The obsessive character of Félicité's passion for Fernand, and the enormous egotistical drive for continued self-satisfaction has so distorted any remnant of the instinct to love that a change to selflessness is impossible for her.

The monolithic presence of Félicité is not the solid structure it might appear to be. Some sense of culpability regarding Mathilde's death makes her vulnerable, and her awareness of this unusual state cannot be easily brushed aside. It becomes imperative to reassure herself frequently, even as she closed the door on Mathilde who lay dying.

> Elle n'a rien à se reprocher. (p. 60)
> ... elle se répétait pour la centième fois, errant à travers la pièce: "Voyons, réfléchissons, je suis montée, j'ai frappé à la porte...." (p. 90)

Félicité is literally haunted by Mathilde:

> Non, non, les morts ne se vengent pas. ... Elle se força à rire, elle ne croyait qu'à ce qu'elle touchait. (p. 111)

She tries to convince Fernand, at least, of her innocence,

> Elle allait et venait dans la pièce, parlant pour se convaincre soi-même autant que son fils; et elle élévait la voix comme si elle eût souhaité d'être entendue par quelque être invisible, mais aux écoutes. (p. 138)

Left speechless and paralyzed by a stroke, Félicité is nevertheless relentlessly driven to consume her son. According to Marie de Lados, "Elle se le mange des yeux."

In analyzing the motivations and purposes of Fernand in relation to the other characters, it must be kept in mind that his behavior has always been that of reaction, even when it appears that he is taking the initiative. That does not mean at all that he is unmotivated, but that his behavior is prompted by response to a stimulus, which is unfailingly provided by Félicité. We can only imagine that a stolen cigarette or melon was all the sweeter for having been forbidden. There is no evidence that Fernand wanted either, however, once he is no longer spied upon by his mother. But that he did have some latent instinct toward liberation and self-expression is evinced by the fact that Fernand did marry Mathilde, over what must have been formidable opposition.

> "Quelle femme aurait trouvé grâce devant toi?"
> La fureur joyeuse de la vieille dame éclata:
> "En tout cas, pas celle-là." (p. 23)

At least part of Fernand's purpose in marrying Mathilde was to have possession of "ce jeune corps parmi les guêpes ... cette proie charnelle et qui sentait le miel." Although his appetite had been whetted by frequent observations of Mathilde through the hedge, "ce grand buste de Cazenave, comme celui d'un dieu-terme moussu, divisait les branches..." (p. 46) why at fifty years of age would he embark on such an unfamiliar and hazardous journey? Just as Félicité was heir to a set of attitudes and values which affected immeasurably her concept of love, so Fernand was indoctrinated with an exceptionally contemptuous attitude toward women, of whom he knew only two kinds: " 'celles qui veulent vous mettre le grappin,' " and " 'celles qui donnent des maladies' " (p. 124).

His boastful insecurity in this connection had made him believe, or at least profess that, "on a toujours la femme qu'on veut à condition d'y mettre le prix." Women, he maintained, knew where they stood with him, "... pas de fleurs, pas de cadeaux, pas de faux frais." With this little litany of pretended satisfaction, for most of his adult life, Fernand stemmed the tide of desire and accommodated himself to Félicité's need to possess him.

In an intuitive realization, actually a spiritual discovery, following Mathilde's death, Fernand examines for himself possible explanations of his relationship with Mathilde. The young wife learned that she was only a temporary weapon between the mother and son, and Fernand comes to understand that all his actions were not gestures toward self-fulfillment, but exercises of resistance and rebellion against Félicité, his jailer. "Crois-tu [he asks himself] s'il ne s'était agi que de t'armer contre ta mère, crois-tu que tu te fusses hasardé à écarter les branches..." (p. 125). That he had doubts about his mother's motivations in her excessive solicitude was revealed even before his marriage: "Tu as voulu que je vive ... près de toi. Voilà le vrai" (p. 49). "Pour mieux me tenir, tu n'as pas voulu que je me marie. Tu ... tu as organisé ma solitude" (p. 50).

Was it true that, as Félicité believes, "c'était son [her son's] plus cher plaisir de faire souffrir sa mère"? Was there an unconscious desire on his part to retaliate against the involuntary servitude he only rarely challenged openly? Fernand will eventually agree that going to visit his "habitude" was a self-inflicted painful pleasure, and a punishment for Félicité. The enjoyment of subsequent ecstatic reunions were, too, all part of the motivation behind what was, in purpose, a demonstration of personal adult liberty. "Il savait qu'elle sécherait d'inquiétude et que jusqu'à son retour, elle ne vivrait plus. Sans cette angoisse qu'il laissait derrière lui, peut-être ne serait-il jamais parti" (p. 186).

As for his motivation in marrying Mathilde, his self-questioning lets him confess that this undertaking was intended at least in part as a torment to Félicité, although other provocations, then unidentified, played a role. "Oui, certes, la faim de vengeance d'abord t'excita — mais elle dissimulait une autre faim plus secrète..." (p. 126). In spite of spasmodic efforts to persuade himself that Mathilde loved him, " 'puisque je la faisais souffrir,' " he must admit: " 'non, non, il ne s'agissait pas d'amour....' "

The closest thing to love which was shown to Mathilde by her husband was in the period of her pregnancy, in a kind of veneration of her as the Chosen Vessel carrying his child. Fernand takes comfort in the fact that he supported Mathilde against Félicité's cruelties. "Mais, elle a cru que c'était à cause de l'enfant." And so it was in part, since Fernand "crevait d'orgueil" in his role as prospective progenitor of an heir to the family name. But there is evidence again of a self-serving satisfaction in addition to the joy of this achievement, in knowing that Félicité had no part.

Fernand's resentment toward Félicité, once he has made the discovery of the possibilities of love and of his thwarted capacity for loving, a world still within his grasp, appears to make him indifferent to Félicité's pain at his continued liaison with the spirit of Mathilde. "Fernand s'irrite de la petite part de sa vie dévolue à l'épouse, alors que la mère couvre de son ombre énorme toutes les années finies" (p. 183). Self-pitying desolation occasionally overtakes him. " 'Je suis plus à plaindre qu'elle, parce que je n'ai rien eu, et elle m'a eu' " (p. 163). A suggested theme of motivation, that Fernand's actions have been the result of a desire to inflict pain on his mother, is confirmed in his own analysis: "Fallait-il que cet immense amour obsédant de sa mère le cernât de ses flammes pour que, traqué, il descendit en lui-même jusqu'à Mathilde?" (p. 184). Thus the resuscitation of Mathilde, this re-creation of a love object who will aid Fernand in his liberation, is also a reprisal against Félicité.

Relating the discovery of love to his future, Fernand is prompted to think of further efforts which will exploit with another "la découverte délicieuse." "Quoi de plus remplaçable qu'une Mathilde?" Alas, no substitutes suggest themselves to Fernand, who had never been "un être aimant." He has been effectively isolated from meaningful human contact. This new desire is destined to frustration, and Fernand strains to escape the sticky web woven around him by Félicité: "... il se débattait, grosse mouche prise" (p. 131).

This theme of self-assertion toward independence is correlative by contrast to that of repression of another. "Il existe des hommes qui ne sont capables d'aimer que contre quelqu'un. Ce qui les fouette en avant vers une autre, c'est le gémissement de celle qu'ils délaissent."

Thus Mauriac underscores the motivation, not known to Fernand until his wife's death, in much of his behavior. In contrast, without the vitalizing, although paradoxically destructive pressures exerted by Félicité, Fernand is passive and eventually inert. A visit to Rue Huguerie, the purpose of which is to take advantage of newly-discovered appetites and a sense of well-being, simply cannot be envisioned or undertaken without the accompanying pleasure of pain and torment to both Fernand and Félicité. A search for renewed calm and peace with Mathilde's memory is unsuccessful for the same reason.

As violent conflicting emotions and a sense of loss had produced a *crise de santé* in Félicité, leaving her paralyzed in her *fauteuil* by the kitchen fire, so Fernand is paralyzed by his sense of loss in a *crise d'esprit* which reduces him to rancorous indifference and a sense of futility. Although the specific motif of surrender never completes the range of military battle terms, it is exactly that which is found in Fernand's resignation to a loveless existence:

... Plus rien à faire. (p. 187)

He concedes defeat to Félicité whose powers beyond the grave emerge intact. She who was intolerant is triumphant.

... elle n'avait souffert la concurrence d'aucun travail, d'aucun divertissement, d'aucune espérance, d'aucun amour, elle pouvait du fond de ses ténèbres, se glorifier de l'œuvre accomplie. (p. 187)

Fernand is motivated, in the abandonment he feels following his mother's death, by a desire for peace and tranquility where no demands will be made upon him and where some rays of love can reach him. He makes tentative approaches of affection to Raymond, Marie's handsome grandson. The boy snatches the bait of a tidbit offered and struggles to escape his grip, as well as the "même regard lourd dont l'année précédente l'avait couvé sa mère taciturne...." The harrowing discord introduced by Marie's family into his house, and the violation of Fernand's property interfere with the attainment of his goal. It is his unexercised latent sense of authority derived from Félicité which enables him to drive out the intruders from his temple where his search for accord was disrupted.

Fernand appears to be left without motivation, without purpose at the novel's end. Deprived of the stimulus, the subject has no reason to react. There is not even a sign of despair, which might be seen as a development, however negative it may be. Fernand is instead immobilized beneath "un poids infini," the millstone of his liberty to want and to become.

Mathilde, the third party in the running battle for survival amid the Cazenaves, was motivated in part, like the others, by the need to overcome the hostile environment which was the world surrounding her. By the time Mathilde is old, and bold, enough to attempt her seduction of Fernand, the forces of her unhappy lot have shaped a personality and character that can respond to circumstances only by seeking some kind of escape.

Her main resource in evading the painful nature of her situation has been her cultivation of a profound capacity for mockery, by which Mathilde can isolate herself from pain and emotional stress: "elle a dressé la moquerie entre le monde et soi" (p. 34). This theme of self-protection allows Mathilde to smile privately at her family's preference for Jean, her sly, night-prowling brother. It permits her to participate obliquely in his nocturnal escapades as she welcomes at dawn, "avec une moquerie sèche, cet ange fripé."

Her need to avoid emotional commitment becomes a way of life, and it colors her judgments, often to her disadvantage. In order to remain detached and free from obligation to her generous cousins (who, after all, could have left her to find her way as an orphan), Mathilde scorns them for their simple sensual pleasures and material values. She views them "avec une cruauté forcenée et sourde." She despises their qualities in a secret diary, "...comme ceux qui ne sacrifient jamais ce qu'ils mangent à ce qu'ils disent" (p. 44).

Her compulsion for detachment has resulted in her perpetual role as observer. The minimal emotional demands in her life as an adolescent are met principally by living vicariously through her brother, Jean. It is as "l'espionne" that Mathilde derives satisfaction and pleasure as she watches the tormented son of Félicité writhe in his mother's smothering embrace. It is her taste for mockery that has her see their contestations as "les ébats." Correlative by contrast is the view she must have of them as a couple after mother and son have excluded her from their circle of intimacy. Voluntary detachment was her source of pleasure; involuntary solitude was to be her punishment.

Although her protective device does enable Mathilde to endure painful childhood experiences with reduced stress, it is "ce goût

de moquerie, chez les Cazenave, [which] devait la perdre." Her
spying on Fernand is done with an infantile sense of malice, in
contrast with Félicité's close observation of him to assure possession and control. The taunting return of Fernand's melon-rinds
(discarded in fright directly into her hedge-hidden face) in order to
see "la tempête déchaînée" between mother and son, was an
audacious step. Mockery also lay just below the conscious level
as Mathilde bought a railway ticket to sit opposite Fernand on
his furious way to "l'habitude" in Bordeaux.

The decision to do so was taken with calculation, requiring that
she lie about her purpose in going to the city. Her mistake in
judgment was in believing that Fernand in his angry departure
really did want to leave Félicité behind forever. She would exploit
his vulnerability (overestimating her skill in the face of Félicité's)
in order to use Fernand to escape her loathsome life as a poor
relation. Having observed the maniacal quality of his desire for
her, "... cette gloutonnerie du regard ... cette attention goulue,"
Mathilde mocks herself in "... avoir su attiser le désir de ce
quinquagénaire timide."

It is Mathilde's desperation in her life-rôle that prompted her
rendezvous with destiny on the train. She blames only herself for
her later, even more disastrous, circumstances in marriage:

> Tu as voulu ton malheur. Rien de tendre ne t'attirait vers
> ce vieil homme. Un instinct de taupe te faisait chercher
> partout une issue à ta vie subalterne. ... Tu poussais
> toute porte entrebâillée — captive qui ne te souciais guère
> qu'elle ouvrît sur la campagne ou sur un abîme. (p. 53)

Mathilde's use of Fernand to serve her own purpose is presented
in such a way that we conclude her behavior to be an instinctive
mechanism to insure her survival. As with Félicité's and Fernand's
inherited characteristics, Mathilde is forced by the harshness of
life to eliminate the resource of tenderness and love, and to regard
people and events for their utilitarian value in escape. With the
exception of her relations with her father and brother, both ending
inconclusively, "... elle se défendît d'être expansive ..." (p. 39).

Mathilde's devious personality is her response to life. Like
Fernand and Félicité she is not free to develop to the fullest her
emotional or spiritual life. It could be said that for her too, any

level of moral maturity beyond the expediency of self-serving, short-term decisions is unattainable. What she has known of love is what she had believed to see in Jean, "sous les traits fraternels de l'ange aux plumes sales..." (p. 43). It was for her to experience only the negative counterparts of love, the humiliation and pain, but never the joy. Was it to afflict Mathilde that her brother sang as he commandeered their *médianoches*, " 'Non, tu ne sauras jamais — ô toi qu'aujourd'hui j'implore — si je t'aime ou si je hais" (p. 40).

Mathilde's dream of escape as she lies dying, removed from the defensive tactics of daily survival, is a gentle one. She would have secluded herself with her child, the two of them alone in a kingdom not of this world, where "Ceux qui la haïssaient n'auraient pu l'y poursuivre." Security and freedom from fear are the goals she seeks. Reality is transposed into revery: "Je serais resté assise dans le noir près de son lit [her child] jusqu'à ce que fût passé le rapide qui souvent lui aurait fait peur" (p. 28).

In the lucidity that precedes the darkness of death, Mathilde formulates a new purpose, a new resolve. Unaware that she is at the threshold of eternity, Mathilde determines that she will be victorious over Félicité. She plots another pregnancy to thwart the jealous *génitrix*. The same error, however, prevails in her judgment as it had before her marriage. She overrates her own capabilities and falls short in her evaluation of Félicité. "Alors l'ennemie serait forcée de rendre ses armes. Il suffisait de mâter sa belle-mère..." (p. 32). Mathilde, "fixed" in her approach to life, cannot cope with reality except by dependence on an instinct for manipulation and intrigue.

Mathilde is heiress to her father's innocence and her mother's culpability. She remained untouched by corruption, seeking ever greater refuge in solitude while, like her mother, she took easy advantage of a vulnerable man.

Fernand and Mathilde used each other as a means of fleeing an intolerable existence, what Fernand calls "sa vie atroce," while giving little in return. Because in each of these characters their discoveries concerning their potential for love come too late to be implemented, each ends his appearance in the novel confined, with no appeal, to the exile of death or a loveless life.

RELATIONSHIP OF THEMES OF THE STORY AND THEMES OF THE PLOT

Two principal themes of the story, the capacity of the individual for self-fulfillment, and the negative, destructive force of possessive love may be seen reflected in the changing motivations and purposes of Fernand, and his failure to achieve the goals he desires once given the awareness of his potential. He asserts himself after Mathilde's death as an individual to live independently of domination and restraint. He enjoys the freedom from bonds and his newly-discovered ability to dream of what his life might be as a whole man. His pleasure is so real and intense that it is his purpose to re-create the dream-like state, and perhaps even implement his dreams, once the practical matters of Félicité's estate have been concluded. Unlike Félicité who had known what she wanted to do with her freedom when she was left a widow, Fernand is perplexed by his liberty. His freedom is not an opportunity, it is a burden which he cannot assume. He has found his free will, but free will to do what?

When in a flash of self-recognition he realizes that his peace of mind has been dearly bought, at the expense of Félicité's life, he perceives that there has been fundamentally no change in his motivation. He had let her die, in retaliation for her imprisonment of him, by displaying a fantasy love and tranquility which excluded her. It had been merely another facet of the sense of reprisal shown in the trips to Bordeaux, where he also killed her a little each time he left. The contingent incident of Félicité's death makes this self-deception apparent to Fernand.

The theme of the awareness of the individual's freedom to develop as he chooses is negated in the development of themes of the plot which provide motivations which are intrinsically opposed to creative behavior. The latent potential in Mathilde, for response through desire, is obliterated by other fundamental motivating forces toward, not development, but survival. "Dieu seul sait s'il n'y eut pas chez Mathilde un moment de détente, d'abandon, un germe secret, une imperceptible inclination ..." (p. 128). If there had been such, her competing instinct for self-preservation repressed it immediately. This is emphasized in the last moments of her life, after a glimpse of a happy kingdom of selfless love with her child. Her motivation stifles such a softening, to enable her to hold out against Félicité in a resurgence of destructive behavior, planning a pregnancy to defeat Félicité.

Even if we are successful in diagnosing the "why" of human behavior, and if, like Fernand, we come to know what lies at the root of our actions, that knowledge in itself is not sufficient to propel the psyche into new paths of motivations. Fernand has done a thorough job of dissecting his motivating forces, yet finds there no release from the bondage of the past to create a future. These cerebral probings merely provide an additional burden to be borne, another obstacle for which a motivation is needed to overcome and make changes. In Fernand's case, having lost the counterforce which was the fuel of his motivating power, no new means are provided for correcting his course. Self-knowledge is not power, or at least not enough power in itself to change irremediable characteristics.

A projection of these analyses can reveal that man, who denies, and is thereby denied, the love of God, is doomed to an apathetic existence, a slave to forces over which he has no control. There is no liberty in the godless state of lovelessness.

GENERIC COHERENCE

Brooding over the entire work, *Génitrix*, is the imposing figure of Félicité, whose name, like the title, was surely chosen with ironic intent. Emphasizing the gluttonous, voracious quality of her maternal love are motifs which concentrate on her physical conformation and mass. A sense of mammoth immobility is revealed by the strain required to exert herself in the emotional crisis, for example, following Mathilde's death. Repetitious labels are found which emphasize such traits, and linking phrases as well are used to carry the themes.

> A bout de souffle, elle éventait avec son mouchoir sa face bleuie. (p. 51)

Her huge body is a burden to move; but obsessive determination propels her:

> ...elle... glissa dans des savates ses pieds enflés. (p. 58)
> Mme Cazenave... dressée sur ses jambes gourdes.... (p. 93)
> Elle repartit soufflante mais soulagée.... (p. 86)
> Furibonde, la vieille femme roulant sur ses hanches gagne l'escalier. De marche en marche elle perdait le souffle, mais tout de même, se hissa jusqu'à la chambre de l'ingrat. (p. 100)
> Elle en fut émue au point de lourdement se soulever, de passer le bras autour du cou de son fils. (p. 165)

No effort is too great to be an obstacle to pursuing her prey. That this mass had a terrifying quality is indicated by Mathilde's fright on her death-bed:

> Quelle était cette masse noire, près de la fenêtre, cette bête couchée et comme repue — ou tapie peut-être? Mathilde reconnut l'estrade que sa belle-mère avait autrefois fait dresser dans chaque chambre.... (p. 13)

The association is completed by the linking phrase which reinforces this impression of a beast, ready to pounce on an unaware victim.

> C'était sur une de ces estrades... qu'un jour de ses fiançailles Mathilde avait vu se dresser l'énorme femme furieuse, piétinante et criant,
> "Vous n'aurez pas mon fils. Vous ne me le prendrez pas!" (p. 14)

Having thus established a theme of animality in Félicité, other component motifs appear which substantiate the suggestion. Consider the letters from Fernand, so unhappy on his honeymoon:

> ...cette lettre vint inonder à la fois d'inquiétude et de bonheur la vieille mère louve. (p. 166)

Her protective reaction toward Fernand in his remorse after his threat to strike her was instinctive:

> ...du même geste qu'en ces jours où, jeune mère animale, elle flairait avidement le nouveau-né.... (p. 142)

When she first tastes fear that Fernand may truly be leaving to love the spirit Mathilde, she lies in Mathilde's bed.

La vieille s'aplatit comme une bête. (p. 104)

Fernand's perspective of his mother transforms these over-powering characteristics into those of a reigning, all-powerful monarch, "dans une attitude majestueuse, puissante" (p. 106). She does become, in fact, "vieille reine dépossédée," as her private kingdom of love is invaded by Mathilde. But the power of memory is also a considerable force, and Fernand's subjection to Félicité after her death is intensified. The boy who had found security under his mother's cape, as though tucked under "une aile noire," draws strength from her as a spirit, reigning on her throne, "sa mère majestueuse, dominatrice."

Félicité's slow-moving bulk is recalled rather in the form of a goddess; indeed as two deities both of whom reveal aspects of his mother's nature which are important to Fernand. The first implied in the passage: "Vieil Enée, près de sombrer, il tendait vers la 'génitrix' toute-puissante ses mains de suppliant" (p. 198). If it is kept in mind that Aeneas was the son of Aphrodite, his plea to her as a source of love is unmistakable. But Félicité is more. She is also indirectly seen as Juno, a female all-powerful Jupiter, with formidable bolts of lightning and thunder. Juno also is the patron-ess of the female sex and implicitly the goddess of mothers. These component motifs bear correlative themes of Fernand's sensual adoration, and his awe of his mother. "Vaincu, il adorait celle qui avait été forte."

Correlative by contrast is the view held concurrently of Mathilde, of whom Fernand says, "... la mort ne te déifiait plus. Mais Fernand se rappelait ce dos rond, cet air battu, ses yeux de chatte pourchassée" (p. 198).

Also correlative by contrast to his adoration of his mother is Fernand's hostility toward Félicité, based, not on regret for the needlessly dead girl, but rather toward his mother as a source of deprivation and loss. Like the indulged child he has been for 50 years, he reacts to Mathilde's absence:

> Si sa mère était entrée, il lui eût crié: "Je ne veux pas que Mathilde soit morte!" du même ton qu'enfant il exigeait que tout le monde se couchât quand il était malade, ou que le jour de la fête, on dévissât pour lui l'un des chevaux de bois. (p. 79)

A linking image in the scene which follows his and Félicité's harsh encounter, reasserts this theme, but with the difference that his meditations on his own nature and that of love made him aware of his childishness.

> ... tandis que lui, l'enfant pourri, qui pendant un demi-siècle a brisé l'un après l'autre tous ses jouets, il a perdu le dernier au moment qu'il venait d'en découvrir le prix incalculable. (p. 143)

This concludes a theme which had first appeared at the beginning of the novel, as Mathilde lay dying, and she understood in the sensation of "ce brisement... éternel," what had happened to her.

> Corps rompu, non par la maladie, songe-t-elle, mais sous les coups de cet homme et de cette vieille femme.... (p. 48)

The insensitive man who, as noted earlier, could not visualize a frightening image his mother sought to conjure before him, "faute d'imagination, il ne le vit pas," experiences something of a miracle as he stands at Mathilde's bier. He *is* able, in a contrasting component motif, to see in the flawless face of Mathilde what she would have been:

> Heureuse, adorée, peut-être Mathilde vivante aurait-elle eu la figure que voilà, inondée de paix, cette figure dé-livrée. "Aveugle... aveugle...." (p. 76)

This question of what both Fernand and his wife might have been, had they not been fixed in their orbits in life by circumstances and conditions, inherited attitudes and values, is treated in several ways. We have already touched upon these qualifications in reviewing themes of the plot as affecting the source of motivation and direction of purposes. What they individually, optimally, might have achieved had they been granted the liberty to do so, was their transformation into sexually responsive people, generous and loving, in selfless concern for each other.

A central theme of the story, the capacity of the individual for achievement — in this case speaking of loving sexual fulfillment — is carried by motifs pertaining variously to thirst, water, and the

sea. The unsatisfied state in which Fernand has passed his first
fifty years is suggested in the parched earth, "De seconde en
seconde augmentait la soif de la terre tourturée" (p. 117).
In a linking image the connection to Fernand is clarified:

> ... sa vie était devant ses yeux, désert morne. Comment
> avait-il peu, sans mourir de soif, traverser tout ce sable?
> Mais, cette soif qu'il n'avait pas ressentie pendant des
> années, voici qu'il en découvrait la torture. (p. 130)

The mounting tension of Fernand's increased awareness and
desire finds release in the arrival of long-awaited summer rains.
"Il se rapprocha de la fenêtre. Quelques gouttes de pluie avaient
dû choir, car il sentit l'odeur de la terre violentée" (p. 132). The
brief burst of rain is not the answer to the need of the consumed
earth's surface. Another linking image suggests the onset of a
rainy period but of a different character:

> ... un chuchotement éveilla la mère et le fils. Les feuilles
> aspiraient ... si avidement qu'il fallut près d'une heure
> avant que la pluie touchât réellement la face consumée
> du monde, et que la terre en fût transpercée, et que
> montât son odeur — odeur du désir loin encore de l'as-
> souvissement mais déjà transmuée en joie. (p. 145)

The violence resulting from repressed sexuality which seeks its
outlet in rare assaults is unrelated to contented fulfillment, and is
more closely identified with frustration. In yet another linking
image, Fernand continues to ponder his loss ever more profoundly,
watching the rain.

> ... de nouveau [il] colla à la vitre sa face. Ainsi demeura-
> t-il longtemps dans une torpeur douce, écoutant le bruit
> répété, obstiné d'une seule goutte sur une feuille de
> magnolia qui touchait la fenêtre. (p. 172)

In contrast to the theme of peace and tranquility to be found
in satisfied love, or even by extension, the search for peace in the
certainty of death, is the theme of violence erupting from repressed
sexuality. What might be called the "Michelet" leitmotif is presented in the following component motifs, when Félicité looks on
Mathilde's corpse with such hatred that "Mathilde vivante ne

pouvait soutenir le regard dont la vieille couve son corps à jamais indifférent" (p. 68). Félicité, in a rare moment of shame, realizes the monstrosity of the desire contained in her fury as she recalls an illustration in her Michelet history. "... un Pape, ayant fait déterrer son prédecesseur, le juge, le condamne, s'acharne sur sa momie" (p. 68).

This theme appears again in the linking image of Félicité's looking at Mathilde's photograph set apart in a frame by an adoring Fernand:

> Elle s'arrêta, puis fit un pas vers le guéridon, ébaucha, les mains en avant, le geste d'un Polyeucte briseur d'idoles. Cracher sur cette image, la déchirer, la piétiner.... (p. 103)

If there is any doubt that this anger derives from a sexual rage, one need only recall the aqueous motifs already associated with sensual pleasure. Here we find, "une marée de fureur de nouveau la souleva..." (p. 102); she angrily finds Mathilde's photo set "dans un cadre de coquillages (souvenir d'Arcachon)," a seaside resort visited by Fernand and Félicité in their happy private past. Following these moments of nearly intolerable stress, we read, "Le sang chuchotait à ses oreilles comme si, dans une coquille, elle eût écouté la mer" (p. 104). The frenzy ends when Félicité takes her daughter-in-law's place, and lies on the bed where Fernand now finds his pleasure in dreaming of the delights which might have been possible with Mathilde: "... une invisible main la poussa vers le lit, l'abattit sur cette couche où Mathilde avait souffert, était morte" (p. 104).

In contrast to the theme of exploitative pagan sensuality which has been proposed in the component motifs of love goddesses, gods and idols, is the Christian theme of One Love. This concept, drawn from Mauriac's attachment to the writings of Lacordaire, implies that all human love emanates from a single origin, the primary generator and reservatory of love being the One God. Separation from this eternal source, as a consequence of original sin or by willful exclusion of the divine presence, results in the loss of man's ability to participate in the gift of Love. He cannot offer or receive its benefits. Although a case could be made in *Génitrix* for a Platonic doctrine of Love and Beauty originating in a single source, there are specific motifs which make the link secure with Chris-

tianity. It is young Raymond, learning his catechism, who in a kind
of chorus effect, recapitulates the nature of love. "Il répétait:
'Il y a donc trois Dieux?' comme s'il n'avait pas su qu'il n'y a
qu'un seul Dieu — qu'un seul amour" (p. 163). Félicité's assurance
that such is the case is tenuous. This child of les Landes, where
"...la Terreur en avait chassé les prêtres," and whose mother
received her First Communion only as part of the marriage cer-
emony, is less a daughter of Christ, than a kind of savage soul:

> Les enfants landais... n'adoraient que le soleil impla-
> cable... cette toute puissance du feu — dieu rapide et
> qui court insaisissable....

Adoration, in Félicité's sense, is seen thereby in its destructive
nature. Exploiting the love object for pleasure, and the continual
"taking," is essentially at odds with the concept of One Love,
which depends on constant giving to provide happiness to another,
and to the giver. It is part of Fernand's discovery, too late, that
"notre corps lui-même cherche, découvre son plaisir enfoui hors
de lui, tout mêlé à la chair d'un autre corps que nous rendons
heureux." Therein is translated into the simplest terms of volupté,
the fundamental Christian teaching: to give is to receive.

Two themes — solitude and fear — appeared as important but
secondary themes of the story, as consequences or negative out-
growths of the exclusion of man from God's love. The universality
of such effects is underscored as each of the characters shows
similar vulnerability in his isolated exposure to unknown dangers.
Nearly identical component motifs can be illustrative of these
themes. Mathilde in her agony hears familiar, often frightening
sounds:

> Le chien sous le perron, gronda, puis son aboi furieux
> éclata parce que quelqu'un marchait sur la petite route
> entre le jardin et la gare. Elle se dit: "Hier encore, que
> j'aurais eu peur." Dans cette maison immense, toujours
> tressaillante, et dont les portes-fenêtres n'étaient pas même
> défendues par des volets pleins, elle avait connu des nuits
> de terreur folle.... (p. 15)

Félicité shares such an experience as she lies unaccustomedly alone
in her room without the protection of Fernand's sleeping nearby:

> Soudain elle se dressa:
> —On a marché dans le jardin.
> Avait-on vraiment marché?... Félicité fit craquer une
> allumette, n'entendit plus rien, éteignait de nouveau. Mais
> en esprit elle vit, au milieu des ténèbres, cette grande mai-
> son sans défense, les portes-fenêtres sans volets. (p. 109)

Fernand is left alone, at the end of the novel, conscious of his
isolation, in a silence "plus profond que les autres soirs,"

> Rêvait-il que quelqu'un marchait dans le jardin? Non,
> puisque Péliou hurla furieusement.... Fernand songea
> qu'il avait oublié de tourner les verrous. Il entendit que
> cédait, sous une simple poussée, la grande porte, mais il
> n'éprouvait aucune peur. (p. 219)

In such cases, the fear had been a generalized one, emanating
from the silent darkness outside the house and the lack of emotional and personal security of those within. Mathilde was finally
protected by the tide of fever which rendered her untouchable,
while Fernand's spiritual and physical lassitude prevent full response to the stimulus of fear. Félicité is the only one of the three,
characteristically, to take the offensive at once. She will have
shutters installed by Fernand, but in memory of Mathilde (for
whom she had not been so obliging in the girl's frightened lifetime).
Cynically, Félicité will make the request in Mathilde's name in
the knowledge that Fernand, "le comblerait par dévotion."

A similar trio of linking phrases recalls the fear of death, with
none of its promise, which haunts the characters. None of them
fears le néant of death, but all of them greedily seeking to hold
on to life, fear dying. Frightening physical conditions provide the
common motif.

> Mathilde, dans un geste d'exécration, avait levé les deux
> mains... les tint un instant devant ses yeux, stupéfaite
> qu'elles fussent violacées. (p. 61)

> Fernand s'approcha, puis s'éloigna de l'armoire, ayant vu
> dans la glace sa tête effrayante — comme si déjà était en
> lui la corruption que, à trois mètres de là, travaillait
> Mathilde. (p. 82)

Félicité eut peur dans la glace de ses joues violacées. (p. 100)

* * *

Mauriac's dexterity is evident in the creation, in a relatively short novel, of a remarkable variety of linking images to support a single generically coherent theme. The theme of a universal fear of the unknown is revealed in what are nightmarish qualities of grotesque faces. Each of the three characters in *Génitrix* is a victim of such terror.

"L'épouvantail," which Félicité tried to create before Fernand's eyes will be recalled in the opening pages of the novel. Mathilde sees a body washed up on the shore, in the *cauchemar* of her fever, and on approaching it, finds it to be a faceless mass of corruption (p. 56). Even Félicité experiences the same infantile fright as she senses her vulnerability in the unshuttered house. "Elle imagina une face sournoise aplatie contre la vitre" (p. 110).

That is not nearly so terrifying, however, as a real shock she experiences. Hoping to restore their relations to a pre-Mathilde status, Félicité approaches Fernand as he stands in the garden. His face is in shadow beneath the brim of his *canotier*. He removes his hat when she reaches him, and she must hold back a cry "devant les ravages de cette face" (p. 118).

Other similar motifs appear as Chapter XII concludes, when the cold winter rain is pouring down. The spirit of Mathilde has usurped Félicité's pre-eminence, and amid motifs suggesting the dead girl's presence in the room, it is read. "Dans l'ombre, une bassine de cuivre étincelait comme une face brûlante." The following chapter ends as grotesquely, but more concretely. Fernand was watching the continuing January downpour, "et de nouveau colla à la vitre sa face" (p. 172). He has not heard his mother's strangling sounds, and turns to find her face contorted: "La langue sortait un peu de la bouche du côté gauche qui était immobile; l'autre se contractait, grimaçait" (p. 173).

* * *

Such terrifying moments, so much a part of the lives of the unloved and unloving, call for some kind of antidote to their spiritual sickness. Mathilde's solution to the deprivations and persecutions of a lifetime, and to the loss of her child, is a tender dream of escape. She imagines the safety and calm of a final refuge: "Ce royaume où se fut enfermée avec la petite enfant n'aurait pas été du monde. Ceux qui la haïssaient n'auraient pu l'y poursuivre" (p. 28). A similar component motif, that of a beatific retreat, appears at the end of the novel when Fernand seeks relief from the immediate pressures caused by the presence of Marie's discordant children:

> Un apaisement lui venait, un détachement comme s'il eût pressenti au delà de sa vie atroce, au delà de sa propre dureté, un royaume d'amour et de silence où sa mère était une autre que celle dont il venait d'être possédé... où Mathilde tournait vers lui un visage détendu... un sourire de bienheureuse. (p. 203)

Fernand's climactic vision at the end of the novel where all is ordered into a happy, blessed sphere of contentment comes after he has been drinking some wine. His experience of a first glimpse of eternity following Mathilde's death, when life was seen for the first time in all its potential, had also been "un peu touché d'alcool...." Even Mathilde's dream of celestial satisfaction was interwoven with the delirium of fever, as Félicité had been "ivre de sa défaite" when she saw a blessed life of renunciation ahead in selfless love of Fernand. Mauriac speaks when he tells the reader "...il suffit souvent d'une ivresse légère pour que nous pressentions l'éternité" (p. 216).

Motifs supporting cyclical themes of life and death, of death and rebirth recur frequently. As Fernand and Félicité "regardaient mourir et renaître la flamme d'une bûche" in their office, Fernand was seeking in books, "le secret de la vie et de la mort" (p. 19). As he selects an apothegm of Spinoza on the desirability of meditating on life rather than death, *la mort* is entering Mathilde's room upstairs.

Félicité did not hide successfully her satisfaction on her husband's death, at freedom from "cet attachement d'habitude" which was her marriage. She instead turns to Fernand, and is overjoyed at the prospect of a future of passionate devotion to him alone:

... elle répéta en l'embrassant: "C'est une nouvelle vie
qui commence." (p. 65)

She has the same hope when Fernand, after his initial compulsive
visits to Mathilde's grave, stops the daily pilgrimages:

> ... voici qu'il se relâchait enfin! Félicité se dit en elle-
> même: "C'est le commencement."

She determines in a final convulsive effort after their serious quarrel to regenerate vitality and purpose in Fernand's withdrawn,
indifferent existence:

> ... elle lui rendrait le goût de la vie, l'enfanterait une
> seconde fois.

Fernand's preoccupation is similar, but more successful, in that
he does indeed revivify Mathilde and derive the rewards of tranquility from his creation. "il aimait Mathilde au point de l'avoir
ressuscitée et se persuadait de sa présence en lui, hors de lui"
(p. 166). A background litany in close textual proximity to these
contemplations is heard in Raymond's rote-learning of the Credo,
"Résurrection de la chair ... résurrection de la chair" (p. 170).

* * *

The interesting figure of Marie de Lados, servant in the
Cazenave household, provides the substance of two sequentially-
ordered, textually apposed motifs which embody the redemptive
themes of death and rebirth. Materially they are unrelated to the
linking phrases which made a clear pattern in the generic coherence
discussion on this general theme. They could stand independently
in illustration of the theme just cited.

Marie, as her name befits, is first revealed as a Virgin Mother
figure, suggestive of the flight into Egypt, as she carries the sleeping
child, Raymond:

> ... un sourire ineffable fit resplender son visage taillé dans
> du vieux buis, sa face de Vierge noire ... elle le prit
> dans ses bras. La tête charmante était inerte, les jambes
> égratignées et sales balançaient des souliers ferrés comme
> les sabots d'un petit âne.

Immediately following is a continuation of the description which is a second, complementary motif:

> Elle l'emporta sans fléchir: elle avait été à douze ans servante de métayer... et on l'obligeait à tenir dans chaque main, la main d'un enfant, et on attachait le nouveau-né sur son frêle dos: s'il pleurait, elle était battue....

This cruciform image of one who is punished, in effect, for the sins of others completes a picture of redemption. Marie de Lados thereby bears the child like a Madonna and like a Cross.

* * *

In contrast with the pagan overtones of sensuality already touched on may be indicated other motifs of crucifixion, with the implications of the redemptive qualities of suffering. Félicité sees a haggard son emerge from his retreat in Mathilde's room, "Lèvres plus blanches que s'il s'était abreuvé de vinaigre..." (p. 118). Again textual proximity, although in a changed setting, takes Fernand to Mathilde's bed where beneath the white, shroud-like curtains, supported by "une flèche," Fernand lies, "couché sur le dos, les yeux fermés, les mains jointes sur le drap, les pieds droits, comme était Mathilde morte..." (p. 120).

The motif of "une flèche," the spear in Christ's side, is repeated in the pain endured by Félicité on hearing Fernand's injurious remark that he is kind to her only for Mathilde's sake, moments before her stroke. Once stricken, Félicité realizes in Fernand's reluctant willingness to stay near her speechless, motionless person, that

> C'était près de la troisième heure, l'instant de l'éponge offerte à la victime. Ah, plus amer que le fiel sur ce visage tendu [of Fernand] était tant d'amour dont une autre qu'elle recevait l'offrande. ... elle ne savait pas qu'elle était crucifiée. (p. 176)

Correlative by contrast to the theme of the story which revealed the individual's capacity for self-realization, and by inference the exercise of free will to achieve moral maturity, is the theme of a controlling, predisposed destiny. This might be seen as a non-Christian counterpoint which frees the individual from responsibility for the formation of his own character. We recall that Félicité abdicates her ultimate responsibility in her daughter-in-law's last moments, inwardly yielding: "Que les destins s'accomplissent." An implication remains that Félicité's shrill, brutal "Bon Voyage" catapulted Fernand on a final trip to Bordeaux over which he had no control, and "par quoi fut fixé son destin" (p. 52). It is this same presumably hostile, omniscient force which hounds Fernand from his final refuge near Marie de Lados at the end of the novel: "Mais, il fallait que le destin poursuivît Fernand Cazenave..." (p. 192). Not instinct, not a gift of God, but "le destin jouait ce jeu étrange d'éveiller dans ce vieil homme des eaux enfouies à quelles profondeurs."

No opportunity is afforded whereby these characters might have created their own destinies from their own substance. Their dreams, however belated, of a potential as yet untried are cruel tricks by which all human endeavor to love is suspended and all such hopes are doomed to disappointment.

These larger cosmic games are seen in microcosm as the unloving characters avoid the generosity of self needed to generate and sustain love. There is the inference to be drawn that individuals are puppets, incapable of initiative, fated to respond to human and supernatural manipulation. Mathilde's mockery, for example, which allows her to play on the reactions of those she is involved with, is part of her anticipation that handling Fernand will be no problem after her recovery. "Ce ne serait qu'un jeu de lui passer la bride" (p. 32). She pledges not to make the same mistake as formerly of overplaying her hand. "C'était croire au gain d'une partie pas même engagée." The ritual jousts of Fernand and Félicité have already been noted as "les ébats d'un autre couple...." Fernand knew well that Félicité often acted out responses she did not necessarily feel: "...elle crut l'entendre enfin et déjà se composait un visage indifférent." Knowing of her own predilection for acting, Félicité attributes the same qualities to Fernand: "Elle y discerna... un air détendu, presque paisible, que d'abord elle voulut croire joué" (p. 148). The time does come for an end to role-playing, and Félicité does not hide her coldness as Fernand moves to Mathilde's room: "Fernand pensa qu'elle voulait jouer serré. Non, elle ne jouait plus aucun jeu" (p. 107).

The characteristic of individuals to use such *persona* to create a role is a theme which parallels the use of others for our own purposes. It is self-aggrandizement at the expense of another, and not unrelated to the theme of meanness by which Fernand takes what he wishes with no consideration given, and at minimum expense to himself.

It is never known whether Mathilde's death-bed prayer was answered:

> Souvenez-vous, ô Vierge toute pleine de bonté, que jusqu'à ce jour on n'a point entendu dire qu'aucun de ceux qui se sont mis sous votre protection ... ont imploré votre secours, ait jamais été abandonné. (p. 30)

Nor is it known whether Fernand so prayed, but when transposed to the temporal level, the arrival of Marie de Lados in the closing phrases of the book, the "vierge noire," who also was never known to refuse requests for help, under whose protection Fernand will henceforth live, assures that he, too, will not be abandoned in this world. A prayer, perhaps unuttered, has been answered, following Fernand's visit to the shrine of Marie de Lados in the *soupente* where in a shaft of pure, brilliant moonlight, a plaster statue of the Virgin Mary, hands outstretched and welcoming, looked kindly down on Fernand's frozen tears.

CHAPTER III

LE DÉSERT DE L'AMOUR

THEMES OF THE STORY

Le Désert de l'amour is told in retrospect, triggered into conscious recall by a contingent incident: the meeting in a Paris nightclub of Raymond Courrèges and a woman he knows as Maria Cross. This chance encounter brings to conclusion a story which began twenty years earlier, the components of which, presented in their linear progression, will be seen to yield the themes of the story.

Raymond Courrèges, 17, a day student still in the unkempt awkwardness of adolescence, returns daily by tramway to his home where the solidly established family of his father, Dr. Paul Courrèges, lives. Although his abrasive personality makes him "la plaie de la famille," the other members are more importantly involved in their individual concerns. The doctor, overworked and distracted by outside commitments, wants a closer relationship with his son but is inarticulate. Lucie, his bitter, neglected wife sees Raymond automatically as something needing better grooming and manners. Their daughter, Madeleine, her husband, Gaston, and their two children, live communal, yet separate lives under the family roof. Mme Courrèges, the doctor's mother, is tactfully self-effacing in her daughter-in-law's home, but passionate in her love and understanding of her son.

The name of Maria Cross, a local minor celebrity as mistress of a prominent married Bordelais, becomes a topic for family discussion on the occasion of the meningitis death of her son, François. The doctor reveals to his astonished family, that the child had been his patient and the mother has become thereby an acquaintance.

Raymond has accumulated funds and gifts of money to flee Bordeaux and pass the summer in Spain. Adolescent inner turmoil incapacitates him, and he spends instead an anguished, turbulent summer in the burning city. Paul Courrèges' interest in Maria Cross leaves the professional level, and his visits to her, ostensibly as her physician, in the home provided by her lover, become obsessively the focal point of his existence.

With the resumption of the fall season, Raymond's life is restored to some equilibrium by the supportive structure of school discipline. His father, however, is increasingly anguished as Maria Cross fails to respond to his unspoken offering of love. He divines painfully that her classification of him as a "saint," covers a fundamental, bored disinterest in him. In succeeding weeks, every effort is made to obliterate his agony in work and research, but the doctor cannot rid himself of desire for the languid, indolent woman. He does observe a dramatic change in his son. Raymond now devotes considerable time to his appearance, following his attraction to a fellow-passenger in the tram, the beautiful Maria Cross, who makes daily visits to her son's grave. His interest is reciprocated, and by silent common assent, the boy and the woman never approach each other among the exhausted, grimy workers.

After a long period, Maria Cross invites the doctor to a Sunday tea while her lover is at the bullfights. Delayed in arriving, Paul meets her as she is leaving. Her exhilaration alerts him that she has a love interest elsewhere. He does not declare his passion (a scene carefully rehearsed), but goes home disillusioned and determined to make amends to his wife. His efforts to restore closer relations with Lucie are disappointing (to her as well) while Raymond grows in assurance regarding his seductive charm.

It is a power failure on the tram which unites Raymond and Maria Cross. His excitement is intensified when he learns her identity. She invites him to her home, justifying doing so in chaste and maternal terms. His objective, especially with what he knows to be a "kept woman," is explicit sexual conquest. Father and son share a desire to talk of her once Raymond reveals his awareness of her identity, but their discussion only drives them apart.

Raymond's first visit to the Cross establishment is disappointing; the second is profoundly humiliating as Maria Cross, in fear and revulsion, rejects his forceful amorous advances. The boy does not recover from the episode, while his father rises from a sickbed to attend Maria Cross, victim of a fall from a window. Paul Courrèges is professionally detached in his care of her. He leaves her house in a state of collapse, to find his wife waiting to take him home and nurse him. Raymond disappears on a six-day debauch in the port of Bordeaux.

Seventeen years later, Raymond Courrèges sits alone in a regularly visited nightclub, with a letter in his pocket from Paul Courrèges, who is in the city for a few days and who is at his son's disposition to visit. Raymond's discomfiture at this prospect is not at first increased by the arrival of a couple—an overbearing, sclerotic man and his female companion. Raymond remembers the man as Victor Larousselle from by-gone Bordeaux days, and his companion as Maria Cross.

She recognizes Raymond and only gradually lets him realize it. It is the arrogant Larousselle who forces a greeting from Raymond and brings him to Maria's table where Raymond is amazed to learn that the couple is married. Raymond and Maria Cross take Larousselle, in drunken collapse, to the couple's apartment. Worried about appearances, Maria thanklessly accepts Raymond's offer to have his father come to attend to Victor.

Paul Courrèges, now old and feeble, attempts to reestablish a relationship with Maria. Her indifference shows itself as in the past. Raymond sees his father to his hotel and once alone, the son roams the Paris streets till dawn, wondering how he can exploit his reacquaintance with Maria. He evaluates his seventeen-years of numberless conquests, and highly developed science of debauch, as a failure. A final gesture of filial affection takes him to the train where he has what is implied to be a brief and final visit with Paul Courrèges who is returning to die under the solicitous protection of his wife, Lucie.

Raymond's tram-rides from his school to his home are a period of deliverance from harassment. "Chassé de la classe," he delights in finding himself "seul enfin parmi des êtres indifférents." Numerous motifs emphasize his removal from familiar life during these adventurous moments. The winter night cuts the tram occupants off from the rest of the world. They are riding in something like a "feu de bengale mouvant," and are as isolated from humanity as are the passengers of "le Titanic." Class and caste differences between him and the workers around him allow him to feel tenderness toward their grimy fragility without danger of obligation or commitment.

The motif of the family group clustered around a single, inadequate lamp, in hostility and suspicion, suggests the meanness of this family circle. His sister, he notes, is less interested in him than in the dog. Bitter words are unleashed on his arrival; an atmosphere of petty recrimination pervades the group. Mealtimes bring into focus the harshness of life in the intimacy of the family. Against a minor-key chorus of domestic complaints, the late-arriving doctor brings medical journals to read at the table. Madeline Basque and her husband, with the four children like "des oiseaux apprivoisés sur un bâton," stay apart, "... un îlot de méfiance et de secret ... indifférents à ce qui ne les touchait pas ..." (p. 22). [1] Lucie Courrèges is the one who feels most acutely her isolation amid the others. Of her relationship with her daughter's family, "Ils ne me disent rien," is a repeated motif. She is as well, "l'épouse amère" who hopes for little recognition in her husband's life: "... il n'y aurait jamais ... un intervalle de repos pendant lequel ... il lui‚ eût accordé le don total de quelques instants" (p. 42).

The theme of distance—in this case, separating Paul Courrèges from his wife—is reiterated in her incredulity on learning that he knows Maria Cross well. His plans to attend the funeral of the Cross child stupefy his wife, and he leaves, "... comme s'il ne l'avait pas entendu, comme s'il ne la voyait pas" (p. 35).

Each morning sees Raymond taken toward school by his father in their carriage. Paul Courrèges, in what should be optimum conditions for confidences, cannot make contact with his son. This is the same man "... qui, quelques instants plus tard, parlerait d'abondance, avec autorité ..." (p. 24).

---

[1] François Mauriac, *Le Désert de l'amour* (Paris: Grasset, 1925). Subsequent references are to this edition and are placed in the text in parentheses.

A description of Paul Courrèges as "un enterré vivant" will be a motif to appear again in other areas of interpersonal relationships. His efforts at guidance of his son, or at camaraderie, were repudiated when the boy "feignait de dormir" and "... insensiblement, l'enfant a délivré sa main" (p. 28). The doctor is making other approaches toward igniting loving response, in his relationship with Maria Cross. His defense of Maria against the vindictive comments of the Courrèges women arouses Raymond's interest in hearing more: "... la jeune proie s'offrait à lui..." but the doctor has turned his attention elsewhere. The obsessive nature of the doctor's attraction to "cette femme étendue" entirely drains his interest in family concerns.

Maria Cross has violated the code of acceptable bourgeois behavior in being the mistress of a rich Bordelais whose wife is dying. She is "une drôlesse," says Lucie Courrèges, who calls the death of François, a young, legitimate son of Maria, "la justice de Dieu." The Bordeaux community deplored Maria Cross' decision to have an elaborate, expensive funeral. "Quel manque de tact! ..." it is called, in view of her irregular standing in the social hierarchy and her particularly undistinguished family background.

At seventeen, Raymond's adolescent turmoil is at its most agonizing. Motifs of a burning, rainless summer under "un ciel intolérable," parallel those of the "flamme intérieure" of Raymond. As in the sandy pine woods around Bordeaux, heat concentrates and accumulates, so it does in "la jeune forêt humaine" of Raymond and his contemporaries. His preoccupation with salacious literature and pictures earns him the disapproval of his masters: "Il a perdu la foi" (p. 38). This theme is supported by such a motif as: Raymond Courrèges jetait aux orties l'uniforme et la casquette qu'ornait le monogramme de la Vierge" (p. 38). This in its turn carries the implication that his virginity, too, was thrown into the nettles as he carouses "avec un catin sans âge."

It is a joyless period for Raymond who is convinced of his ugliness: "Raymond Courrèges était beau et ne doutait point d'être un monstre de laideur, de saleté. Il se faisait horreur.... Il avait honte de son corps" (p. 40). The boy's frustration reaches such an intensity that he plans suicide. Locating his father's hidden revolver, his intention is thwarted since "... Dieu ne voulait pas qu'il en trouvât les balles" (p. 45). A contingent incident—the appearance of a swollen, putrifying animal carcass floating in the lake—ends in disgust his thoughts of drowning himself. Correlative by contrast is the theme soon to be encountered, following his first views of Maria Cross, when as a result of her approving interest, he becomes "sûr de plaire et occupé à séduire" (p. 72). The supportive framework of school discipline reorganizes the diffused emotional mass that is Raymond, and he finds comfort in familiar routines and the renewed rides in the tram.

His father, conscientious physician and scrupulous researcher, has rearranged his life to accommodate late afternoon visits with Maria Cross. He is indifferent to her tawdry surroundings: "...une allée mal entretenue ... aucun domestique ... chaise cassée ... luxe et misère ... déchirures des tapis ... les plis des rideaux dissimulaient des trous..." (p. 52). The compassion shown by Paul Courrèges for a stricken mother and child turns into passion: his desire is not to cure but to caress Maria Cross; not to protect her but to possess her. "Dévoré de désirs," his original contentment with "silence amoureux" (p. 52) fades with the summer, and subsequent visits embolden his ambition. The doctor's aspirations reach a climax in his determination, carefully elaborated, to leave his family and ask Maria to follow him, in spite of her repeated attempts to cast him in an avuncular role. He reluctantly recognizes that she has created for herself the role of disciple, and has relegated him to that of spiritual director. "C'est difficile à introduire ... une allusion amoureuse ... avec une femme déférente ... qui le revêt d'une paternité spirituelle" (p. 52). His discouragement is profound when her wishes are clumsily and insensitively transparent. She writes him: "Votre exemple, vos enseignements me suffisent: nous sommes unis au-delà de toute présence ... vos lettres me suffisent, mon cher directeur de conscience" (p. 78). Yet Paul Courrèges cannot control his desires or even his imaginings: "...comme un chien retrouve l'os enterré, il revenait à ses imaginations dont parfois il avait honte" (p. 86). The discrepancy between these reveries, in a man of science, and his professional commitment is revealed as he pompously rebukes his assistant: "Non, mon cher, chez le vrai savant il est impossible que, sauf éclipses passagères, la science ne l'emporte sur l'amour" (p. 125). He has the grace to blush, as the worshipful young man, complimenting the devotion of the doctor to science declares:

"...je n'en vois guère [savants] qui aient été de vrais passionnés"
(p. 125).

The theme of the limitations imposed by a practical reality on
fantasy is underscored by repeated references to the unchecked, ir-
rational soaring of man's expectations: "il ... ne se croyait pas
différent des autres hommes qui ... étaient fous dès qu'ils se
trouvaient seuls avec eux-mêmes et hors du contrôle d'autrui"
(p. 87). The pain caused by the distance between the ideal and the
attainable is emphasized in the doctor's realization:

> ...lorsqu'il était loin de Maria Cross... il n'existait point
> d'obstacles qu'un amour comme le sien ne pût traverser...
> mais dès qu'il retrouvait la jeune femme... il se rendait
> à l'évidence de son malheur irrémédiable. (p. 54)

Raymond enjoys a kind of fantasy life in the impersonal vessel
of the tramway, which carries its human cargo in steerage. Motifs
which reinforce the idea of fantasy are seen in the train cutting
through the winter evening shadows as would a ship through
waves of the sea. It passes among trees of coral and through
gardens of the deep. The appearance of a beautiful, well-groomed
woman in the rush-hour, working class train, fits smoothly into
his visionary voyage. Her calm, steady observation of him, "Comme
elle l'observait pourtant!" (p. 62), arouses none of his recent
stress about his appearance. He does not know that unkempt
though he is, his disreputable appearance is not of the same sort
as it is of their fellow-passengers. Maria sees it at once, however:
"Cela n'est rien que la terre qui souille le fruit intact, soudain
détaché de la branche, et que, d'une main précautionneuse, tu
ramasses" (p. 62).

Motifs of thawing earth carry the theme of Raymond's ef-
florescence into manhood. "...la brume recelait cette douceur
secrète de la saison qui approchait. La terre était nue, mais elle
ne dormait plus" (p. 64). Surely this land is the same "pays inconnu" which Maria Cross sees beneath its coating of school-boy
grime and ink. A linking image compares the emergent young man
to a goddess in a tree, and under Maria's continued gaze as the
trips continue, "un être neuf" is born. Earlier motifs had included
Raymond and his schoolmates among "...ce troupeau d'enfants
près de mourir, et d'hommes près de naître" (p. 38).

Maria can now do without the crutch of Doctor Courrèges' support. "Mon cher docteur, qu'importe en somme de ne plus nous voir?" (p. 78). Although such an anticipation is incomprehensible to him, Paul is revolted by her complacent insincerity. He embarks on a regime which will require thinking of her as "à une morte," and will "... attendre soi-même la mort, en doublant la dose du travail" (p. 81). He will survive by the use of "... l'opium d'une besogne forcenée." He will save himself by "... une fatigue immense ... une lassitude sans nom" which will enable him to bury himself. This theme is in contrast with the fantasies which seek to liberate this "enterré vivant" from a living tomb. The motif of work as a life-saving, death-giving drug is used repeatedly as the physician uses one narcotic to free himself from addiction to another.

That he is not successful in making a complete break from Maria is evident in his rationalization he must continue his visits, but on a professional basis. "Mais lui, qui se scandalisait de ce que les autres se mentaient à eux-mêmes, il se dupa encore: 'Elle a besoin de moi: je me dois à elle comme à tout malade...'" (p. 81). The torture of awaiting a reply to this proposal is merely a substitute for the former anguished intervals between rendez-vous, and is relieved by an invitation to tea, while Larousselle is at the Sunday bullfights. He determined that the visit will be one he will control. He will set a tone "plus intime, plus confidentiel," so that "... il pourrait déclarer sa passion." He justifies his frenzy to rid himself of his family. "A cinquante-deux ans, il est temps encore de savourer quelques années d'un bonheur..." (p. 86). "Un enterré vivant a le droit, s'il le peut, de soulever la pierre qui l'étouffe" (p. 88). He calls for comparison with the animal world where mate and young are abandoned when the rearing function ends. He recalls that Christ preferred as disciples those who had left their wives and children.

A lingering sense of hypocrisy pursues Paul Courrèges as he makes his way through the bullfight crowds to Maria Cross. Buffeted by an approaching storm and the intoxicated spectators, he recalls his insistence to a patient that the man conquer his emotions and assume control of his life. Hurrying past the parade of bullfighters, he sees "les cochers ... sordides et glorieux" as he presses on to the "luxe et misère" of Maria's house. He is impressed by the sense of integrity he sees in the faces of the matadors, in contrast to the cheap sentimentalism and false culture he lamented in gifts from his patients in the office he just left. The doctor's anticipated control of the interview is gone immediately he sees Maria, not "sur la chaise longue," but leaving her house, without her usual mourning attire. He is seized by "une lâcheté immense" at losing this round with destiny. Jealousy, in his certainty that she was leaving to meet a man, is met with teasing incredulity on her part: " 'Ah ça, docteur, seriez-vous jaloux?' . . . elle n'aurait pu même imaginer que le docteur éprouvât un sentiment de cet ordre" (p. 100). He is so defeated by her obsequiousness and thinly-veiled rudeness that on departing, he refuses an umbrella, in the fear that it might become an excuse to see her again. Although he had but recently declared, "il n'y a rien que mon tourment," he now asserts: ". . . rien ne devait plus compter pour lui que [son] travail . . . renonciation totale. . . ."

As he had planned after earlier renunciations of Maria Cross (like the renunciations by all the characters in this work, they come only after failure, negating any redemptive value), Dr. Courrèges intends to compensate his wife for past slights and neglect. Lucie responds eagerly and quickly to his suggestion of a stroll after dinner. She runs "avec une hâte inaccoutumée," to join him, and he is touched at memories which assail him. ". . . la chair de Lucie avait la même odeur qu'autrefois quand ils étaient fiancés . . . le parfum même de ses fiançailles que cette odeur de chair et d'ombre" (p. 106). Motifs of "un rossignol parcimonieux" and "le parfum d'amande amère" foretell the theme of pettiness and bitterness which have pitifully overtaken the life of Lucie. After a numbing discourse on domestic problems, she is aware ". . . qu'elle l'avait déçu." He feels drowned in defeat. "Il sentit en lui descendre une marée—un reflux qui entraînait des confidences, des aveux, des abandons, des larmes" (p. 108). He meets the anguish head-on with his own prescription for relief of pain: "Travail, opium unique . . ." (p. 135).

It is the contingent incident of a power failure on the tram that brings Maria and Raymond into communication. The lack of power in the lines is more than compensated for in the current of excitement running between Maria Cross and the boy. While discussing a suggestion of walking home together, Raymond identifies himself. A mild panic is added to the sentiments "de scrupule, de honte et de délice" circulating in Maria. She fears that revealing her name will repel Raymond. Motifs of Psyché or Lohengrin, on the sad consequences for a too-curious lover, provide a melodramatic background for this theatrical development. It is interesting to note that, in contrast to these romantic epithets, Raymond will come to hear "...les anneaux de Dalila et de Judith tintaient à ses chevilles..." (p. 159).

Throwing herself into the hands of destiny, Maria Cross quickly murmurs her name, and is surprised when he proposes a meeting the next day. She is unaware that he is not at all revolted, but rather proud of a conquest, and one of which he can boast to his incredulous friends: " 'Maria Cross a le béguin pour moi" (p. 119).

His body and soul seem to have literally expanded under the impact of such an unlikely and dazzling possibility. "Il respirait le soir comme si l'essence de l'univers y eût été contenue, et qu'il se fût senti capable de l'accueillir dans son corps dilaté" (p. 119).

Contrasting with this approach of infinite pleasure is Raymond's awareness of his home as within "...l'épaisse prison de feuilles où les membres d'une seule famille vivaient confondus et séparés...." He escapes to a pine wood, where it has been said, "...la chaleur s'accumule, se concentre," and where he embraces the earth, "plus chaude qu'un corps."

Raymond's desire to confide regarding Maria Cross is joined to that of his father. "Une force, à leur insu, les approchait." The two men, so long the victims of incommunicability, now share an instinctive interest: "Comme deux papillons séparés par des lieues se rejoignent sur la boîte où est enfermée la femelle pleine d'odeur ... se posaient côte à côte sur Maria Cross invisible" (p. 124).

The linking of sexual attraction to animal instinct had been touched upon earlier. Madeleine Basque, sensing her husband's return each evening long before there is any sound, hurries through the dark garden to meet him:

> ...guidée par une connaissance infaillible, comme si elle eût appartenu à une espèce différente des autres animaux, où le mâle et non la femelle eût été odorant pour attraper la complice à travers l'ombre. (p. 21)

Not because Raymond represents "un rival inconnu," but because he sees Maria from a different point of view, father and son are driven further apart. For Raymond, Maria is a *femme entretenue*, admirable for "... sa hardiesse, pour son ambition sans frein, pour toute une vie dissolue qu'il imaginait" (p. 126). Paul's defense of Maria Cross, of her "humilité extraordinaire," her indolence, her "nonchalance désespérée," prompts ridicule in the son. This turns to open laughter as Paul innocently explains her righteous virtue in taking the tram as a means of avoiding the gift of an auto from Larousselle. Just as the doctor had argued that his son was wrong to believe that all men are evil, "... il existe des hommes sans calculs ni ruses," so does he now insist that the boy is wrong to believe the world about Maria. " 'Tu me trouves bien sot .... De nous deux, c'est toi pourtant le naïf. Ne croire qu'au mal, c'est ne pas connaître les hommes' " (p. 130).

Father and son have lost themselves in a maze of contradictory declarations. To emphasize Maria's helplessness, the doctor says that she is deceived daily by a faithless Larousselle. Raymond boasts knowing that she consoles herself with other men. A cry " 'Menteur!' " escapes Paul. Raymond, considering this response, has to suppress the notion that his father loves Maria: "... lui, non plus, ne pouvait introduire l'amour dans l'image ... de ce père ... sans passions, sans péché, inaccessible au mal, incorruptible, au-dessus de tous les autres hommes" (p. 131).

Paul Courrèges' frustrated desire to touch Maria finds its only physical expression as he embraces, in the dark, a chestnut tree where the initials of another love, his daughter Madeleine, are carved. " 'On croit que tu es ma femme, ..' " he rejoiced in telling his daughter as a girl. It is not surprising, then, too, to see motifs carrying a theme of jealousy on the doctor's part, not only toward Larousselle, who has established prior claim on Maria, but also toward Gaston Basque, who has taken from the doctor another important love.

In their first furtive, but public, rendezvous, Maria maintains a perspective of an angelic Raymond, in spite of "un rire, une allusion, un regard en dessous ..." and "ce corps puissant" which make her tremble as she notes "la candeur de ce regard." While Raymond dreams of rented hotel rooms, she sees him as "cet enfant farouche," "un oiseau sauvage," and as "un faon."

While she insists on the virtue of her intentions, Maria yields to feverish imaginings which drain her physical energy. With nothing to do but smoke and read, "il y avait cela aussi: cette mollesse de son corps en dépit de l'imagination la plus fiévreuse." As she dreams of "des baisers calmes," Raymond exults in his contemporary's advice that "avec ces femmes-là, la brutalité, il n'y a que ça..." (p. 150).

It was Victor who asked the doctor if Maria's (to him) disinterested attitude toward sex could have come from her readings, from "un bouquin." Replying in the negative, the doctor finds that " '... bouquin éveilla dans son esprit le mot bouquetin, et il vit se dresser auprès de Maria Cross un chèvre-pied" (p. 141).

The connection is made soon with Raymond, as he celebrates the prospect of the conquest to come: "... le garçon ... se mit à courir ... sauta un massif, aussi agile qu'un bouquetin ..." (p. 150).

A brief visit to Maria's home is an immense disappointment for Raymond, although it leaves Maria with "une impression de sécurité, d'innocence." Maria, faced with the reality of Raymond's arrival, evades him by various feints. She prevents his taking action ("... ne la laisse pas manœuvrer ..." his friends had urged) by weighting down his knees beneath an album of her son's photos. Raymond endures her control: "... elle ne voyait pas la figure furieuse du garçon.... Il haletait, il tremblait de violence au repos." She escapes into a fantasy about her son now idealized in the perfection death provides. "... rien ne distinguait à cette minute ce que François avait été réellement pour elle, de ce qu'elle avait espéré de lui" (p. 159). Raymond is cheated of the anticipated excitement of possessing a "fallen woman," as Maria Cross creates a Madonna-like role of purity. The "tête-à-tête périlleux" that Maria feared is avoided but she is left with "... une paix qui peut-être était de la déception" (p. 160).

The theme of the discrepancy between dreams and reality is indicated again in her unconscious disappointment when the longed-for hero materializes and reveals himself as an awkward lad with a too-short haircut. Faced with the damp hands, sweating brow, and bad breath of the determined boy, — "Je me suis juré qu'aujourd'hui je ne serais pas manœuvré" — Maria's sentiments are revealed in the recurring motifs. "... d'abord qu'il s'éloigne" and in the same sense of disgust she recalls experiences with

Larousselle. Her indication to Raymond, " 'J'ai besoin d'être seule, Raymond... il faut me laisser seule...' " (p. 174) prophesies her intention to thwart Raymond's efforts to take her by force. She maneuvers him to the opposite side of the *chaise longue*.

The great abyss gapes before Maria once Raymond has gone, as she admits the hollowness of her visits to François' grave as a device to meet, less maternally, "un autre enfant vivant." She has the leisure to dream of her ideal of love, which fills the gulf between two people yet which does not need "...cette brève étreinte que la honte dénoue." It was Gaby Dubois, a friend from the *demi-monde*, who cried in protest "Il n'y a que ça de bon... la seule consolation." Maria's refuge would rather be that "...son désert intérieur se confondît avec celui de l'espace."

Her desire to lean infinitely into space to become part of it, is denied as a death-wish on her part, after she is found fallen from the window. " 'Je n'ai pas voulu mourir... mais dormir' " (p. 197). Like the many antithetical themes of the novel, the theme of escaping the void of life by seeking another *néant* is correlative, for example, with that of the doctor's using one drug to overcome addiction to another.

Raymond impulsively plans to unleash on his father, his anger toward Maria. Finding Paul Courrèges ill, but content to be lovingly shared as "proie" by a devoted wife and mother, Raymond spares his father pain, and, instead, gives the doctor assurance once denied him, that he was indeed the only person to know Maria Cross well. The doctor is certain of his detachment from the woman he loves without hope. He resigns himself to obeying "son destin solitaire." His peaceful acceptance of wifely and maternal attentions finds him a willing dupe of their optimistic kindness. "Mais que ce fût la main de sa mère ou celle de sa femme sur son front, le docteur retrouvait cette sécurité [d'un enfant malade]..." (p. 184).

It is a kind of *tableau vivant* anticipating his later words to Raymond, " '...à la fin, comme au commencement, il faut qu'une femme nous porte' " (p. 237).

So ill that he believes that he can not stand, Dr. Courrèges leaves his sickbed when word comes that Maria Cross has fallen from a window. Confident in his new-found innocence, he allows his wife to prepare him for the visit on foot to Maria's house.

Motifs supporting the theme of his innocence are the simple tastes of bread and chocolate which recall "son bonheur" of childhood. Only at this moment, as he shrugs off his wife's concern as a sign of jealousy, does it occur to Lucie that there might have been an extra-professional relationship between doctor and patient. " '... ma pauvre Lucie ... je suis très attaché à cette malheureuse, mais ça n'a rien à voir....' "

Raymond had envied his father's privileged professional familiarity with Maria Cross' body. Paul Courrèges, even now, must remind himself, "Tu n'es qu'un médecin à son chevet!" His integrity and discipline are such that he does not notice as alluring the object lying before him. References to her body are offset by ethical and rational refusals to desire it: "Cette source charnelle ... de ses délectations ne suscite plus en lui qu'une curiosité intense" (p. 197).

A mild delirium induces involuntary comment from Maria Cross who speaks openly, and probably honestly, of her incapacity to find pleasure in love, or love in pleasure. " 'Hélas, le plaisir n'est pas à la portée de tous.... Je ne suis pas à la mesure du plaisir' " (p. 199). The doctor who had cried out to his son: " 'Je la connais.... J'ai été son meilleur ami' " rejects her assertion that her approaches to love were "misunderstood" as solicitations to voluptuous adventure. He calls her "femme menteuse," who is like all the others on the sad road to love, and who seeks only pleasure. She amends her remarks to agree that she had, perhaps, sought pleasure but " '... en moi, le plaisir et le dégoût se confondent, comme l'éclair et la foudre ... Il n'est pas d'intervalle entre le plaisir et le dégoût' " (p. 200). Doctor Courrèges has learned from experience that love invariably, if not inevitably, does become a source of displeasure. Worn by life, one finds, " 'Plus de désir: des habitudes sales' " (p. 201).

Seventeen years later finds Raymond alone in a familiar night-club. The evening has gone badly. Abandoned by a young man he had invited to dinner in the hope of dominating and influencing him—(Raymond "... avait la passion de l'influence ..."), he is distracted by the arrival of a couple in the bar. Occupied as he was with egotistical musings on his conquests and discomfited at the prospect of seeing his father, who is visiting Paris, Raymond notes first that the man he sees is familiar: " 'J'ai vu quelque part cette tête-là ... c'est une tête de Bordeaux.' " He only then realizes the woman's identity.

Seen objectively, he had noted about her that "la quarantième année avait touché de ci — de là, ce bas de figure, tiré la peau, amorcé un fanon." He recognizes Maria Cross "... malgré ... le corps épaissi, et cette destruction lente ... qui montait vers la bouche et les joues" (p. 14). As he reviews the painful experience of her repudiation of him at seventeen, and becomes once again "l'adolescent hérissé, honteux" of that time, and the "homme nouveau" that she had created, his responses toward her change subtly. "Mais elle, cette Maria Cross, qu'elle avait peu changé ... le visage ... baigné d'enfance; c'est peut-être leur enfance éternelle qui fixe notre amour et le délivre du temps" (p. 17). He continues to watch her, but only gradually does her attitude toward him soften.

Maria begs Victor not to insist on greeting Raymond, but resigns herself to Raymond's enforced presence at her table, speaking "sans regarder le jeune homme." She is determined to be silent but Raymond's astonishment that she is married goads her to explanation.

She at first refuses to recall Raymond's humiliating visit seventeen years earlier, saying: " 'Il me semble que vous me parlez d'une autre femme' " (p. 214). Her desire to obliterate that part of her life as *femme entretenue* is now repeated in a similar motif when Maria Cross asserts to the doctor, who has come to care for the drunken and injured Larousselle: " 'Je ne suis plus la paresseuse que vous avez connue...' " (p. 229).

Paul Courrèges, who had at one time seen Maria Cross as part of his destiny, tries to combine optimism for the future with resignation to the vagaries of destiny, which he believes directs their relationship: " 'Peut-être faudrait-il aider la chance...' ... 'Ne croyez-vous pas madame, qu'il nous serait possible d'aider un peu la chance?' " (p. 229).

As she had wounded him in the early days of their acquaintance, the same evasion comes to her in the false cheerfulness of politeness: " 'Savez-vous ce qui serait gentil, docteur? Nous pourrions nous écrire?' " The proposal is refused angrily and sadly as creating an artificial life. The doctor does not perceive the artificiality of the suggestion he himself was making.

It is the sound of the name of Larousselle's son, Bertrand, which gives context and substance to Raymond's appearance at Maria's table in the bar. Just hearing the name itself, leaves her "détendue, apaisée, attendrie." Maria Cross is so essentially indifferent to Raymond, except for dreading a revival of the past, "... qu'elle ne s'aperçoit pas qu'il a rapproché son genou du sien: elle ne sent même pas le contact" (p. 220). Her preoccupation with Bertrand and his achievements is so intense that Raymond realizes his retaliatory conquests and long-plotted vengeance are left to him as a barren hoax: "... elle ne le méprisait même pas; il n'existait pas à ses yeux."

Awareness of the empty folly of his existence is emphasized as he looks in the same mirror that had comforted him earlier in the evening. Now he sees that without "la splendeur éphémère du printemps de l'être humain," he has no attractions to arouse "... d'antipathies, de préférences, de pudeurs, de remords ... de curiosités, d'appétits" of "une femme usée."

Correlative to themes depicting the attrition of life on love, motifs depicting the erosion of youth and its companion, physical attraction, are present as well:

> ... il [Raymond] touchait à l'âge où, seuls, ceux qui s'addressent à l'âme peuvent asseoir leur domination. Mais, les plus jeunes souhaitent des complices de leur génération, et sa clientèle s'appauvrissait. (p. 9)

His contemporaries, if they survived the war, fell to the onslaught of life: "... ils fussent enlisés dans le mariage, ou déformés par le métier." Raymond feels himself set apart, in a kind of timeless vacuum, untouched by the ravages of time. "... [il] les accusait d'être les assassins de leur jeunesse et avant qu'elle les renonçât, de la trahir."

Raymond's jealousy of his all-too-capable successor, Bertrand, turns to mockery as he sees the "lit de fille, de séminariste" of Bertrand's austere, cell-like room, where Maria asks him to wait. Spiritual works line the shelves on the bare walls above a desk, "ordonnée comme une bonne conscience." Raymond pleases himself in comparing it to the stage-set of seduction which is his own bedroom and interprets this ascetic chamber as a clever denial of pleasure which intensifies and prolongs the delectation of the voluptuous pursuit. Maria Cross is outraged, as at witnessing a sacrilege, to smell Raymond's residual masculine odor and his thick tobacco smoke in this little chapel of a bedroom. Sensual overtones of adoration are noted as she kneels at the bedside as though praying, and finally places her head on the consecrated pillow. The nature of her adoration is emphasized as there is recalled an almost identical motif of Paul Courrèges, who had also paid homage to his goddess of love, Maria Cross. "Il s'était levé, et rapproché de la chaise longue, s'était mis à genoux; après avoir craintivement regardé du côté de la porte, il avait enfoui sa tête dans les coussins" (p. 66).

An amended version of childhood carriage trips with his father is seen as Raymond accompanies Paul Courrèges in a taxi to the hotel. On this occasion, however, he supports the old man's body, holds his hand, and initiates conversation. Two views of love and passion pass through Raymond's mind: the brittle surface of love reflected by a mistress:

> "En amour, quand je souffre, je me mets en boule ... sûre que l'homme pour qui je souhaite de mourir, demain peut-être ne me sera plus rien; l'objet de tant de souffrances ne vaudra plus un de mes regards." (p. 235)

and the consuming, smouldering passion of a dutiful man like his father, where "... la passion se conserve, se concentre ... elle s'accumule, croupit, se corrompt, empoisone, corrode le vase vivant qui l'enferme" (p. 235). In close textual proximity to this definition of disaster, is Paul Courrèges' urgent appeal that Raymond protect himself in marriage. The care of others is offered as the greatest distraction from our own expressions of passion and voluptuousness. The responsibility for the well-being of dependents, " '... nous défend contre la foule des choses désirables.' " That death will be sweet for him is his reward (unlike his own father who had suffered a stroke while on a debauch and was brought home, robbed of his possessions, by two *filles de joie*). Lucie is the ministering angel who will assure his peace in the days that remain to him, " '... nuit et jour, elle me couve' " and this "excès de soin" is Lucie's sweet revenge.

A look at Raymond's calendar, which yesterday seemed so importantly full, shows a long day ahead cluttered only by a few inanities. "Il se penchait sur cette journée comme un enfant sur un puits... comment combler ce trou?" (p. 234). Raymond regrets he has not arranged further meetings with Maria Cross. He could exist in anticipation, and like his father before him, breathe new hope in "le vide infini de sa vie," should she postpone the date. His dream of intimacy with Maria is not only an escape. It is nourishment for his passion. It is his punishment that everything feeds this "bête féroce" within: "...le jeûne l'exaspère, l'assouvissement la fortifie, notre vertu la tient éveillée, l'irrite.... Quelles échappatoires? Que peut Dieu?" (p. 241).

Raymond remains a prisoner of his passion and, like Paul Courrèges, will be willing to live a fantasy life of perpetual "absence et attente" for the privilege of loving and desiring an inaccessible woman. An impulsive last-minute visit with his father, "...qu'il ne devait jamais revoir," seems to leave Raymond alone, free to determine if he will remain victim "...de l'incendie qui maintenant ronflait, s'avançait sur un front immense..." or if he will find again his faith: " 'Il faut d'abord que vous ayez foi en votre volonté....' "

THEMES OF THE PLOT

Maria Cross, as her name suggests, might be viewed by those who loved her as a kind of malign inversion, in which she represents, like the crucifix, the burden to be borne, and the medium on which they perish in love. Although the motivations and purposes of all are important, it is an examination of those of Maria which can illumine the responses of the others named. The futility of their efforts in reaching this ambiguous woman is emphasized in the realization that there is no constant quality in her to which another individual can attach his hopes. Lacking an identity, or at least uncertain of that identity, Maria Cross never presents a consistent character which can be grasped, literally or figuratively. She changes form, like the original Proteus, as a defense mechanism. She is thereby free to remain untouchable, unseizable. This elusiveness is the quality which in her case, gives rise to the notion of inaccessibility, and it is because of this remoteness that Maria Cross can indulge in the role-playing that presents a different version of her personality to everyone who approaches.

The superficiality of her make-up is indicated in numerous motifs. In contrast to the motif of her ostracism from Bordeaux society, is her rejection of a possible social life among the *demimondaines* of the city. She is pretentious in an assumption of superiority:

> "Pensez-vous que je sois femme à me commettre, tout d'un coup, avec les maîtresses de ces messieurs — moi qui les ai fuies jusqu'à présent comme la peste? Je suis seule à Bordeaux de mon espèce...." (p. 99)

She knows, but does not admit that the same half-world of kept-women looks scornfully at her in return: "...elle avait entendu... des lambeaux d'injures proférées.... 'Cette traînée qui joue à l'impératrice... cette... qui fait à la vertu...'" (p. 153). Having overheard these biting comments in a theatre, Maria waits until the "faces de bêtes" are riveted on a nude dancer before making her escape, a motif which subtly dissociates her from the world of the garish and the explicit.

An important consideration in Maria's allowing the doctor to continue his interest in her, in spite of his profound capacity for boring her, is seen in the social advantage and esteem she attaches to his visits. "Elle était fière d'intéresser le docteur et, dans sa vie déchue, prisait très haut ses relations avec cet homme éminent: mais qu'il l'ennuyait!" (p. 55).

Her days are spent in idleness, with no interests beyond the perimeter of her limited social activity. She is noted most often reclining on a *chaise longue,* smoking innumerable cigarettes, in a dressing gown and slippers. Why does she choose to stay in this shabby half-lit world of dependence? Her reason is, she says, that once having made a better-then-hoped-for marriage, when left a widow she is still victim of " '...le désir d'une belle position, la certitude d'être épousée...'" (p. 80) and importantly, in its substance and her recognition of it, " '...cette lâcheté devant la lutte à reprendre, devant le travail, la besogne mal payée'" (p. 80). Maria Cross follows "le chemin de velours" even though in her case, the velvet has become slightly soiled.

The reading she undertakes is rarely completed, as the doctor methodically notes indications of her habits: "Que de livres! Mais aucun dont les dernières pages fussent coupées" (p. 65). A satisfaction with the appearance, or the beginnings of things reveals the lack of depth and purpose, but is a characteristic she feels helpless to change; "Que de plans d'évasion, de purification, échafaudés et détruits!" (p. 148) although she knows a cure might be found in a change of routine: "... se lever, faire des démarches, voir des gens."

Her pretentiousness is illustrated by her protestations that her visits to the cemetery are a joy to her because, " '... je suis heureuse d'être là, au milieu de ces pauvres dont je ne suis pas digne' " (p. 78). " 'Je regarde ces hommes; ils me paraissent aussi solitaires que moi-même ... aussi déracinés, déclassés.' " This stated purpose is at odds with a contrasting observation of her reasons for staring at Raymond. "Ce visage va me consoler des minutes misérables qu'il faut vivre dans une voiture publique. Rien ne peut m'offenser. ..."

Once married to Victor Larousselle, however, Maria Cross wants to efface from her own, and every other, memory the images evoked by discussions of her years in Bordeaux. She begs him not to talk with Raymond in the bar, appealing to his social judgment, but actually to avoid resuscitating that nearly-forgotten era. Although attempting to appear indifferent to Raymond, even after he has come to her table, she denies as much as possible, the occurrences he describes. To his specific recollection of the incomplete seduction scene, "Elle feignit de ne pas le comprendre ..." (p. 214). Once recalled, however, she insists: " 'Vous ne sauriez croire comme c'est loin de moi " (p. 214). In her last meeting with the doctor, she tries to remove, forever, the impressions of her he has carried for seventeen years. " 'Je ne suis plus la paresseuse que vous avec connue, docteur. ...' "

In contrast, her emphasis is on the fact that she is indeed married, and on the reasons for her marrying. It is Victor's son " '... qui nous a suppliés de conclure ce mariage.' " As for herself, she pompously adds: " '... je n'y tenais guère ... j'ai cédé à des considérations très hautes ...' " Recalling her original "désir d'une belle position," these contrasting motifs reveal the gap between motivation and purpose.

Of critical interest and thematic importance is the theme of sexual indifference or hostility, particularly as it is revealed in a woman whose ability to attract men sexually is her means of physical and psychological survival. Dr. Courrèges realizes, that in the face of his obvious but unspoken passion, "... un comble d'indifférence à son égard pouvait seul expliquer qu'elle ne s'en aperçut pas" (p. 55). But it is not only in relations with the loving doctor that Maria seems indifferent. Victor Larousselle confides to Paul Courrèges, " 'Entre nous, elle n'aime pas ça... vous me comprenez...?' " He turns this coolness to his advantage, since Maria can safely act as his hostess to business friends. There is no likelihood of sinning in her case, since she experiences no temptation. He asserts that she is "une innocente, docteur." " 'Personne qui connaisse moins les choses de l'amour que Maria et qui y prenne moins de plaisir' " (p. 141).

Virtue obviously would lie in the successful overcoming of temptation. Maria Cross is rather like an empty canvas, on which each person who knows her paints another and different portrait. In contrast to the theme of role-playing and insincerity is Maria's admission, " 'Je ne suis pas à la mesure du plaisir' " (p. 199).

Maria Cross is seen, at least, to want to respond to the lure of *volupté*. Her attraction to Raymond is unquestionably a sensual one, and the motif of his being a fruit waiting to be picked up supports the suggestion. It is reinforced when their first meeting ends in disappointment and she dreams of him as "ce fruit... écarté de sa soif...."

A series of materially similar motifs is used to suggest her own questioning of motives in inviting Raymond, alone, to visit her home. There will she seek, in purpose,

> ...les caresses les plus proches, les plus chastes.... (p. 137)

> ...elle ne l'attirait chez elle que pour la douceur, le réconfort... une contemplation.... (p. 148)

> ...de propos confiants, de caresses maternelles, de baisers calmes.... (p. 149)

Yet the warning flags are up, which signal a more profound sexual motivation, growing in intensity:

> ...rien de trouble en elle, à la naissance de ses désirs et pourtant tous ses actes offraient un aspect monstrueux. (p. 147)

"...qui nous défend le bonheur? ne saurais-je le rendre
heureux, ce petit?" (p. 149)

"...aie donc le courage de t'avouer que tu pressens au-
delà de ce pur bonheur, toute une région interdite et à
la fois ouverte." (p. 149)

The range of her vacillation reaches its widest, from a determination to be out (but where?) so that the feared seduction will
not take place, to the willingness to throw herself into the arms of
destiny once the boy does indeed appear: "...aucun remords
n'empoisonnait donc son bonheur. Au destin qui de force lui jetait
l'enfant en pâture elle protestait qu'elle saurait être digne de ce
don" (p. 156).

Destiny is her crutch as well. Condemned forever to knock on
unresponsive doors (p. 177) she resigns herself to a sense of
futility. "...à quoi bon cet effort vers la perfection lorsque c'est
notre destin de ne rien tenter qui ne soit louche en dépit de notre
bon vouloir?" Just as she cannot be praised for her virtue, she
cannot be blamed for her faults. She is the determinant of neither.

There is a discrepancy, though, between Maria's instinctive
confidence in her seductive charm to direct Raymond's responses,
and her desire to absolve herself from responsibility by calling upon
Destiny.

"Je me fusse vite fatiguée de le contempler si je n'avais
su qu'il répondait à mon manège...." (p. 149)

...le petit Courrèges avait reçu sa lettre; elle connaissait
assez sa timidité pour être sûre de son obéissance.

As he stands dripping rainwater in her living room, on his first
visit she admits: " 'Je savais bien que vous viendriez tout de
même' " (p. 157).

Paul Courrèges is Maria Cross' staunchest defender. He risked
his son's ridicule in maintaining: " 'Oui, tu as dit le mot: chez
une Maria Cross... une sainte se cache...' " (p. 130). Yet the
doctor knows it may be a woman playing at being a saint. Was even
the grief at her son's death-bed genuine? "Le vrai est qu'elle était
sincère mais que tout de même il se mêlait à tant de grandeur une
satisfaction — oui, elle satisfaisait son goût de l'attitude" (p. 140).
Believing her first meeting with Raymond to be the last, her taste

for "situations romanesques," overtakes her: "... [elle] cède peu
à peu à l'attrait d'un amour sans espoir" (p. 163).

In addition to her distress at having to tell Raymond her name,
risking his leaving her at once, she enjoys "une satisfaction obscure" to find herself in such a dramatic situation. " 'C'est tragique...' " is the dimension she assigns to their meeting.

She was wise in not introducing Raymond to her melodramatic
daydreams, since Raymond realized that she exploits her son's
death to enhance her own image, "... il doutait de cette douleur
et... devait se répéter. 'Elle se prend elle-même à son jeu... ce
qu'elle joue bien du cadavre" (p. 159).

In one of her rare and reluctant insights, Maria Cross admits
to the hypocrisy inherent in exploiting the image of her dead son to
her advantage, especially in dissimulation of her desire to see
Raymond in the train.

> "... avoue que tu ne cherchais, près de ce cadavre, qu'un
> alibi. Elle n'avait été si fidèle à visiter l'enfant du cimetière
> que pour les retours si doux aux côtés d'un autre enfant
> vivant." (p. 177)

She uses him, too, as a "protection," in showing his photographs
to Raymond, to "purify" the room where Raymond had come for
their presumably chaste meeting, revealing some hesitation in her
thought that Raymond was both an angel and a child. "Puisque
l'enfant [François] est là, c'est le signe qu'il n'y a rien que de pur
en tout ceci" (p. 157).

Her use of the dead boy to emphasize her own pitiable state
was even more flagrant with Dr. Courrèges, originally appealing
to him as the mother of a desperately sick child. She is able to
transfer, with some success, her searches for perfection in François and Raymond to the son of her second husband, Bertrand,
who at thirty-one, lives an austere and pristine life with Maria and
Victor Larousselle.

Bertrand eventually becomes her "destiny," the source of direction in her life. She willingly accepts his dictum, " '... que nous ne
commençons à vivre de notre vrai vie qu'après vingt-cinq ou trente
ans.' " Accepting such an approach to life not only serves as
contrast to dispute Raymond's belief that the latent forces within
him were irremediably shaped in his adolescent experience, but

also exculpates Maria from responsibility for her actions in her early years. Those years can then be truly seen as of another being — as of "une autre femme" as she longs to believe.

Maria's actions are now motivated by her desire to please Bertrand who has assumed reponsibility for directing her life, and who has urged that she yield reasonably to Victor's vulgar lifestyle. " 'C'est Bertrand lui-même qui me conseille de céder ... aux goûts de mon mari.' " She owes more to Bertrand than she cares to indicate: " 'Mon mariage, en effet — mais ce ne serait rien. Il m'a révélé ... mais non, vous ne pouvez comprendre' " (p. 218).

The pretentious nature of her character having been established, it can be questioned whether Bertrand has in fact helped her on the way to inspired living, or whether this unfinished state (like all those unfinished books) is not just a spiritual glitter which serves to distract from her main goal — marriage — an objective she tries to deprecate.

Paul Courrèges is buried alive in a cheerless, relentless routine of work and research, a prisoner of his goodness: "Cette bonté du docteur Courrèges n'était célèbre que parce que ses actes en témoignaient; seuls ils rendaient témoignage à cette bonté enfouie en lui ..." (p. 25). That he expects integrity in others is revealed in numerous motifs. Although he cannot sway Raymond from his cynical views, he enjoys idealism in his own convictions, and has persuaded himself of the existence of the guileless man. "... il existe des hommes sans calculs ni ruses, ... les plus habiles souvent sont les Machiavels d'une cause sublime ..." (p. 27). He rejects as vulgar his wife's priggish comments regarding Maria Cross and her situation, and urges charity. " 'Ce n'est pas nous qu'elle offense' " (p. 30).

It has been said that there is not an outward sign of politeness which does not have a profound moral foundation. The doctor's consistent courtesy, which does not belie entirely his deep frustration, is a projection of his sense of responsibility. Unable to tolerate Lucie's cruelty toward a Maria Cross she does not know, he conceals his repugnance: "il ... gagna la porte d'un pas qu'il s'efforçait de ralentir, mais la famille aux écoutes l'entendit monter l'escalier quatre à quatre" (p. 31). He replies to her queries about his presence at the funeral of Maria's son with controlled emotion: "... de sa voix la plus douce, qui témoignait chez lui d'une exaspération à son comble mais jugulée" (p. 35).

Paul Courrèges detests his own hypocrisy in requiring self-discipline and self-control in his patients. " 'Il faut d'abord que vous ayez foi en votre volonté.' " He knows that his own is ". . . une foi morte . . . une foi qu'il avait perdue." He must concede that he cannot control the "bête somnolente" within himself (p. 94).

It was a sense of obligation, or even guilt, that prolonged Dr. Courrèges' contact with Maria Cross after her son's death. The image of her as grieving mother at her child's bedside, yields to that of her reclining casually on her own *chaise longue*. The doctor begins secretly to seek free moments in his crowded days to join her in a brief respite ". . . de contemplation et d'amoureux silence où un long regard contentait son désir" (p. 43). The change in motivation is in thematic contrast with the doctor's idealism and integrity, as he abuses the confidence of his wife who believes him occupied with " '. . . sa clientèle de pauvres. . . . Et puis son laboratoire, l'hôpital, ses articles . . .' " (p. 42). His reputation as a saintly man, incapable of sin, untouchable by corruption, leaves him free to plot his "moves," like a clever chess player, to make time for his secret life with Maria Cross. His need to see her becomes compulsive, and if she should break an appointment, ". . . le docteur n'aurait plus eu la force de vivre si . . . Maria Cross n'eût proposé un autre jour" (p. 43).

He becomes so strongly motivated to possess Maria Cross that he tries to convince himself that he can imitate other men who have left their family responsibilities to start new, more pleasure-oriented lives. He imagines a new existence, far away, where he can escape, with her, "le morne ennui" of his marriage. He would enjoy release from the burden of his goodness: "Ah, être méprisé enfin . . . il serait un homme qui aime une femme et qui la conquiert avec violence" (p. 90).

The doctor's quest for possession of Maria Cross is concomitant with an unrealized desire to prolong interminably the years of possible pleasure. His purpose in making a definitive declaration of his love, following prolonged dream-like preparations, is stricken by the cruelty of reality. Over her *chaise longue* hangs a large mirror which disarms him as it reflects, not the eager lover about to succeed in conquest, but ". . . une figure rongée de barbe, des yeux

sanglants et abîmes par le microscope, ce front déjà chauve..."
(p. 53). To touch her suddenly seems as mad as hoping to wipe the
ravages of age from his face. "Pourquoi à chaque fois... cette
stupeur désolée s'il se fût comme attendu à voir sa jeunesse lui
sourire?" (p. 98). Two reactions are to be noted following these
frequent, involuntary encounters with reality's reflection. A sudden
perspective of himself as an aging man, inarticulate with desire for
a young woman, causes him to retreat into "ce ton paternel et un
peu grave," while "il... se souvint des paroles brûlantes qu'il avait
préparées" (p. 99).

A second, perhaps involuntary, response is to think of his wife,
Lucie. " 'A partir de ce soir, je rendrai Lucie heureuse,' " is his
determination, although the image of Maria Cross efface his efforts
to think of his wife.

The doctor's stated purpose to restore relations with his wife
is understandable as a remedy to relieve and deflect his pain in
failing to arouse the interest or affection of Maria Cross. It is also
a support of the theme of the story which was revealed in his
theoretical premise that a family serves as a protection against
too-desirable things. The doctor's instinctive resort to consideration
and courtesy is almost like a penance for having aspired to the
unattainable.

Seventeen years later, without having met Maria Cross, in the
contingent incident of his visit to Paris, the same distance prevails
between his dream and the actuality. His desire is rekindled that
Maria will want to keep him with her forever: " 'A présent que
je vous tiens, docteur, je ne vous lâche plus' " (p. 228). The same
indifference and impersonality, however, is encountered. " 'C'est
vrai que le monde est petit.' "

The doctor's purpose in plunging into a whirlwind of work and
numbing fatigue is at odds with his strong desire to possess Maria
Cross. He makes rational use of the weapons available to him
— the acquired habits of work and discipline — to fight an addiction which is not his to combat; a battle which he is doomed
by inheritance, or destiny, to lose.

> "Je n'ai hérité... qu'un cœur capable de passion, mais
> pas le don de plaire...." (p. 105)
> C'était la loi de sa nature de ne pouvoir atteindre ceux
> qu'il chérissait. (p. 187)

The glances in the mirror above Maria Cross, he acknowledges, were not really necessary to explain the solitude of his life: "... il avait obéi à son destin solitaire" (p. 188). It is on the basis of helping "la chance" that he makes his final appeals to Maria to start together afresh after their years of separation.

Rationalization is the tool of compromise which allows modification of the man himself and of his image of those around him to permit his pursuit of the ideal in love. Paul Courrèges first had to create a suitable basis for his desire to end, "cette pauvre vie recluse et besogneuse, pour renaître avec vous [Maria Cross]'" (p. 89). His need for her is greater than the need of his family for him:

> Sa présence ne servait même pas à rendre heureuse l'épouse la plus amère.... Sa fille, son fils? depuis long-temps il avait renoncé à être aimé d'eux. Quant à Raymond, ce qui est inaccessible ne vaut pas qu'on s'y sacrifie. (p. 87)

The fact that Maria Cross, too, is inaccessible, is unrecognized in these justifications. It has been noted that such evaluations of his wife and family are reversed in direct proportion to his inability to win the love, or at least the affection, of Maria Cross. The family is both his burden and his haven. When all hope must be abandoned of achieving his goal of possessing Maria Cross in this life, he will say to Raymond: " 'Tu ne saurais croire comme il fait bon vivre au plus épais d'une famille ... mais oui!' " (p. 236). He begs Raymond, "Ne reste pas seul," in his final conviction that man must create his own safeguards and refuges against the pain of unsuccessfully reaching for fruits beyond his grasp.

Mauriac is reiterating that it is the inaccessibility of those we need, and want to love the most, that makes them more precious, more valuable than possession might have done. The loss of a loved one in death encourages a worship of the cherished memory in all its perfection. Paul Courrèges has removed Maria Cross from the vulnerability of routine living in his determination to "... ne plus penser à Maria que comme à une morte ..." (p. 81). His dream can be maintained without the tarnishing contact of reality. Its very unattainability is a propelling force generating hope, which can, after seventeen years, encourage Paul Courrèges to renew his attentions to Maria Cross as though there had been no interval.

He comes to realize that in love, man creates an object which is in itself unreal, and which is molded to meet his own needs. Disappointment is suggested as the only possible outcome of the perpetual quest which is love. Paul knows the disappointment is not limited, in his case, to Maria Cross. He recalls the many occasions, "... où il ramenait contre soi l'objet tant convoité, et soudain diminué, si appauvri, si différent de ce que le docteur avait éprouvé, de ce qu'il avait souffert à son propos" (p. 187).

Yet the man has the right to try to remove the weight of loneliness which is suffocating him, although after doing so, he will find himself still alone, desiring the one he loves, who remains inaccessible forever.

By a recognizable recurrence of phraseology which jogs the reader's memory that he has heard something similar expressing the same idea in a previous location, Mauriac reinforces the theme. The linking of the theme of detachment through antecedent motifs becomes apparent, and provides a simple thread of continuity. Raymond is always touched by the tenderness of the exhausted, drained working-class passengers around him in the tram, a sentiment which he indulges only in circumstances where he is certain of his invulnerability in isolation.

> ... tramway plein d'ouvriers à qui la fatigue du jour donnait *une expression de douceur.* (p. 18)

> ... ce long voyage du retour en tramway ...; cette femme en cheveux levait vers les lampes le feuilleton et *sa bouche remuait comme pour une prière.* (p. 19)

> ... le tramway toujours essailli d'un peuple accablé, *sale et doux....* (p. 49)

> Raymond dans le tram d'ouvriers, si brutal au collège, ici ne repoussait pas la tête ballottée d'un garçon de son age, à bout de forces, et dont le sommeil défaisait le corps, le déliait *comme un bouquet.* (p. 61)

> ... rien ne comptait dans sa vie, hors ces minutes où ils furent assis face à face, au milieu des pauvres dont le sommeil renversait les faces charbonnées. (pp. 221-222)

The words are not duplicates, but with variety, Mauriac says virtually the same thing five times, recalling on each occasion Raymond's comfort in the disinterested solitude among the workers.

* * *

Paul Courrèges had felt that he was somehow relegated to anonymity by his own father, who in his preoccupation with pleasure referred to his son always as "le petit." Raymond Courrèges might have enjoyed such a friendly negligence. Happiest among "des êtres indifférents," whom he sees daily in the tram, he becomes sullen and withdrawn on meeting the face of family rancour and bitterness, where he shows "... le front durci comme au collège, les sourcils rapprochés... le coin droit de la bouche un peu tombant..." (p. 20).

He has "cette prescience des adolescents pour connaître qui les aime," which distinguishes his father from other family members. Raymond responds intuitively to "cette bonté... enfouie," in Paul Courrèges, although without giving any outward sign of his appreciation. He knows he intimidates the doctor, that he "le rendait de glace," by ignoring his father's unspoken appeals for affection. It is at first suggested that Raymond avoids the need to reciprocate his father's attempts at communication by pretending to sleep: "L'adolescent avait fermé les yeux qui peut-être eussent trahi malgré lui une faiblesse le désir de plier, — " (p. 27).

The complexity of Raymond's make-up is confirmed in later recollections of these early morning moments in the carriage when Raymond was "... tout livré au plaisir cruel de se taire — son plaisir des aubes d'automne dans le coupé..." (p. 169). Revealed herein is an innate desire to inflict pain on the only member of the family who can claim his respect or love.

Further motifs will be examined, suggesting the inherent trait of cruelty in Raymond, although there can be seen as well motifs which present ostensible purposes of tenderness or kindness. The need for a deeper satisfaction often underlies these overt actions. Raymond, for example, plays affectionately with his nieces and nephews, a sight his grandmother mentions to prove that " 'Ce n'est pas un mauvais drôle.' " But also indicated is that he uses them, "n'importe quoi de frais, de tiède et de vivant, comme une défense contre ceux qu'il appelait les cadavres." It will be recalled that he taunted and pursued as a small boy Bertrand Larousselle until the child sobbed on the ground. Raymond picks the child up, dusts his clothes, and wipes his eyes. He then wounds the boy by asking, " 'Dis, tu l'as vue quelquefois Maria Cross?' " The boy flees, ashamed but unharmed.

Raymond attributes his life of angry, impersonal conquest to the humiliation suffered at the hands of Maria Cross. It is revealed at the novel's end that "...toutes ses passions, depuis dix-sept ans avaient été à son insu allumées contre Maria" (p. 240). Yet, this taste for perpetual pursuit was evident before her rejection of him. The "... goût de blesser, de faire crier la biche — sa merci," which will be his for seventeen years was preceded by the "jeune mâle bein armé, sûr de sa force ... indifférent à ce que le corps ne peut pas pénétrer." He was the reprehensible boy at school, known for his lewdness. His desire for vengeance against Maria Cross takes him from adolescent experimentation to a calculated indulgence in *volupté*, where "tout sert la passion." He is the same boy who in his youth, enjoyed the aftermath of a nosebleed before a mirror, where he "... s'amusait de sa figure barbouillée, feignait d'être à la fois l'assassin et l'assassiné" (p. 60). In his manhood, he voluntarily submits to an assassination of his personality by Maria Cross, while he exults leaving his partner of any night's lovemaking "... en travers du lit, un corps recru, comme assassiné ..." (p. 220).

Raymond, in recalling that he was doubtless born "avec cet instinct de chasseur," may have been right, since the predatory instinct was alerted before Maria Cross' invitation to visit her. He had already resented his father's early proposition that Maria was a helpless innocent, "honnête et molle," since such a victim could "... abîmer sa conquête." Motifs of petty cruelty are repeated as Raymond torments his father, first by suggesting he knows of promiscuous behavior on Maria's part without any such real knowledge; and secondly, by walking so quickly to avoid his father's persist questions that the older man cannot keep pace. "Et même il avait hâté le pas méchamment, parce qu'il s'était aperçu que son père avait peine à le suivre ..." (p. 169).

His need to wound the one who, by loving him, creates a bond or obligation, is revealing of Raymond's conflicting motivation toward freeedom from responsibility or commitment. Never having grown with the developing experiences of the acceptance of responsibility or love, Raymond will always pursue for impersonal and immediate satisfaction. Maria Cross, too, failed to recognize "cette rage du peureux... du lâche résolu à l'action" which supports the themes of meanness and pusillanimity.

Raymond's intention to avoid the responsibilities of commitment — whether to a profession, a person or a cause — is a correlative theme with his need to dominate or manipulate both friends and mistresses. He cannot endure the burden of what another might contribute to a relationship. He intends to have the freedom to begin and end, at will, whatever connections he has established. The other party merely serves a need and must be dispensed with at Raymond's convenience. It is an exercise of power which is required to reinforce Raymond's battered self-identity. This need to own any person he has favored with his attentions, rendered him "...jusqu'à trente ans, incapable de ce desintéressement que la camaraderie exige..." (p. 9). Without friends, his acquaintances serve only as "...témoins... confidents... une paire d'oreilles" (p. 9). A key indicator of the fragility of his personality is seen: "Il aimait aussi se prouver à soi-même qu'il les dominait, les dirigeait; il avait la passion de l'influence et se flattait de démoraliser avec méthode" (p. 9). Prompted, doubtless, by his need to obliterate the painful memories of himself as a boy at the mercy of school, family, and a mistress who treated him as an angry mother might have done, Raymond's adult life is spent in proving to himself and the world that he is not the child he used to be.

The author intercalates the suggestion that Raymond could have been a surgeon, a priest or a doctor, "...s'il avait été capable d'asservir à une carrière ses appetits..." (p. 9). Raymond is capable of, and does curiously employ a systematic self-discipline, but it is geared entirely to the delectation of passion. Even the goal of immediate satisfaction is clinically achieved in "cette science dans la débauche, patiemment acquise et cultivée" (p. 241). Thus his appetites are controlled as the author might have wished, but the unanswered question lies before Raymond: "Le tout est de savoir

si la débauche l'eût délivré de sa passion; tout sert la passion..."
(p. 241). Raymond's scientific exploitation of his appetites, motivated by a desire to liberate himself from his obsession with Maria
Cross and the humiliation she had caused, are ironically the
wellsprings of renewal of his compulsion.

The sense of predestination, of fatality, is implicit in Raymond's
yielding, at the end of the novel, to a life of "dépendence et solitude." Having inherited an inextinguishable capacity for passion,
he is resigned to life as a miserable satellite, circling endlessly and
unproductively around "cet astre," the unattainable Maria Cross,
or "d'autres Maria Cross." "Et s'il veut échapper à cette gravita-
tion, quels autres défilés s'ouvrent à lui que ceux de la stupeur
et du sommeil?" (p. 243).

The similarity of theme, man doomed to aimless existence,
looking for exits from the hell of solitude, is seen in Maria Cross'
repeated question: "Où aller?"

Once more it is a mirror which relentlessly cracks the image
of eternal youth and attainable love which Raymond enjoys. For
him, the mirror hangs over the nightclub bar, scene of his anticipated conquests: "Il regarde ardemment... son visage... ce
visage que la trente-cinquième année épargne encore. Il songea que
le vieillissement, avant de toucher son corps, touchait sa vie"
(p. 10). After his last conversation with a Maria Cross, so indifferent that she did not even notice his knee pressing on hers, the
view in the mirror seems altered: "Il leva les yeux, regarda dans
les miroirs sa jeunesse décomposée, vit poindre les signes de la
décrépitude... le temps d'être aimé n'est plus" (p. 221).

Raymond is spurred to a final effort to reach the heart of Maria
Cross: " 'Vous vous souvenez du tramway?' " Her insolent reply,
" 'Quel tramway?' " sounds a death-knell to his unrealizable hope.
He has been abandoned "... n'ayant plus d'avenir... tout son
passé fourmille." His social calendar reveals empty days ahead
while his mind concedes: "Ce qu'il avait eu ne comptait pas; rien
n'avait de prix que ce qu'il n'aurait" (p. 242). As his father had
done before him, Raymond will settle into an orbit of suspense,
awaiting word from Maria Cross, without finding the substitute
comfort of family affection which will at least temper the remaining
days of Paul Courrèges.

It is not only three principals who are victims of a fatally-imposed solitary confinement. That it is the lot of every man to reach vainly toward the object of his love is revealed in motifs pertaining to Lucie Courrèges. Lucie is strongly motivated by deep and trusting affection to be a helpful, faithful wife. Se has limitless sympathy for the doctor's crushingly heavy work load, but a bitterness has developed in her inability to maintain an intimacy with Paul Courrèges. Her impulsively biting words, which she instantly regrets, serve only to widen the gap. " 'Qu'est-ce que j'ai dit d'extraordinaire?' " is her wonderment at how she has wounded him. As in a nightmare, "chaque effort vers son mari l'éloignait de lui" (p. 34). "Empêtrée d'une maladroite tendresse, elle avançait comme à tâtons, mais de ses bras tendues, ne savait lui donner que des blessures." Her anxiety and longing to care for him surround her husband with "rappels plus harcelants que des mouches." She has finished hoping for open affection or attention. It is her protection to believe it is the character of her husband and the characteristic of his profession to leave no room for self-indulgence or pleasure. "Elle ne savait pas que l'amour, dans les vies les plus pleines, sait toujours se creuser sa place.... Cette ignorance l'empêchait de souffrir." That the old, the poor and the sick could be deliberately neglected by the doctor, or that he could be "... différent pour une autre femme" is suspected only months later. Her remonstrations that he is too ill to answer from his sickbed a call to Maria's "suicide" elicits her husband's naïve response: " 'Mais non, ma pauvre Lucie, tout cela est loin de moi maintenant. Tout cela est bien fini...' " (p. 192). She accepts generously and courageously the inadvertent revelation that there was "tout cela": " 'Je ne te reprocherai rien, mais je veux savoir' " (p. 192).

Although inarticulate, Lucie Courrèges has remained alert to Paul's sufferings. She cannot control what has become a domestic commonness in her, but her sensitivity is keen in matters concerning her husband: "... Lucie Courrèges entendait l'appel étouffé de l'enterré vivant... elle percevait ce cri de mineur enseveli... une voix répondait à cette voix, une tendresse s'agitait" (p. 108).

Her helplessness in dealing with intimate problems of sensibility has reduced her ability to relieve the invisible torments possible in one who lives at her side. It is as though through paralysis of her mechanism for delicate response, her capacity to imagine such a facility in another has lessened as well. "Mais l'épouse, elle ... ne croyait pourtant qu'au mal physique" (p. 51). This is in particular contrast to the elder Mme Courrèges, who murmurs in the background: " 'Il n'est pas malade, mais c'est vrai qu'il souffre' " (p. 49).

Lucie Courrèges enjoys a hollow triumph, yet it is the nearest alternative offered in Mauriac's novel to the fulfillment of love. Old age and resignation on Paul Courrèges' part allow her to bind him to her in affectionate obligation. She now has his total devotion and attention, only to wait with him for the approaching end. Not life, but "la mort sera douce" in her loving hands.

Beyond considerations of delicacy are posed the complacent, greedy figures of Victor Larousselle and Gaston Basque. Nearly identical motifs are offered for both which reveal themes of arrogance and overbearing mannerisms. Larousselle suppresses Maria's wishes to leave the nightclub, so that she might avoid Raymond. He is determined to remain: " 'Et puis je le veux, hé, ça doit te suffire" (p. 211). Gaston Basque similarly dismisses Madeleine's opposition to his and Lucie's diagnosis of Paul Courrèges as a sick man: " 'Mais puisque je te dis que ta mère a raison! Cela ne te suffit pas?' " (p. 64).

Victor is motivated to possess Maria Cross with the relentless determination of a collector of desirable properties, above all, one which is unavailable to others. His intention in keeping a mistress — to add another enviable possession to his acquisition — had not foreseen marriage. Proud of her as a hostess, he professes to himself that her fidelity to him makes her indifferent to other men. As a man "... qui aime que la galérie l'admire" (p. 15), he is known to maintain Maria Cross "pour la montre." Failing to seize the essence of the elusive Maria, he agrees to their marriage, although he remarks publicly, " 'Je fais un mariage morganatique,' " thereby holding as his own the form, if not the substance of the mysterious woman. These outward gestures of pride and bravado do not reveal the true situation: "Maria demeurait la passion du grand Bordelais, sa défaite secrète et dont il crevait de rage. Il l'avait achetée tout de même, il était seul à la posséder" (p. 84). Only Maria Cross has seen him in admission of failure to win her: "... Larousselle s'écartant, le sang aux joues, maugréant: 'Qu'est-ce qu'il te faut? ...' " (p. 179).

RELATIONSHIP OF THEMES OF THE STORY AND OF THE PLOT

A central thematic unit of the story, illustrated by motifs of solitude, is reinforced by certain thematic elements in the plot. Particularly relevant are those components which stress the imaginative and fantasy lives of the characters as more satisfying than actuality. The dissociation of the individual from reality, finds a correlative theme, for example, in man's inability to achieve intimacy with those closest to him, while he remains articulate, or even voluble, with strangers. The theme of solitude, too, is correlative with that of inaccessibility. Whether by destiny or design, the man who withdraws from the initiation of human relationships renders himself unavailable to the approaches of others.

The proposal that it is only the presence of other human beings which limits the extent of man's envisioned paradise is a further indirect confirmation of the focus on human desolation. "Les autres" are not contributors to the enrichment of experience, but are obstacles to private manipulation and interpretation of the reality faced by the character. The dream-like unattainability of love is also emphasized by the shattering effect upon it of the processes of life. Love, which should be the motivating force of all human behavior, is instead eroded by practical existence and is doomed, by this as well, to rapid extinction.

Themes of the story which pointed up the mystery of the relationship between love and pleasure, are reiterated in the plot in the search for sexual identity, in the passion for possession, and in the substitution of domination for magnanimity. The evasion of the troubling enigma is made possible by that behavior which is motivated to seek a "nothingness," and also by other efforts to nullify the torment this basic uncertainty introduces.

The compromise in self-delusion which is so easily made in the omnipresence of failure in love, as noted in the story, is counteracted in some measure by motivations based on idealism and integrity, seen in the themes abstracted from the plot. Man seems to be endowed with unlimited capacity to deceive himself and others. It is idealism which prompts the attempt, as in the case of Paul Courrèges, to elude this quicksand of self-deception. Yet the novel closes with each character retreating for a last time into his preferred dream: Maria into chaste and sensual adoration of her stepson; Raymond into eternal anticipation of an end to the absence of love; and Paul, into the reassuring comfort of his wife's attentions. Correlative to the themes of fear of aging and loss of love, which were touched upon in the story, is the search for immortality in the presence of, and preservation of, youth.

Throughout the story themes appear which concern the powerful influences brought to bear, consciously or not, by one partner in love on the other person. The involuntary response of the beloved to the needs of his lover suggests the loss of individual capacity for controlling his own development. Correlative are themes of the plot which stress manipulation of other people, surrender to destiny, and resignation in failure. At odds with the responsibility each man has for the control he exercises over another is the motivation which urges detachment from all obligation and commitment. Such submission to exterior forces, and such evasion of responsibilities, imply a further incapacity to achieve moral maturity.

Man's uncertain role, by implication due to his lack of divine guidance, leaves in doubt the nature of his relationships with fellow human beings, and the nature of their exercise in love. The lack of self-love is evident as well, as the individual psyche must rely on fictive personalities created to be imposed on reality.

GENERIC COHERENCE

There are a number of major themes which derive their coherence from those component motifs which occur throughout the work. It is from the interweaving of these motifs and themes that the unity of the thematic fabric is assured. The author will develop as principal themes some ideas suggested by the component elements of the title. The barrenness of life without love is a theme which receives considerable attention, but motifs will be presented which will show the desert as well, as the barren space between groping, loving individuals, and also as the fruitless disillusioning expanse of love itself.

The human quest for love, which is a key thematic element of the novel, is graphically and touchingly implied in the leitmotif

of hands reaching through some barrier. Several linking phrases
contain motifs which are in turn component motifs in correlative
themes, representing the many facets of love and the routes man
takes to reach the destination of satisfaction.

The image of a green park, lush with the few trees of Bordeaux
where the burning sun is consuming their very substance, appears
in the summer of Raymond Courrèges' turbulent, sexually-aroused
seventeenth year. The cool refreshment of the verdure — which in
a public park should be available to all — is cut off from those
young people, like Raymond, who are thirsting for fulfillment of
newly-awakened desires.

> ... Bordeaux, ville pauvre en arbres, hors de ce Jardin
> public où il semblait aux enfants mourant de soif que,
> derrière les hautes grilles solennelles, achevait de se con-
> sumer la dernière verdure du monde. (p. 37)

Doctor Courrèges hurries to what he hopes will be a climactic
visit with Maria Cross, the meeting which will put an end to his
longing to possess her, as storm clouds lower overhead: "Entre les
grilles de petits jardins, des branches de lilas poussiéreux attendaient la pluie comme des mains tendues" (p. 96).

Raymond shares similar hopes, and experiences, as he recalls
his longing for Maria in the days of their tram rides together, underscored in the motif: "Des feuillages poudreux ressemblaient à
travers les grilles à des mains qui cherchent l'eau" (p. 222).

The boy's greedy grasping of Maria, when their final rendezvous
takes place, leads her to distract him with refreshments to drink.

> "Vous avez soif?"
>
> ... ...
> "En tout cas, pas soif de sirop."

It was the reaching movement itself which removed Maria
Cross from the ardent Raymond forever: "... et tout à coup, le
geste de ses bras tendus avait suffi pour éloigner cette Maria
vertigineusement.... Il savait d'une science sûre que désormais
il ne la toucherait pas plus qu'une étoile" (p. 173).

Gestures which seek to span a distance toward those who are
beloved are expressed in motifs which underlie themes of the inac-

cessibility of love of any kind. Has it not been noted that Lucie Courrèges' lifelong nightmare is to strain to touch her husband, only to find him always beyond her reach? "... elle avançait, comme à tatons, mais de ses bras tendus, ne savait lui donner que des blessures" (p. 34).

Silent, almost impersonal rides in the family carriage saw Paul Courrèges take his son's hand when words do not come to bridge the void between them. The boy gently frees his hand to prevent development of intimacy and its obligations. In contrast, the same gesture signals, at the end of the novel, the establishment of some communication between the two men, as Raymond willingly holds the old man's hand courteously.

The importance attached by Mauriac to the theme of inaccessibility is indicated by his use of other component motifs which project the sense of universal distance between individuals in a variety of relationships.

Just as the bars of the garden grill held overtones of prisons, Raymond approaches his home and sees: "... l'épaisse prison de feuilles où les membres d'une seule famille vivaient, aussi confondus et séparés que les mondes dont est faite la Voie Lactée..." (p. 119). Maria Cross sees Raymond further away than ever as an attainable love: "... aussi loin de son amour que le chasseur Orion, brûlait cet enfant inaccessible" (p. 164). The very idea of love remains suspended for Maria Cross, unrewarded, and so distant that its light may not be enough to guide her through the desert below: "Mille idées confuses s'éveillaient en Maria, disparaissaient, comme au-dessus de sa tête, dans l'azur désert, les étoiles filantes, les bolides perdus" (p. 180). Her inability not only to experience, but to comprehend the nature of love leaves her conscious of profound loneliness, without family or friends to distract her: "... mais qu'était cette solitude, au prix de cet autre isolement dont la plus tendre famille ne l'eût pas délivrée..." (p. 180).

It would have been self-delusion, however, to expect that a compromise in love—the exploitation of a family for comfort's sake— would resolve the riddle of love and pleasure. A correlative theme stresses the belief that a family, like the prison of this planet, is a miniaturized world, inhabited by persons whose power to communicate has been short-circuited. Component motifs specify

Lucie Courrèges' resentment of her husband: " '... tu ne me dis rien.' " That their son is a near-suicide is not observed by parents self-preoccupied by their particular torments. Survival is insured by taking the offensive in disarming other members of the group. "... les membres d'une même famille ont à la fois le goût de ne pas se confier et celui de surprendre les secrets du voisin" (p. 33). How else to explain a family which does not notice an unkempt, maladroit boy becoming overnight a polished, sophisticated young man, confident of his ability to please and determined at seduction: "... les membres d'une famille trop unie ne se voient plus les uns les autres" (p. 72). Maria Cross has only confirmed to Raymond what he had already learned of family life: " 'Nos proches sont ceux que nous ignorons le plus.... Nous arrivons à ne plus voir ce qui nous entoure" (p. 171).

* * *

The value of the linking image is found to be not only in the expression of the major theme which it consolidates through its motif component clusters, but also in its linking quality with other major thematic interests. For example, the music-crazed dancers in the bar, at the end of the novel, make the same gesture of vain aspiration, in a motif of yet another substance. "... les hommes se détachèrent des femmes et ils battaient des mains, puis le tendaient vers les nègres, avec le geste des suppliants—comme si leur vie eût dépendu de ce vacarme..." (p. 216).

It can be appreciated that such a leitmotif is especially meaningful since the futile gesture of the hands stretched out leads in this case to another generically coherent theme, that of, not a thirst, but a *goût du néant*. The void of nothingness, like the annihilation in death or love, is later cited to be just another form of drug. Some one of these is essential to make endurable the human condition of solitude.

The three fundamental human relationships—one's ties to the family of man, the bonds of consanguinity, and the regenerative impulse toward some complementary individual—are illustrated in motifs depicting the human passage toward love as a journey, oriented by the winds of chance. Raymond finds contentment among the strangers in the tram: "Bien loin de souffrir... dans cette cargaison humaine; il [Raymond] se persuadait d'être émigrant; il était assis parmi les voyageurs de l'entrepont, et le vaisseau fendait les ténèbres..." (p. 61). Threats to the family are treated like a fire in the hold of a ship. Some instinctive response of survival seeks to preserve discipline in the family vessel, where mutiny of a few threatens all, even the prisoners who are aboard. "L'instinct de conservation inspirait à cet équipage embarqué pour la vie sur la même galère, le souci de ne laisser s'allumer à bord aucun incendie" (p. 76).

As helpless as a rudderless craft, Paul Courrèges must watch Maria Cross leave the course of his destiny forever. "...les amarres sont rompues, les ancres levées, le vaisseau bouge, et l'on ne sait pas encore qu'il bouge, mais dans une heure ce ne sera plus qu'une tache sur la mer" (p. 202).

Correlative to the theme revealed by hands reaching vainly through the grill is the explanation of attempts toward *volupté*. It is Maria Cross who speaks of sensual pleasure as a kind of escape hatch in man's effort to fill the abyss between individuals and of the pursuit of voluptuous pleasure itself as evidence of the essential paucity of profound human contact. The objective becomes so desperately remote, that sensuality which was to be the path toward fulfillment, becomes itself the object of man's larger, futile endeavors. "Toute caresse suppose un intervalle entre deux êtres" (p. 179). She professes a belief that a mystical kind of communion might be produced in an intimacy more profound than physical: "...cette étreinte n'aurait pas été nécessaire, cette brève étreinte que la honte dénoue..." (p. 180).

The drive to find expression of the creative human energy is revealed to be an irresistible one, which follows an unmarked road toward an ill-defined land of satisfaction. The theme is indicated by use of motifs using a "route" image, a route on which several of the characters embark in futile march.

Dr. Courrèges can look back over a lifetime of experiences, initially as hopeful, and ultimately as hopeless as his inarticulate pursuit of Maria Cross.

> Elle rejoignait toutes ses autres amours depuis son adolescence.... Suivant cette piste, le docteur s'avisa qu'un sentiment l'avait toujours occupé... pareil à celui dont il finissait à peine de souffrir. (p. 187)

He can at last look at the prostrate body of Maria Cross without desire, a professional man whose will can impose itself, ethically, on his soul in ferment: "... il regarde ce corps ardemment, de toute son intelligence, son esprit lucide barre la route au triste amour" (p. 196). He makes thereby a radical detour from the road on which Maria Cross has set out, the distance of which extends over the horizon to undisclosed possibilities of love. The progression of her amorous expectations of Raymond Courrèges is revealed in the motifs:

> Elle entrevoyait une longue route ... et se défendait de songer aux étapes devenues brûlantes — à la forêt enfin dont les êtres qui s'aiment écartent les branches pour s'y perdre. Non, non, ils n'iraient pas si loin. (p. 137)

Although she terminated the voyage in rejecting Raymond, nevertheless Maria Cross recognizes reluctantly that advances made toward the unknown quantity of another human being are the sole means of attaining a goal of satisfying love. " 'Songez qu'il n'est aucune autre route entre nous et les êtres que toucher, qu'étreindre ... la volupté enfin' " (p. 198). The enormity of the problem—how to reconcile love as a passion and metaphysical aspiration with the institution of marriage—is suggested as Maria continues:

> "Nous connaissons bien pourtant à quoi mène ce chemin, et pourquoi il fut tracé: pour continuer l'espèce ... et pour cela seulement. Oui ... nous empruntons la seule route possible, mais qui n'a pas été frayée vers ce que nous cherchons. ..." (p. 198)

When pleasure is there to be enjoyed, and while the loved one remains unattainable, " 'Quelle folie d'espérer atteindre cet objet. ...' " Sensuality becomes the distraction from the pain of the unhappy search.

Confirmation of the failure to achieve even this goal is seen in Raymond's desolate observation of his seventeen years of concentration on the pursuit of pleasure:

> Pourtant, ce qui, du passé confus, lui appartenait en propre n'était qu'une mince route vite parcourue entre d'épaisses

ténèbres; le museau à terre, il a suivi sa piste, ignorant toutes les autres qui croissaient la sienne. (p. 208)

Motifs proclaim that a human being's hope to find fulfillment in loving pleasure requires self-delusion to the point of madness. As a student, it will be recalled, Raymond did not conceal his adolescent interest in the delights of the flesh, thereby posing a threat to his contemporaries, "... comme si, dans un asile de fous, le bruit eût couru que le plus furieux, ayant rompu sa camisole errait tout nu...."

Paul Courrèges recognizes that any gesture to embrace Maria Cross, while on his "professional" calls to her, would be "un geste aussi dément que de briser ce miroir." Repetitious labels indicating the madness of his expectations as a lover suggest the hopelessness of his cause: "Certes, il avait été fou de croire qu'une jeune femme pût avoir le goût sensible de sa présence. Fou! fou! Mais quel raisonnement nous préserverait de cette insupportable douleur?" (p. 81).

Indulgence in romantic and erotic fantasies provide "un enchantement ignoré," "un beau songe." " 'Je suis un fou, et pourtant...' " (p. 89). Seventeen years later, father and son are still victims of the same mania. The doctor lapses only momentarily to denounce Maria Cross' denial of a search for pleasure, as he insists: " 'Comme les autres vous ne cherchez vous aussi que ça; le plaisir,' " and appalled at his own behavior in the recurrent fever of passion, he declares, " 'Mais qu'est-ce que j'ai? Je suis fou.' "

At the same time, Raymond, too, recognizes that he is in the grip of a seizure he cannot control. His mind throbs with tantalizing visions of future conquests of Maria Cross, which are as empty as images on a movie screen. The projections and his responses are so alive that Raymond "... s'étonne de ce que les premiers passants ne s'aperçoivent pas de sa folie" (p. 240). Forced always to run after the unattainable, Raymond asks himself if he was yielding to "... cette folie qui oblige de courir ceux dont les vêtements sont en feu" (p. 242). Fleeing the searing pain of the flames, of course, intensifies the burn to be endured. The flight, as well, causes the flames to burn more cruelly than ever. Every step away from the original small flame finds the fire of passion shining more brightly.

Two component motifs, repetitious in their phrasing, provide the correlative link with another significant, generically coherent theme. It is Paul Courrèges' considered belief that

> Dès que nous sommes seuls, nous sommes fous. Oui, le contrôle de nous-mêmes ne joue que soutenu par le contrôle que les autres nous imposent. (p. 66)

> Non, il ... ne se croyait pas différent des autres hommes qui, selon lui, étaient tous des fous qu'ils se trouvaient seuls avec eux-mêmes et hors du contrôle d'autrui. (p. 87)

There are raised herein the fundamental questions of man's ability to shape and direct his present and future life, and of his responsibility for the consequences of his behavior in view of the unknown effects each individual has on others. It is an inference that man's moral perspective is determined not by aspirations toward some beatific being, but in consequence of the limiting presence of his fellow creatures, which results in the adaptation of personal behavior to obtain general social acceptance or loving approval. The suggestion that man makes himself in the image created by those who love him—an image which in itself is subjective and self-serving to its creator who is meeting his own needs— raises as well questions of "sincerity" and "authenticity." A lifetime of involuntarily restructuring one's identity and character to meet conceptions artificially established by another obviates the salutary maturing process of self-determination, and the exercise of free will.

Unquestionably, the unformed adolescent is easy prey to those who yet have hopes of imposing a final and different cast on the product of their efforts. The hostile, critical atmosphere of Raymond's family—"ses ennemis"—makes him accept an image of gross ugliness. "A dix-sept ans, il arrive que le garçon le plus farouche accepte bénévolement l'image de soi-même que les autres lui imposent." The boy's malleability is seen in his reaction to the uncritical, interested observation of him by Maria Cross in the tram. She has brought thereby to life "un être neuf," and the attribution is made: "... une femme, sans prononcer de paroles, par la seule puissance de son regard, transformait leur enfant, le pétrissait à nouveau ..." (p. 72).

Although this change appears to be a radical one, imposed from the exterior, contradictory hints are offered that the man he is in the process of becoming is, in germ, already in existence within. There can be noted the motif of a goddess emerging from a tree where she has been buried. Or, the question is posed, "...avant que l'inconnue l'eût regardé, n'était-il réellement qu'un écolier sordide?" His change from unkempt brute to polished seducer is decribed as "l'apparence d'une résurrection invisible" —resurrection implying a re-appearance of qualities deeply buried, but certainly already present. "Nous avons été pétris et repétris par ceux qui nous ont aimés... nous sommes leur ouvrage" (p. 73).

This is a key motif carrying the theme of the responsibility each individual must bear for the influence he has in affecting the lives he touches, a theme recurrent in the thinking and behavior of the characters of the novel. "Le Raymond Courrèges de ce soir... ce garçon de trente-cinq ans, serait un autre homme si en 19...... il n'avait vu s'asseoir en face de lui dans le tramway du retour, Maria Cross" (p. 73). It was her encouraging, even flattering attention that wrought the positive miracle of emergence in Raymond. Her responsibility for his later negative development is fixed as well: "Si elle l'avait créé par son amour, elle achevait son œuvre, en le méprisant: elle venait de lâcher dans le monde un garçon dont ce serait la manie, de se prouver à soi-même qu'il était irrésistible" (p. 176).

The deprivation of man's moral right to free himself from destructive forces within himself, by this conception of the all-powerful rule of others, produced at thirty-five a man fated to remain frozen at the emotional level of his first disappointment. Just seeing Maria Cross again causes a regression to "...l'adolescent qu'il fut: timide, empêtré d'un désir sournois" (p. 208).

Because the image one person holds of his fellow being is necessarily a subjective one, and not necessarily accurate in its perceptions, the chosen love object is condemned to strain futilely to meet an impossible, unrealistic standard: "C'est notre douleur de voir l'être aimé composer sous nos yeux l'image qu'il se fait de nous.... Et il nous impose sa vision, il nous oblige de nous conformer... à son étroite idée" (p. 209).

But Raymond is not the last link in the chain of human experience. Self-conscious and self-preoccupied as he is, he sees, in the correlative theme to others' shaping him, the responsibility he must now bear for those he in turn has affected, as he reflects: "... que de créatures à qui son approche fut fatale!" (p. 242) "Encore ne sait-il pas combien d'existences il a orientées, il a désorientées; il ignore qu'à cause de lui, telle femme a tué un germe dans son sein, qu'une jeune fille est morte..." (p. 242).

The detachment from obligation and commitment which he has steadfastly maintained is unacceptable with the realization that human beings must rejoice and suffer on behalf of another: "... la douleur pour la première fois l'obligeait d'arrêter sa pensée sur ces choses à quoi il n'avait jamais réfléchi."

It is the realization that he is a prisoner of his past experience that causes Raymond's astonishment: "... il fut stupéfait de ce qu'un être, sans le vouloir, puisse peser d'un tel poids dans le destin d'un autre être" (p. 242).

The participation of destiny, as the force which moves the pieces of the chess-game — placing one person here and another there to produce a fatal outcome — is developed generically as a theme, touching each of the principal characters. One might almost see the contingent incident as a messenger of destiny, dropping onto the path of existing characters and situations to bind their destinies forever.

Raymond is spared the ignominy of suicide by shooting or drowning: "... il allait être sauvé — non par ses seules forces." And so he is, with the assistance of a benign God who "... ne voulut pas qu'il en trouvât les balles," and the appearance of "... une bête crevée... blanche." He is saved for the chance meeting in the tram which will alter irrevocably, it is suggested, the shape of his years to come.

Maria Cross, too, it is affirmed, rode the same public carriage to visit her son's grave, but toward an unknown purpose: "... sur la route qui mène à l'enfant mort, il a fallu qu'elle rencontrât cet enfant vivant." Having already yielded to destiny, she accepts in the attraction to Raymond, "son destin inéxorable," as part of a larger fatality which condemns her to present her actions to the world with "une face abominable" (p. 147).

The loss of individual power to make one's own destiny has been indicated in those component motifs which show man at the mercy of unidentified forces. Raymond's unhappy recognition that his life is nothing more than "... une absence qu'il faut balancer par une attente," reveals the lack of control of the resource of his brief stay on earth. He feels he must be content to live on his expectations only, a vicarious life, substituting the hope for the deed of meaningful action. It is the punishment of all those in the novel who spend a lifetime seeking, with little thought to giving, in love.

Lucie Courrèges had abandoned hope ever of receiving from her husband "le don total de quelques instants" although she pleads for the reward of a few intimate words. Her husband's days are of even greater emptiness. He cannot endure if Maria Cross does not set a time for a meeting. "Par un miracle instantané, toute son existence s'organisait autour de ce rendez-vous nouveau." Raymond undergoes a nearly identical experience when he accepts his role as a perpetual satellite in orbit around this or another Maria Cross. "Même eût-elle remis le rendez-vous, Raymond s'en serait consolé pourvu qu'elle en eût proposé un autre, et ce nouvel espoir eût été à la mesure du vide infini de sa vie" (p. 240). Even Maria Cross knows that for her, the vitality of the present is encompassed in the expectation of a future joy: awaiting the first spoken contact with the ever-more intriguing boy in the tram, she dreams as she listens to his father:

> Mais, demain, demain il y serait sans doute et déjà elle était toute tournée vers cette joie future, vers cet espoir chaque jour déçu et renaissant qu'il se passerait peut-être du nouveau, qu'il lui adresserait la parole enfin. (p. 98)

No word that they speak ever meets these glowing expectations. Once the relationship is established, the hope prevails but is doomed to everlasting disappointment: "... Maria Cross ... attend cette heure unique du rendez-vous, brève flamme dans sa journée terne. Mais cette heure, qu'elle est décevante!" (p. 136).

Rather like the abstract tension just discussed — living in a present absence anticipating a future presence — is the equally enigmatic theme of those living in emptiness, seeking a "néant." Although Raymond Courrèges may have recognized his life as "vide infini," or "vide atroce," the abyss is not deep enough or empty enough to dull the pain of his certain knowledge that his passionate quest is to be eternal and self-perpetuating: "... passion toute puissante, capable l'enfanter jusqu'à la mort d'autres mondes vivants, d'autres Maria" (p. 243). He has inherited not only this capacity for passion, but his father's systematic approach for negating its power. He will accept some advice at the novel's end, " 'en attendant que ce soit fini, drogue-toi; fais la planche,' " since he has already seen that no other exists from the torments of his nature, and the nature of love, exist than "de la stupeur et du sommeil."

Paul Courrèges had survived the enucleation of Maria Cross from his life by, medically speaking, anaesthesia and therapy. With an established life pattern of overwork, he is assured a numbness to what seems intolerable. The same technique is his salvation once his obsession develops for Maria Cross. The excessively generous giving of himself which earns him accolades of saintliness is, in truth, the narcotic used to deaden his suffering in love.

The leitmotif of a man injecting himself with morphine is a focally placed motif, resounding in linking phrases, always in dynamic tension with a failure regarding Maria Cross. "Comme il se fût fait une piqûre de morphine, il s'inocula le souci quotidien" (p. 102).

> ... le laboratoire surtout lui était un havre; il y perdait conscience de son amour; la recherche abolissait le temps, consumait les heures.... (p. 44)

> ... oui, se rosser, se tuer, atteindre la délivrance grâce à l'opium d'une besogne.... (p. 81)

> Travail, opium unique.... (p. 135)

Although those few linking phrases represent a weapon against the chagrins of love, there is a kind of insurance policy held by Paul Courrèges, of which he is not the sole beneficiary, in the family he has established. That, too, is an escape but in complete contrast with the emotional paralysis induced by psychological drugs. The doctor urges Raymond to try this treatment as a means of diverting his grief:

"Tu ne saurais croire comme il fait bon vivre au plus épais d'une famille.... On porte sur soi les milles soucis des autres; ces mille piqûres attirent le sang à la peau, tu comprends.... Elles nous deviennent indispensables." (p. 236)

Although death seems the simplest way out for the suicidal boy, Raymond, or his father, who would like to "se terrer dans sa vieillesse," the business of living continues its pressure and attractions. Man's dreams invariably become his hopes, and as Raymond asks himself of his empty days ahead, "...comment combler ce trou?" the challenge of living prompts a response however evasive or inauthentic.

It was Mme Courrèges, perceptive mother of the doctor, who first realized that although he was not sick, he was indeed suffering from some internal torment. It is only when Raymond and his father meet for the last time in the novel that the son realizes his father's unending anguish. "Pourtant ce vieillard, voilà dix-sept ans qu'il saigne" (p. 235). Paul Courrèges repeatedly thought of his agony for Maria Cross as a malady, for which, by determination and resignation, he could affect a cure. Each time he believes himself to have mastered his need for Maria, he is amazed, "...pareil à ce faux miraculé qui voit soudain la plaie se rouvrir qu'il avait crue guérie" (p. 124). "...sa passion n'était plus qu'un mal engourdi, dont il gardait une conscience sourde; il aurait pu le réveiller s'il l'avait voulu: en touchant l'endroit sensible, il était sûr de s'arracher un cri" (p. 135). Maria Cross, to whom discipline and control are vitually unknown qualities, enjoys the gnawing pain she feels. The suffering is at least a diversion from the emptiness of her idle days: "...elle irritait sa plaie, entretenait son feu...." The cares of a family will, for Paul Courrèges, be the therapy to make a cure possible — an essentially selfish, exploitive view of the function of this group, yet their small, continuous concerns allow little time for introspection: " 'Elles nous détournent de notre plaie secrète, de notre profonde plaie intérieure...' " (p. 236).

The conflict in the role of sexuality is seen in the views of it held by father and son. Paul Courrèges believes that man needs protection "contre la foule des choses désirables." He attributes his safe passage through life to Raymond's affection for him;

turned often by it from " 'une sollicitation délicieuse, peut-être criminelle....' " His son can only mock him in exasperation: " 'Quelle folie ... de croire qu'il existât des plaisirs défendus' " (p. 237). Also antithetical are the personalities of Maria and the doctor, who is characterized in a frequent repetitious label of a particular gesture: the motion of sweeping away impediments before his face. The physician, an exacting man of science whose attention to detail allows no obscuring of vision, and whose overladen days can tolerate no obstacles is observed as "... il déblayait sa route encombrée..." (p. 43). To wipe the indifferent Maria from his mind, "sa main fit, dans le vide, le geste de déblayer" (p. 101). To drive out memories of tears and separation, "Il ébauche encore le geste de déblayer, de faire place nette" (p. 103). He obliterates painful moments with Lucie when "il fit encore le geste de déblayer..." (p. 109). Even in his old age, he makes the same gesture to eliminate traces of his final meeting with Maria Cross before returning to his home and wife.

No other description seems so significant of Maria Cross than the repetitious label which underscores her indolent sensuality. Like a personification of the passion which is in the doctor's mind and which "s'étire, et bâille, et se redresse," Maria is almost invariably depicted as reclining. No less than eleven times does Mauriac present her in some languourous representation of "femme étendue." So habitual is the attitude for her that having changed her position in Raymond's presence, he asks "pourquoi elle ne restait pas étendue."

Raymond's despair at satisfying his burning adolescent longing is typical of motifs used to underscore the burning, parched aridity of unfulfillment and the soothing alleviation of satisfaction.

> ... il traversa les vignes assoupies, descendit vers le vivier, au bas d'une prairie aride: il espérait ... qu'il ne pourrait se dépêtrer de cette eau bourbeuse et qu'enfin sa bouche, ses yeux seraient comblés de vase.... (p. 45)

A suicide is equated, in effect, with a wishful self-dissolution in the moist, steaming stagnancy of sensuality.

Maria's desire, kindled by feverish imaginings, is described in recurrent motifs of unfed fire: "... cette flamme à qui tout aliment

soudain faisait défaut mais tout de même inextinguible. De quoi
se nourrissait ce feu?" (p. 175).

The connection between the nourishment of passion, or the
slaking of thirst, is revealed by numerous component motifs relating to the actual tasting of sensual experiences: "Maria Cross,
Maria Cross, ce nom l'étouffait comme un caillot de sang; il en
sentait dans sa bouche la douceur chaude et salée ... le tiède flot
de ce nom gonfla ses joues ..." (p. 121).

In the absence of more direct expression, a certain voluptuousness is achieved in shaping words about the loved one. "Faute
d'éteindre ce qu'elle désire, elle [la passion] s'assouvira de paroles"
(p. 125). Raymond experiences a related pleasure in regurgitating
his loathing of Maria Cross after her rejection of him: "... déjà
le goût était dans sa bouche de ce qu'il allait vomir" (p. 185). There
is little of the abstract in matters of physical satisfaction for
Madeleine and Gaston Basque, who in the regular format of their
lives, find gratification, on a schedule, in "le lit immense." "Ils y
allaient comme ils se mettaient à table à midi et à huit heures:
le moment d'avoir faim" (p. 60).

Mauriac, in stressing the rampant power of the human sexual
energy, introduces numerous motifs concerning the Baudelaire
phrase, "l'obscur ennemi qui les ronge." Paul Courrèges had
warned his patient that it is essential "de dompter en vous toutes
ces bêtes qui ne sont pas vous-même." Maria Cross, is thought by
Raymond to have "une face étrange, à la fois, intelligente et
animale ... la face d'une bête merveilleuse." This may be a related
expression to the one she found on the faces of men watching her
and a nude dancer at the theatre, "des faces de bêtes." Men in love
are said to be wearing masks: "'... les hommes pleins de leur
amour ont aussi, collée à la figure, cette apparence souvent hideuse,
toujours terrible de la bête qui remue en eux" (p. 179).

It is interesting to note, too, that when Maria enters the little
nightclub she does so: "Aveugle comme au soir du toril...."

As Maria, filled with the turbulence of her confused desires for
Raymond, paces beneath the whirling, storm-filled clouds which
mirror her own state of mind: "Dans ce livide ciel, une bête féroce
est somnolente, rôde, gronde, se tapit."

Not unlike the bull in the arena he passes, who struggles to
escape his suffering, Paul Courrèges hurries toward his critical

meeting with Maria. The skies are again reverberating with pent-up energies: "Non, l'orage n'éclaterait pas avant que le dernier taureau eût fini de souffrir." The storm does indeed burst, and coincidentally it is read of the doctor, "Il ne souffrait plus; il jouissait de l'orage finissant — pensait à lui-même . . . comme à un ami dont on accepte la mort en songeant qu'il ne souffre plus" (p. 101).

CHAPTER IV

LE NŒUD DE VIPÈRES

THEMES OF THE STORY

THE NARRATOR OF THE NOVEL, Louis, is reared as the only child of a scrupulously thrifty bourgeois couple. The death of his father, a minor civil servant, lies outside the thematic framework of the story. The grueling pattern of self-deprivation is relieved for his widowed mother only by the boy's outstanding scholastic success. His obsessive competitive drive toward achievement has negative consequences to his health, when he succumbs to consumption, and to his personality, when hypersensitivity in human relations makes him fiercely unapproachable and unloveable. His recovery from the respiratory disorder coincides with his mother's disclosure that on his majority, he will enjoy considerable private means as a consequence of her business acumen, with her persistent direction of her son toward a law career, and with their removal to a relatively luxurious, staffed town house.

Attentions paid him by the glittering, distinguished Fondau-dège family as a suitor for their daughter, Isa, represent an unanticipated compliment for this boy, conscious of his lack of family background. Only his mother realizes that it is his fortune, and not his person, which attracts the luxury-loving family. Her evaluation of that group remains one of an unsatisfactory business risk. After a quiet wedding for the young couple, they in turn reject her, as a too-visible evidence of Louis' humble origins.

Isa's confession of an earlier engagement to a handsome and wealthy man revives Louis' earlier self-doubts and creates suspicion regarding her reasons for marrying him. A new life of silence and alienation begins which will last for forty years.

A series of pregnancies permits legitimate distanciation between the couple, as Louis begins a secret life of amorous pursuit in the city. Also unknown to his wife and children is his extraordinary ability to profit in business affairs. His legal career exceeds all expectations and only in his home is his celebrity unnoticed. His reputation grows as a calculating, covetous man and he rejects opportunities for political success in favor of increasing his private wealth.

Louis becomes an isolated figure in the household, facing fear and hostility in his wife and two older children, Geneviève and Hubert. His youngest child, Marie, innocent, pious and loving, is the single comfort of his days. He almost yields to the temptation of seducing Marinette, Isa's sister and a recent widow, willing to love. The death of the child, Marie, creates a void of unspeakable depth. His grief is assuaged in the appearances of Marinette's son, Luc, who becomes for Louis the son he could admire and love. His objective becomes to bequeath everything to Luc while eliminating from his will, his wife and "her" hostile children. Luc's attraction to the "sport magnifique" of war is fatal and he is soon declared missing at the front, and is presumed dead. Isa's children are desperate, in their marital and business problems, to have access to some of their father's estate, or at least to be assured of some expectations.

Anger drives Louis to Paris to seek an unknown illegitimate son, Robert, whom he has supported since birth. Robert's ignorance and fear defeat Louis' purpose of leaving his entire fortune to the boy and his mother. Unable to endure the stress of financial maneuvering and aware of his helplessness, Robert betrays Louis' plan to Hubert and Geneviève, the legitimate children, who promise a small annuity in return for the information. Detained in Paris by illness, Louis receives, too late, telegrams from Hubert, notifying him of his wife's sudden illness and death.

Louis confronts his children with their intrigue and with their hypocrisy in pretending not to know an exact address where he might have been reached to be present at his wife's death. His fortune and properties cease to interest him, and he seeks only peace from the harassments of his family. He makes complete bequest of his estate during his lifetime to his incredulous children, and his quest for spiritual riches and salvation becomes his preoccupation. His past life of self-hate, and guilt at projecting such an image on his children, are rejected in a spirit of love and concern.

Against the wishes of his children, Louis shelters in his home his granddaughter, Janine, whose humiliated husband abandoned her. She observes Louis' last weeks of life, as he helps to orient her perspectives of marital and personal relationships. Louis' attempts to define or identify a spiritual source become specific, and he dies confessing to his journal that he finally knows who is the One to be adored.

All of the foregoing essentials are revealed through what is begun as a letter, and what becomes a compulsively written journal. Louis' views of his own circumstances and responses to them are substantially refuted by his son, Hubert, in a letter written to Geneviève after his discovery of the journal. Janine, however, although denied access to the diary, is steadfast, as she writes to Hubert, in her vindication of Louis, as a man converted to, and protected by, Divine Love.

This brief outline is a re-ordered view of events, arranged in their linear progression, an order not seen in the work itself. More erratic in its chronological pattern than the two novels previously discussed, *Le Nœud de vispères* is offered as an emotional out-pouring, with all the unevenness and vagaries of uncontrolled, spontaneous expression. The nature of the document itself, which is described at the outset as a letter which would have contained nothing other than expressions of vengeance, "... durant presque un demi-siècle cuisinée" (p. 9), [1] becomes a source of wonder to the writer himself, after the first twenty pages: "Je relis ces lignes écrites hier soir dans une sorte de délire.... Ce n'est plus une lettre, mais un journal rompu, repris..." (p. 30).

The interruptions to the journal are not only daily occurrences which take place in the last years of his life (Louis is 68) and the arrival of death itself in mid-sentence, but are also to be seen in

---

[1] François Mauriac, *Le Nœud de vipères* (Paris: Bernard Grasset, 1933). Subsequent references are to this edition and are placed in the text in parentheses.

recollections of earlier years when events and relationships revealed themes of importance to the development of the story. Facets of his resentment toward his wife, Isa, are often revealed, for example, as springboards they provide to memories from the past. His wife, from the outset, failed to understand the relationship he had with his mother, the nature of the organized, hierarchical society in wich he grew up, and indeed, never succeeded in knowing Louis' mother as an individual. The prodigality of the easy-living Fondaudèges was in the sharpest contrast to the frugal, yet substantively rich life of Louis' parents. The Fondaudèges, for example, kept splendidly-equipped carriages and teams, but had to use uninvested capital to do so. Louis' mother, on the other hand, spent rarely, drawing her first-class provisions from her profit-making lands and farms. "Les métairies de ma mère ... fournissaient à bon compte notre table dont j'eusse été bien étonné si l'on m'avait dit qu'elle était très raffinée" (p. 19).

His parents' self-denial "en se saignant aux quatre veines," had bought the vineyards which Louis owns and will profit from throughout his life. The pine forests were sown by them on wretched land, so that at twenty-one, Louis might claim a fully matured forest awaiting his disposition. It is his mother's prodding which directs Louis into a legal career in overriding youthful, idealistic interest in social justice.

> Un certain désir de justice sociale me tourmentait aussi.
> J'obligeai ma mère à mettre bas les maisons de torchis où
> nos métayers vivaient.... (p. 28)
> Mais, je ne fis rien de plus.

His social conscience is stilled also by a passion shared by his bourgeois contemporaries, even those whose friendship he despised. "Je souffrais de reconnaître que nous avions mes adversaires et moi, une passion commune: la terre, l'argent" (p. 29).

Louis' uninterrupted application to "cette lutte pour la première place," his willing and "haineuse rivalité" with his schoolmates, his inability "de souffrir la plus légère moquerie," his "ton supérieur et doctoral" with women, created a lonely world apart where he could succeed with little interference from others.

The isolation of these adolescent years, when he was imprisoned within the walls of his character and personality, is a keystone in the structure of his early manhood. Convinced by then of his displeasing personal mannerisms, he exaggerates his faults: "Je me hâtais de déplaire exprès par crainte de déplaire naturellement" (p. 24).

The remarkable frugality of Louis' mother in his childhood is offset in manhood by her astonishing generosity, once their fortune is assured,

> Elle que j'avais vue si économe, pour ne pas dire avare, me donnait plus d'argent que je n'en demandais, me poussait à la dépense, me rapportait de Bordeaux des cravates ridicules que je rejusais de porter. (p. 25)

He responds to her overwhelming indulgence with "une dureté atroce." She accepts supinely his furious anger "comme les colères d'un dieu" at her and at his lack of social success. Once she realizes that he is taking an interest in pursuing girls, she has no objection but merely seeks to protect him from damaging excesses. She takes advantage of his confinement to bed with a lung complaint to condition his mind for the career she is about to propose. Louis is shaped and programmed by his mother, lovingly to be sure, for maximum production "pour gagner gros" as though he were, and in truth he was, her most valuable possession. "Elle parlait, parlait, me découvrait, d'un coup, ses plans. Et moi, je l'écoutais, boudeur, hostile, les yeux tournés vers la fenêtre" (p. 23). Her purchase of a relatively smart house in Bordeaux, with a domestic staff, places Louis in an enviable position as he enjoys his private income. Yet in spite of his new advantages, he remains an outsider among the Jesuit-trained, English-mannered young men of brilliant genealogical background: "Je les enviais et je les méprisais, et leur dédain (peut-être imaginaire) exaltait encore ma rancœur" (p. 27).

He does not spare, either, boys of lower social orders, whom he describes as "adversaires" of the *haute bourgeoisie,* and whom he attracts, uses, and then abuses. He treats them with "... une moquerie qui les blessaient mortellement et dont ils me gardaient rancune" (p. 28).

Away from the demanding complexities of urban society, amid background motifs of pure mountain air, fresh foods, and flowering trees, Louis and his mother observe the Fondaudège family on vacation. The level of the Fondaudège standard of living is dazzling. Occupying the royal apartments in the hotel, served by a nun in their *entourage*, driven in magnificent carriages, the sight is a social revelation to Louis. He is at first attracted to Isa's mother, dressed in black, as he dreams of "défis stendhaliens": "La nudité de son cou, de ses bras, de ses mains me troublait" (p. 32). But he finds irresistible the attentions of Isa, "vouée au blanc," who makes the opening, fatal move: "C'est extraordinaire, pour un garçon d'avoir de si grands cils'" (p. 34).

The years of isolation, of hateful rejection, drop away. He can feel his powers of attraction assert themselves, as he sees a response to him in the faces of women generally. Louis interprets as love his warm reaction to the invitation to enter the magic Fondaudège circle. "Cela passait l'imagination, c'était unimaginable..." (p. 29). Even his hatred of organized religion disappears as he gladly welcomes acceptance by the Fondaudège family and joins them at Sunday mass: "C'etait le culte d'une classe." So confident has he become of his power to charm and please that he never questions Isa's family's willingness for him to meet her alone, and receives unthinkingly, "... la confiance des tiens dont j'étais à mille lieues de croire qu'elle pût être calculée" (p. 39). He accepts her explanations for her sobbing tears as they sit together beneath the lime trees, "'Ce n'est rien, c'est d'être près de vous...'" although it is not long before he realizes the reason for weeping is, ironically, just that: "... parce que tu te trouvais auprès de moi que tu pleurais — auprès de moi et non d'un autre" (p. 38). Their engagement was literally a misunderstanding, when Isa chose to interpret a remark from Louis differently from his intention. He was caught forever, as surely as the linking image suggests, by the worn-out, Anglophile snobbery of the Fondaudèges. "Un vieil Anglais de l'hôtel attrapait, avec un long filet, les papillons de nuit qu'ils (les réverbères) attiraient" (p. 38).

Louis is spared the shame of asking his scorned acquaintances of school days to be part of the wedding. The Fondaudèges accept Louis' fortune as "assez belle," although the obscurity of his background prompts them to "supprimer les fêtes nuptiales." In condescending references to this "alliance... médiocre," Louis is spoken of by Isa's relations, "... comme si j'avais été un enfant naturel" (p. 47).

The euphoria of expansiveness, in Louis' infinitely increased awareness of his capacity to please, ended as abruptly as a dream does. Residual sensual desire in Isa provokes repeated thoughts of a young and rich Rodolphe to whom she had been briefly engaged. This girl, who rebuffs Louis' love-making frequently, with pleas of fatigue, uses the darkened intimacy of their bedroom to savour speaking of her first love. Louis later recognizes her need: "Mais toi, misérable, tu avais besoin de libérer par des paroles cette passion déçue et qui était restée sur sa faim" (p. 54). Insult is added to injury as she maintains that she could not have been happy with such a man "moins respectueux" than Louis, and who was as well, "beau, charmant, aimé" (p. 54). This is the phantom lover of whose presence Louis had been aware intuitively: "... il nous semblait toujours que quelqu'un respirait au fond de la chambre ... autour de notre lassitude, une ombre rôdait ... Il surgissait, ce Rodolphe inconnu ..." (p. 50). As incredible as had seemed his good fortune in being admitted to the Fondaudège world, so is it difficult to accept that Louis' liberation was a hoax: "Tout était faux ... je n'étais pas délivré ..." (p. 52).

This man, who prides himself on not being victim of self-delusion, has indeed fallen prey to his dreams, because he persuaded himself that the sentiments he wants to experience and inspire are real:

> L'amour que j'éprouvais se confondait avec celui que j'inspirais, que je croyais inspirer. Mes propres sentiments n'avaient rien de réel. Ce qui comptait, c'était ma foi en l'amour que tu avais pour moi. (p. 35)

Isa's further insensitive confession that Louis appeared as the answer to a prayer said at Lourdes, to save a girl believed by her panicky parents to be "non-mariable," undermines Louis even further. This multiple confession emerges repeatedly as the particular event which was the cause of the breakdown of their relationship: "... tu as détruit, à ton insu, notre bonheur" (p. 46).

Still only vaguely aware of the enormity of her error, Isa does not know that the following morning, Louis watches her "en proie à une haine" which he will taste for years to come.

The first step to their forty years of silence was one of prudence, in avoiding further mention of the name Rodolphe. "... le fantôme de Rodolphe ne naissait plus de notre étreinte et tu ne prononças plus jamais le nom redoutable. ... il avait accompli son œuvre de destruction" (p. 59). Those delicious moments of intimate conversation must end, which were so sweet that "... peut-être l'amour nous était-il un plaisir moins que ces confidences, ces abandons" (p. 16). Their inability to tell each other everything without fear of repercussion a gulf too profound to measure. "Pendant ces quarante années où nous avons souffert flanc à flanc, tu as trouvé la force d'éviter toute parole un peu profonde..." (p. 129). Louis, whose success had shown early promise in "une grande facilité de parole," responds to his desolation with another newly discovered talent, "la facilité de silence" (p. 23).

A series of pregnancies, miscarriages and births reduce the opportunities for privacy, and the family will henceforth realign itself into two opposing forces. Isa and her children gradually present a united front to their father. The children become her reason for living. Numerous motifs reveal the complexity of this withdrawal to the midst of her family as Louis observes:

C'est la maternité qui t'a rendue à la nature.... (p. 50)

... tu n'avais d'yeux que pour les petits. J'avais accompli, en te fécondant, ce que tu attendais de moi. (p. 61)

With the passage of years, hostility and fears intensify. In his old age, Louis will write: "Tu étais mon ennemie et mes enfants sont passés à l'ennemie" (p. 75). He had a moment of hope during an illness when Isa seemed to care about his prospects for recovery. It is only in overhearing her conversation with the doctor that he realizes it is to protect her children's reputation from rumors of congenital illness that she has shown concern: " 'Il [Louis] m'a fait bien peur pendant quelques jours; je pensais à mes petits.... Comme si c'était de lui seul qu'il s'agissait!' " (p. 115).

Louis recognizes in the rigidly conventional society of the provinces that he is condemned to a marriage in which he will always be the outcast. He is, for instance, enchanted by the unspeakable purity of his children's voices singing, but his isolation is indicated in the motif cluster: "Calme bonheur dont je me savais exclu, zone de pureté, et de rêve qui m'était interdite" (p. 80).

His relationship with Isa is intimate but enforced. "Je t'étais uni comme le renard au piège" (p. 59). A related motif reveals Louis' method of escaping the snare. "La vie dans une ville de province développe, chez le débauché, l'instinct de ruse du gibier" (p. 60). A secret life of sexual pursuit intensifies without joy, or possibly even pleasure. He, who as a boy had repelled younger women with his superior, humorless manner, continues to do the same for different reasons. He is disliked for petty meanness, and for creating ugly scenes to save a small sum on a tip or tariff. His relationships in the *demi-monde* can be regulated, in effect, by good accounting practices. He can balance his emotional books for a fee: "Ce qui me plaisait dans la débauche, c'était peut-être qu'elle fût à prix fixe."

In the days of their engagement, Louis' anti-clerical convictions were easily overlooked as he proudly joined Isa's elegant family at mass. "...j'étais fier de me sentir agrégé, une sorte de religion des ancêtres à l'usage de la bourgeoisie, un ensemble des rites dépour-vus de toute signification autre que sociale" (p. 35). He even withholds objection at first to the innocent custom of a husband's accompanying his wife to mass "...la religion ne concernait que les femmes" (p. 48). He is overpowered by the traditions of the Fondaudège family which send the children to religious schools.

But he realizes that in his opposition lies a weapon which can be used to induce personal contact. He has found an issue sensitive enough to produce invariably a reaction in Isa in challenging her religious views. It was "...le seul sujet qui pût te jeter hors des gonds, sur ce qui d'obligeait à sortir de ton indifférence, et qui me valait ton attention" (p. 81). He abhors the lengths to which Isa will go to keep the children as custodians of vacuous ritual and dog-matic practices, "...le dépôt du dogme, cet ensemble d'habitudes, de formules — cette folie" (p. 82). Louis writes that only the prim-itive, irresistible love of the youngest child, Marie, offsets in his wife and her two older children, "...les croyances que tu prati-quais, avec cet instinct du confort que leur ferait, plus tard, écarter toutes les vertus héroïques, toute la sublime folie chrétienne..." (p. 85). He can mock Isa's concept of charity—her niggardly wages to domestic servants, her contemptible haggling with vendors, her anti-Semitic views on Dreyfus — and can force her to say of the Bible: " 'Il ne faut pas prendre au pied de la lettre...' " (p. 89).

Even the young, idealistic seminarian, engaged economically as a summer tutor, is used to sustain a mild, continuous torment of Isa, reminding her frequently of Christ's uncritical hopes for all men. Louis sees a vindication of his views on the institutions of religion, in the overwhelming grief following Marie's death, to which Isa cannot adjust: "Tu ne pensais qu'à cette chair de ta chair qui allait être ensevelie ... tandis que moi, l'incrédule, j'éprouvais devant ce qui restait de Marie tout ce qui signifie le mot 'dépouille' " (p. 110). He can accept without resistance the fact of the finality of man's temporal sojourn. Even the young abbé cannot comfort the bereft mother. " 'Elle [Marie] est vivante, elle vous voit, elle vous attend' " (p. 110).

Such differences are confirmed on the occasion of Marinette's death in childbirth. Isa is righteously complacent about the fate of the girl who had deprived the Fondaudège family of great wealth by violating a clause in her husband's will, and by remarrying. Louis asserts of Isa's heartless satisfaction: "...je n'ai connu personne qui fût plus que toi sereinement injuste.... Il n'est pas une seule des Béatitudes dont tu n'aises passé ta vie à prendre le contre-pied" (p. 111). Isa's complacent equation of moral value and material acquisition is not unlike that of Louis' mother whose assurance was unshakable that a life of thrift and gain is approved by God. She liked to say: " 'Je suis bien tranquille, si des gens comme nous ne sont pas sauvés, c'est que personne ne le sera' " (p. 27).

Having centered his life around the acquisition and accretion of his properties, and believing that these had been his attraction for Isa, Louis seeks repeatedly to deny to Isa and her children the use or expectation of this wealth.

His first and futile effort to do so, in planning an outright gift of all funds and securities to the journalist, second husband of Marinette, and father of Luc, is recorded in the journal:

> Ma pauvre Isa, si vous aviez su... ce que j'ai offert à cet homme ce jour-là! ... Toute ma fortune mobilière....
>
> Faut-il que je vous aie haïs à ce moment-la. En bien, il n'a pas voulu marcher. Il n'a pas osé. Il a parlé de son honneur. (p. 113)

Louis' hatred is outspoken to both his wife and children when the pressures on his financial resources are greatest. "Tout se pas-

sait d'ailleurs en sourdine sauf dans les occasions solennelles:
...au moment du mariage des enfants.... J'ai été plus fort, la
haine me soutenait —" (p. 113). He elaborates plans for hiding his
fortune in the name of Robert, his illegitimate son, but in this
case, encounters the obstacles of petty ignorance and fear. The
timidity of Robert and his mother, and their continual need for
reassurance are vexing to Louis: "Ah, faut-il que je haisse les
autres pour ne pas claquer la porte au nez..." (p. 137). The ar-
rangements become so involved with precautions that even Robert
is uncomprehending of Louis' extraordinary efforts. " 'Mais enfin,
qu'est-ce qu'ils vous ont fait, les autres?' " (p. 164). A kind of
contagion evinces itself in the subtler revenge the children exercise
in maturity on their mother who has failed to turn their father's
intentions in their favor.

> Ils discutaient maintenant comme si la vieille femme n'eût
> pas été présente.... Les enfants ne lui répondirent même
> pas... c'était elle qui devait les embrasser à la ronde, ils
> ne se derangèrent pas. (p. 144)

Motifs are present which reveal greed and acquisitiveness as
characteristics not reserved to any particular social class. Since the
journal is a subjective account of his circumstances, Louis' perspective of his mother's peasant frugality emerges as a double one.
Her financial astuteness, while embarrassing in his youth, is
comforting. It was she who refused the Fondaudège offer of a marriage allowance, insisting on the payment of cash. "J'imagine que tu
[Isa] avais autant de confiance dans le génie de ton père que
moi dans celui de ma mère. Et après tout, peut-être ne savions-
nous... à quel point nous aimions l'argent" (p. 43).

He has come to believe that his "vice de trop aimer l'argent" is
inherited from his mother, and has affected his entire life, including
his choice of a profession: "Elle aurait mis tous ses efforts à me
maintenir dans un métier où, comme elle disait, 'je gagnais gros'....
Je n'avais rien que cette consolation de 'gagner gros' comme l'épicier du coin" (p. 73).

She is the one, however, who guarded his resources in the face
of his marriage to Isa, an alliance his mother opposed as if he had
been "une fille résolue à épouser un débauché" (p. 43).

Louis had been filled with horror when he met the husband of Isa's sister—an old man, corseted, starched, dentured, anxious to be young—to whom the young girl had been sold to save the Fondaudège family the price of a dowry. Following his death, Isa and Louis are unanimous in their disapproval of Marinette's jettisoning, by remarriage, her inherited fortune. Louis is unable to treat lightly the disposition of that inheritance. Aware of his own remote but possible role as a potential heir, sentiments are easily adjusted to accommodate a pragmatic position. Marinette, who had admired Louis' unconventional views toward many subjects, here declares in disappointment at joining her, and his enemies: " '... vous avez beau les haïr, vous appartenez bien à la même espèce ..." (p. 99).

The cynical assumption that greed is the norm among those who have married Louis' offspring and their fortunes, is indicated when the children, grandchildren and their spouses speak rudely of Louis, and of themselves as his victims. A young son-in-law of Hubert denies such an idea, and protests that he, for one, "... avait épousé sa femme par amour ..." (p. 147). A general mockery of such idealistic expression causes the others to shout tauntingly: " 'Moi aussi; moi aussi! moi aussi!' "

In addition to the unflattering, even frightening portrait of himself that emerges from his journal's pages, Louis is forced to look at his progeny as reflections of himself and his characteristics.

Correlative, but by contrast, is his attraction to Marie, to Marinette, and to Luc, as what he believes to be opposites of himself. It is their genuine disinterest in his material goods, their acceptance and love of him without requiring any changes in him, that make him helpless to refuse their love "... ce que j'aimais en lui [Luc], c'était de ne m'y pas retrouver" (p. 120).

His own children, he recognizes, are direct heirs of his own traits in all their repellent force: "... leur âpreté, cette primauté dans leur vie des biens temporels, cette puissance de mépris ... implacabilité...."

Luc, close to nature, a being of "une parfaite grâce," makes Louis conscious, by comparison, of his "difformité." Yet Louis cannot resist giving his hidden gold coins to Luc as the boy leaves for the war front. The young soldier laughingly, and prophetically, refuses the money. " 'Que veux-tu que je fasse de ça, mon oncle?' "

The only souvenir of Luc's entry into the war, that "sport magnifique," is a postcard to Louis, printed by the military, and signed, "Tendresses." The loss of Luc overshadows the death of Louis' mother, which goes nearly unnoticed.

Louis' next effort to deny Isa and her eager children his fortune is seen in his visits to Paris to locate Robert, his illegitimate son. In contrast to the duplicates and opposites of himself already cited, is offered the humiliating issue of Robert. Louis is aware of the extent of his own self-hatred as he views with loathing his disappointing descendant, "ce spectre de moi-même."

> ... entre les trottoirs, je me suis vu moi-même: c'était Robert. ... Ces grandes jambes de Robert, ce buste court comme est le men, cette tête dans les épaules, je les exècre ... tous mes défauts sont accentués. (p. 160)

Instead of the "love-child" he had imagined, endowed with the purity of Luc and the beauty of Phili, he finds a parody of himself.

Each of the principal characters is corroded by a private fear, a corruption inculcated in them by self-serving interests in material goods. The family members are bound together by what they are afraid of losing. Isa is essential to her children as an intermediary between them and the man whose *largesse* could solve their financial and marital problems. "Elle était chargée de leurs désirs. ... Soucis d'argent, de santé, calculs de l'ambition et de la jalousie, tout était là, devant elle ..." (p. 155). She faces their scoldings and reproaches when her efforts at intercession fail. Her granddaughter, Janine, complains, for example: " 'Vous n'avez pas su le prendre. Vous n'avez pas été adroite' " (p. 139). Louis terrifies his children, unintentionally in their youth, and deliberately in his old age. He sees his daughter, Geneviève, tremble as she plans to ask his help for Phili, her son-in-law: "Comme je vous fais peur à tous. ... C'est affreux de faire peur à ses enfants" (p. 64). He not only denies her request, but reveals what he has heard from his sickroom window, as his children murmur against him in the garden: "Vous parliez à voix basse, et c'est cela qui me trouble. ... Maintenant, vous méfiez, vous chuchotez. ... Que me cachez-vous?" (p. 29).

The deeds and decisions of desperation attempted by the children, include the cajoling false concern of Janine and Phili:

"Grand-père, vous avez tort de fumer... c'est bien du café dé-
cafeiné?" (p. 63). They also contain the ultimate suggestion that
he be committed for mental incompetence: "Pauvres imbéciles!
comme si j'étais homme à me laisser interdire ou enfermé" (p. 149).
Louis' privileged position gives him exceptional power, whether in
the situation of his bedroom where he may overhear discussions,
or in the world of business: "Avant qu'ils aient pu remuer le petit
doigt, j'aurais vite fait de mettre Hubert dans une situation désespérée.... Quant à Phili, je possède un dossier...." With the help
of chance he accidentally sees his son Hubert, with Alfred, meet
Robert in St. Germain-des-Près, to betray him. "Une affreuse joie
m'envahit.... Un policier, qui voit le voleur entrer dans la souricière, n'éprouve pas une plus délicieuse émotion que celle qui
m'étouffait un peu à cette minute" (p. 175). "Je n'osais avouer le
plaisir que je me promettais, à jouer, comme un chat, avec ce triste
mulot" (p. 175). His satisfaction in holding his family hostage to
his fortune, and to damaging information which can be their ruin,
is sufficient unto itself "...il me suffira de montrer les dents"
(p. 149).

In contrast to Louis' imposition of fear, and his pleasure in
doing so, is the counterbalancing terror he experiences himself.
Alone, amid a group of people conditioned to respond to him in
fright, Louis awaits retaliation. He draws on experiences observed
in his lifetime as prècedents, whereby the young, to expedite their
expectations, take action against old people who stand in their way.
"...ils doivent nous passer sur le corps" (p. 66).

The first case he had pleaded as a lawyer, was a litigation to
force the children of an old man to take care of their father. Louis'
last reference to such a theme speaks of himself "...comme un
vieillard malade contre une jeune meute" (p. 198). It is used to
torment Hubert, suggesting that the children would leave an old
man to die of hunger, "...Et lorsque l'agonie dure trop longtemps
on ajoute des édredons, on le couvre jusqu'à la bouche..."
(p. 203). Louis has genuine justification for his anxiety, as he
knows that he is "...un vieillard près de mourir, au milieu d'une
famille aux aguets, qui attend le moment de la curée" (p. 38). He
had seen the handsome, lupine Phili verify that Louis was asleep
(he was not) and try to steal from the inert man his billfold. "J'ai

éprouvé cette terreur des vieillards isolés qu'un jeune homme épie. Il me semble que celui-là serait capable de me tuer" (p. 117). Louis writes in his journal that he knows he is safe as long as he controls his money. "Un vieillard n'existe que par ce qu'il possède" (p. 44). Speaking still of his security in his gold, he reminds Isa: "Il vous attire, mais il me protège" (p. 44).

It is his overhearing his children's proposal to have Louis declared incompetent that initiates his first moment of self-esteem. Repeatedly had motifs appeared in the journal in self-justification that he was not "un monstre." Now Louis experiences something new: "Un grand calme... un apaisement de cette certitude: c'étaient eux les monstres et moi la victime" (p. 148). Confronting his children with the knowledge that they in truth had known his whereabouts in Paris, since he had witnessed their rendezvous with Robert, he asserts they could have alerted him to Isa's final illness: "J'éprouvais un état de bien-être, tel qu'un homme qui s'est disculpé, dont l'innocence est reconnue.... je ne sais pas ce qui m'adoucissait malgré moi" (p. 194). Louis' bitterness and rancor ease gradually as he realizes that his hatred has died, and the desire for reprisal has vanished. In the face of Hubert's final request for funds, disguised in moral tones of "protecting the patrimony," Louis feels detached from his fortune, "qui ne me concernait plus" (p. 200). In the face of the ugly quarrel which ensues between brother and sister, he experiences only slight disgust and distaste. "Que cette dispute, naguère, m'eût diverti!" (p. 203). Louis acknowledges that once he has turned over, intact, his properties to Hubert and Geneviève, his children, "témoignent beaucoup de respect et de gratitude."

The pleasure of seeing his children fight for crumbs of their legacies should have filled him with joy. But he can, in his last days, view with a wry humor their "terreur d'être désavantagés," in their willingness to cut a tapestry in two, rather than allow one person alone among them to enjoy it. "C'est ce qu'ils appellent avoir la passion de la justice..." (p. 207).

He experiences a sense of curiosity that he is no longer prompted to protect with his own body his beloved vineyards from a threatening hailstorm. "Rien n'est plus à moi et je ne sens pas ma pauvreté (p. 206).

He compares his disposition of his wealth, so long his *raison d'être,* to an amputation, and like a surgical patient, he awakes to find in surprise that the operation has been painless. The state of numbness he has entered is interrupted by his search among the ashes of papers burned by Isa the day before her death. He has found charred fragments of letters from her confessor, phrases from which reveal her private torment that Louis had loved another women, probably her sister, and that Luc was perhaps Louis' own son. He is filled with a holy joy of discovery. Isa had loved, and been jealous of him. Like a penitent emerging from a confessed life of sin, he runs down the stairs, "mains noires... mon front balafré de cendre" (p. 211).

Released from the bondage of his wealth, and liberated from perpetual negative concerns, Louis becomes desirous, even anxious, to communicate lovingly with his children, Hubert and Geneviève. His joy in self-discovery is a naive one. He feels he must use every available minute to acquaint them with the new person he has become.

> J'étais impatient de leur montrer mon nouveau cœur.... Je brûlerais les étapes vers le cœur de mes enfants, je passerais à travers tout ce qui nous séparait.. ... j'avancerais si vite dans leur amour qu'ils pleureraient en me fermant les yeux. (p. 214)

He even tries to express warmth toward his servants, whose faithful attentions have gone unnoticed over the years. He inquires about their daughter, only to learn that the girl had died ten years earlier. The impassive faces of the domestics reveal no surprise or forgiveness. When Geneviève and Hubert do not come, as they had promised, a cry nearly escapes Louis: " 'Mes petits, pourquoi n'êtes-vous pas venus?' " (p. 216).

The revelation of the mere accessibility of love, of his previously unknown need for another—"Quelqu'un"—to teach him how to love, almost brings Louis to his knees in prayer. The strong affiliation between human and divine love is revealed in Louis' longing for The One who is at the burning center of all love. He experiences, "Désir, qui peut-être était déjà prière" (p. 218).

The lateness of the hour in his life is supported by motifs of the dead and wasted past lying about him. The heavy furniture is revealed as "... épave ensablée dans le passé d'une famille, où tant de corps aujourd'hui dissous, s'étaient appuyés, étendus ..." (p. 219). "Des bibelots morts couvraient les consoles" (p. 216). Only the shutters on a single room left open by chance give promise of escape to some wider world beyond the confines of life and death.

Louis is pleased with his own anxious concern. When no word comes from his son and daughter, he goes to them. It is found that Janine has been abandoned by the weak and handsome Phili. Geneviève cannot comprehend that this grasping boy would depart, now that Louis' fortune is assured. It is Louis' perception that the young husband fled in the final humiliation of his awareness of having sold himself for the promised gold.

Louis, for the first time in his life, is needed by another: "Em-menez-moi ..." the distraught girl cried to him. Her parents plan a punitive annulment for Phili, and blame their father when Janine excuses her errant husband, thereby foregoing possible favorable legal action. Louis realizes that his own children, indeed, had not yet observed the new man born within him, since in a conditioned reflex, they attribute his support of Janine to "malice ... vengeance, peut-être ... méchanceté pure" (p. 227).

His self-confidence is so securely founded now, he can say: "... isolé, sous le coup d'une mort affreuse, je demeurais calme, attentif, l'esprit en éveil" (p. 227). There are motifs indicating a respite from the winter of death—an Indian summer prevails in Louis' life. "Aucune feuille ne se détachait encore, les roses refleurissaient" (p. 227). He is possessed by a profound peace, "qui ... eût été quelqu'un" (p. 228).

His only impediment in his efforts to bring spiritual comfort to Janine is her rigidly conventional relegation of religion to its social ritual. When he asks her, " 'Tu as la foi?' " she indicates a refusal to bring religious considerations to bear as she seeks alleviation to her pain. Although she had asked Louis: " 'Que faudrait-il faire pour ne plus souffrir? ...' " (p. 232), when he tries to approach the subject of reordering her perspectives so that love, as she seeks it may not be found in Phili, but in another, divine object, she indicates that "... elle n'aimait pas à mêler la religion avec ces choses-là" (p. 233). Louis will no longer reject as hateful, "cette caricature grossière ... cette charge médiocre de la vie chrétienne," but will continue to seek the key which can be offered to Janine at this turning point of her life.

The linking image of her search for warmth at the fire, while Louis prowls questioningly around her is indicative of a theme of the attraction to the warm source of love, and man's impatient quest: "Elle laissait mourir le feu, et à mesure que la pièce devenait plus froide, elle traînait sa chaise vers l'âtre, ses pieds touchaient presque la cendre" (p. 234).

Louis' heart is filled to bursting as he writes in his journal that he has finally found the name of the one to be adored, perhaps to be shared with Janine if she will accept it. Death overtakes him in mid-discovery.

The journal is found by Hubert, whose fraternal duty it is, he believes, to send "cet étrange document" to Geneviève, and whose filial duty requires that he share a new view of their father: "je n'ose dire plus noble, mais enfin plus humaine."

He sees in Louis' self-revelation only a kind of fiscal failure:

> La vérité est que le pauvre homme ... n'avait plus le temps ni les moyens de nous déshériter par une autre méthode que celle qu'il avait imaginée.... il a eu la rouerie de transformer sa défaite en victoire morale. (p. 237)

The spiritual exaltation, as he reads of it, is for Hubert only a confirmation of his father's delirium. He would submit such an interesting analysis to a psychiatrist if he did not fear danger to the family name. It is so well written, he concedes, that there is a danger some descendant might publish it. The very extremes of hate and mystical love to be found in the journal are to be mistrusted in themselves. Hubert's *devise* might well be his words to his sister: "La vérité, c'est l'équilibre" (p. 240).

Louis' religious aspiration and new-found convictions leave Hubert untouched, but faith in his father's financial astuteness never wanes: "... nous devons suivre son exemple."

This important letter of transmittal, accompanying the revelations of a lifetime of anguish and self-destruction, concludes with Hubert's cheerful advice regarding movies, and an anisette brandy, as possible investments: "Voilà un type d'affaires que ne souffrira pas de la crise" (p. 241).

A final defense of Louis' behavior is offered by Janine, who presents further evidence in confirmation of the sanctity and magnanimity of his final days. She attests to meetings with the local priest, and Louis' prayerful hopes that he would live until Christmas when he would, like the child Jesus, be born again in a new form and join the community of man.

THEMES OF THE PLOT

It is from Louis himself, narrator of *Le Nœud de vipères*, that we get an important indication of the origins of the anguished, tormented man whose self-examination in his diary rewards us with opportunities to analyze his purposes and motivations. Never one to shirk a fact to be faced, Louis writes: "J'ai mis soixante ans à composer ce vieillard mourant de haine" (p. 184).

Having begun his journal in his sixty-eighth year, the writer is in a position to feel his approaching physical death, and to review a lifetime passed in the shadow of spiritual death. As the rays of the setting sun find difficulty in reaching the routes and buildings of valley villages, so will the light of divine guidance, of grace, find the tortuous way into the shadowed soul of a man obscured in the darkness of life without God's love. Near the end of Louis' diary, he invokes the motif, "nid de vipères," as he perceives the extent of his error in life. His crime, as he calls it, "... ne tenait pas tout entier dans le hideux nid de vipères" (p. 212). This "nœud immonde" is not, as he once thought, to be found only within himself. The implied emotional and moral contortions extend beyond him into his children and family. The "nœud de vipères," as defined by Mauriac through Louis' own words, is revealing of important motivational themes: "... haine de mes enfants, désir de vengeance, amour de l'argent" (p. 212).

As important as those sins of commission may be, it is the sin of omission in his "refus de chercher au-delà de ces vipères enmêlées," which is cited by Louis as the ultimate element of the criminal compound. Completing the image proposed of the day's last rays reaching down through the fog of human resistance to grace, these latter thematic elements are also barriers preventing the final touches of divine love from lighting the buried soul of a sinner.

Some initial observations may be made of the purpose expressed for the creation of the journal itself. It is begun after Louis has ceased to live in active hatred for his heirs, but has not yet progressed to a state of charity or magnanimity. He has not yet forsaken hopes of stealing a bitter satisfaction from the expression of his contempt for his covetous children. Writing a letter to his wife and children, which will be read posthumously, is in itself a pleasure: "... pendant des années, j'ai refait en esprit cette lettre" (p. 9).

The letter does not, however, accompany the disinheritance so joyously planned. "Vous avez eu de la chance que je survive à ma haine ... aujourd'hui du moins, je ne la sens plus" (p. 10).

In the same way that his hatred had been the stimulant of so many years, now the letter, one it is recognized to be in fact a journal, provides a reason for living: "Il faut que je vive encore assez de temps pour achever cette confession" (p. 16).

The confession is intended to attract and hold the attention of his wife, Isa, an attention he felt he had never fully obtained in their long life together. He is confident that she will finish reading it, "... ne serait-ce que par devoir" (p. 18), and the hope that she will do so is essential to continuing: "... tu liras ces pages jusqu'au bout; j'ai besoin de le croire. Je le crois" (p. 18).

His new "fièvre d'écrire," however, is not enough to evoke an open reaction from Isa. Louis must persuade himself: "Aussi peu que tu m'observes, comment n'aurais-tu pas noté un changement dans mon humeur. Oui, cette fois, j'ai confiance que tu ne te déroberas pas" (p. 13).

Louis is aware as he writes that his purpose and motivation have changed. No longer does he address himself to Isa in excited vengeance, or in puerile demands for attention: "Je l'ai commencée [cette histoire] pour toi.... Au fond, c'est pour moi que j'écris" (p. 62).

In legalistic terms, he is compiling a brief, a dossier of damaging evidence, "de ce procès perdu." In more metaphysical terms, he is sitting in moral judgment on himself. What was to be an indictment of his family is apparent to him, on re-reading his completed pages, as a condemnation of himself. "J'ai relu ces dernières pages — stupéfait par ces bas-fonds en moi qu'elles éclairent" (p. 126).

Even psychological considerations are brought to light: "A quoi bon reprendre ce travail? C'est qu'à mon insu, sans doute, j'y trouvais un soulagement, une délivrance" (p. 133).

As positive motivations, like the desire to reach a state of loving peace, outweigh the negative purposes originally seen in writing to Isa, Louis' purpose alters noticeably. It is hoped that the record he is presenting now will reveal him, in all his aspects, to Robert, his illegitimate son, whom he is about to meet: "Par cette confession, je réparerais, dans une faible mesure, l'éloignement où je l'ai tenu depuis qu'il est né" (p. 134).

The journal might also have been the instrument of rehabilitation in Louis' and Isa's marriage. Was he hoping for a miracle in wishing that she would read it through, perhaps in his lifetime, and be affected by its contents? Would their lives be renewed if they then fell to their knees together (p. 129). He, for one, is instead shattered by the portrait of himself which emerges from his own pages. "Moi-même, je ne puis les relire d'un trait. A chaque instant, je m'interromps et cache ma figure dans mes mains. Voilà l'homme.... Vous pouvez me vomir, je n'en existe pas moins" (p. 168).

The moral progression is to be emphasized at the end of the journal when Louis prays for added weeks or months of life in which he can, rather, present his newly-recreated self to his children. A letter from Janine, written after his death, indicates his desire to live until Christmas, which would have signified the birth of his spirit as a Christian, brought into the world in the humble spirit of the Christ-child.

Although listed in secondary position as a component in the *nœud de vipères,* it would seem that Louis' capacity for vengeance —inspired by hatred—is the single most powerful motivational force in his early life. His need to avenge himself for wrongs, real or imagined, which have been done him, has its origins well in advance of the terrible wound inflicted, unfeelingly, by Isa.

We recall that Louis' adolescent failures were a continuing defeat for him:

> ...j'appartenais à la race de ceux dont la présence fait tout rater. (p. 24)

Fifty years later, Louis still burns with envy at the sight of young, beautiful men, like his granddaughter's ne'er-do-well husband, Phili:

> ... ce garçon triomphant, qui a été saoulé, dès l'adolescence, de ce dont je n'aurai pas goûté une seule fois en un demi-siècle de vie.

He had, as a youth, a retaliatory instinct which was instantaneous and deadly. A light joke made at Louis' expense was intolerable.

> ... j'assenais aux autres (sans l'avoir voulu) des coups qu'ils ne me pardonnaient pas. J'allais droit au ridicule, à l'infirmité qu'il aurait fallu taire. (p. 24)

Louis' desolation in these early years, which he describes as "un long suicide," finds relief in his attributing of problems to his mother's excessive care of him. His treatment of her is punitive:

> Oui, j'étais atroce ... je m'emportais brutalement au moindre prétexte et même sans motif. (p. 25)

He acknowledges the innate subtlety of his revenge on his mother in describing a brief winter courtship of a girl she strongly disapproved. She feared that Louis would contract from the adventure at best, tuberculosis, or at worst, a marriage. Louis did not even find his new love-interest a pleasing one. It is in his old age that he concedes: "Je suis sûr aujourd'hui de m'être attaché ... à cette conquête ... pour imposer une angoisse à ma mère" (p. 26). Even though he was impressed by his mother's choice of a house in town and her unusual extravagance in its furnishings and personnel, he showed only, "... la cruauté de ne faire que des critiques." What would he have done in the face of her opposition to his desire to marry into the Fondaudège family, nourishing "une rancune presque haineuse contre ma mère," if the banks had not assured her that though their expenses were high, the Fondaudèges' resources were ample?

Revenge is a weapon which lay not only in the hands of Louis. He sees destiny using it as an instrument of correction, to balance the payment necessary for all deeds. Destiny has made Louis pay for his cruelty toward his mother's overpowering indulgence, by granting him a wife who will crush him with indifference: "Il est juste que je paie" (p. 25).

In a correlative theme, then, Louis is no longer the instigator, but the victim of a larger avenging force. The anger of the gods, in his anti-religious view, demands retribution for crimes he has committed. Louis is, at the start of his examination, aware of a sense of guilt, but not yet conscious that a loving explanation lies ahead, waiting to be discovered.

The key event, at least as Louis interprets it, which releases his capacity for fierce, sustained reprisal, is Isa's sweetly-savoured confession, as she lay in Louis' arms, that another love had preceded him. Louis insists that his objection is not to any casual relationship which might have preceded his acquaintance with Isa. What isolates, terrifies and enrages him is that she still loves this phantom Rodolphe, and finds sensual pleasure in forming words concerning him. Louis intuitively, and defensively, realizes that some other motive, therefore, than love lay behind Isa's acceptance of him in marriage.

She has driven him back, by a single deed, to the hell in which he lived before he had become a pleasing object in the warmth of what he interpreted to be her love. "Je ne crois pas à ton enfer éternel, mais je sais ce que c'est que d'être un damné sur la terre, un réprouvé, un homme dont la route a toujours été fausse" (p. 117). He who had spent his youth in a ceaseless battle "pour la première place," believes himself to be loved, if at all, as "un pis aller." He realizes, eventually, that in reaction he had used her pregnancies and her infants as a series of events, "... qui me fournirent de plus de prétextes qu'il n'était nécessaire pour m'éloigner de toi" (p. 60).

The journal concedes, too, that behind an expressed purpose of exercising paternal rights over his children, Louis is motivated in truth to punish Isa by taking his children from the influence of "une femme bigotte." "Je me donnais de hautes raisons, je mettais en avant l'exigence du devoir.... Mais il s'agissait bien de cela" (p. 61).

Contradictory motifs reveal the vagueness of Louis' understanding of the onset of his burning need for revenge. It has already been noted that Isa's thoughtless revelations in the darkness awakened the next morning her husband, "en proie à une haine," whose bitterness he tastes after forty years. Yet a second reference to Louis' antipathy toward Isa indicates that the root of the destructive emotion is to be found elsewhere.

Il ne me semble pas que je t'ai haïe dès la première année qui suivit la nuit désastreuse. Ma haine est née, peu à peu, à mesure que je me rendais mieux compte de ton indifférence à mon égard. (p. 68)

The latter theme of revenge to compensate for Isa's disregard of his person, and his achievements, is the more particularly stressed. It is surely subtly correlative to her admission of the circumstances surrounding their marriage, however. It could be said that it was a kind of fundamental indifference to the person Louis actually was when Isa "misunderstood" a comment made by him, and an engagement announcement was forthcoming very soon. The possibility of Isa's having made a passionate bid for Louis is negated in the motif: "... ta famille et toi vous étiez jetés avidement sur le premier limaçon rencontré" (p. 53).

The ultimate long-term vengeance, sweely anticipated by Louis, is invariably envisioned as his denial on his death, to her and "her" children, of his great wealth, in "... ce mouvement de marée qui est celui de la haine dans mon cœur" (p. 74). The idea is as insupportable that she might enjoy his money before he is buried, as it is after he dies. He is adamant in his refusals of all requests for help from his family: "Non, non, mon argent m'a coûté trop cher pour que je vous en abandonne un centime avant le dernier hoquet" (p. 100).

The money has indeed been an expensive commodity. His obsession with its accumulation has blinded Louis to other more significant goals and has frustrated possibilities of other routes in life. There is only Janine's comment, written after Louis' death, to give witness that the road to material acquisitions was really only a detour: "Me comprendrez-vous si je vous affirme que là où était son trésor, là n'était pas son cœur?" (p. 245).

Isa is blamed for insisting on the making of money as the primary objective of his career: "La tare dont tu m'aurais guéri, si tu m'avais aimé, c'était de ne rien mettre au-dessus du gain immédiat" (p. 73). Her emphasis on his money-producing abilities is a related idea to that of indifference, especially when viewed in the image Louis offers: "Depuis trente ans, je ne suis plus rien à tes yeux qu'un appareil distributeur de billets de mille francs, un appareil qui fonctionne mal et qu'il faut secouer sans cesse..." (p. 31).

Louis' opportunity to find in Isa's beautiful sister, "une petite sœur, une amie,"—or more—is lost forever when he tries to persuade her to put conservation of her fortune before other, human considerations, such as happiness: "...je lui assurai que personne n'était capable d'être heureux après le sacrifice d'une pareille somme" (p. 99). Marinette might have become, indeed, a double prize if he could both keep her money in the family and find in her, at the same time, his "petite sœur." It would represent a magnificent gesture of hate, and spite, toward Isa. The desire to wound Isa in such a way stems from Louis' conviction that he believes his wife to be too confident about Louis' invulnerability to such a temptation. His wife expresses only moderate interest that Louis keeps Marinette diverted: "...il l'occupe, et c'est sans inconvénient" (p. 103). He admits, with shame, in his journal that in the moments alone with Marinette in the moonlit woods, "...mon infamie... fut de penser à toi, Isa, de rêver d'une vengeance possible: me servir de Marinette pour te faire souffrir" (p. 106).

Even Louis' lifelong antipathy to formalized Christian ritual is subverted and serves as fuel to his harassments of Isa:

> Naguère, l'irréligion n'avait été pour moi qu'une forme vide où j'avais coulé mes humiliations de petit paysan enrichi méprisé par ses camarades bourgeois... je l'emplissais maintenant de ma déception amoureuse et d'une rancune presque infinie. (p. 81)

Louis' drive toward the joyous fulfillment of his machinations, by which he would like to hear Isa cry through her mourning veil after his funeral that the securities are not in the vault, is distracted by the pleasure he might experience in hearing her triumphant call to her children that the securities are indeed there. Louis is torn between the desire for vengeance and his need for a reassurance that he was, after all, right about his family's greed.

That Isa is the principal focus of his anger is revealed not only in his directing the journal to her, but also in his keen realization that when she has died, unexpectedly, before he has, the propelling force of his motivation has died with her. Merely to deny money to his children holds little promise, but to have known of her discomfiture and distress at reading the journal, or at finding no inheritance, was the sweet revenge he had long dreamed. "Il y avait un aspect de ma femme, que je n'avais jamais perdu de vu: c'était ma veuve, celle qui serait gênée par ses crêpes pour ouvrir le coffre" (p. 187). All his "projects, ruses, complots" were directed toward these exquisitely satisfying moments.

Before her death, there were moments when a softening of Louis' attitudes could be discerned. But then, it must be recalled that Louis' attitudes were not always vindictive toward Isa. She had appeared in his life as a presumably loving force which relieved the tensions caused by pride, solitude, and class differences. It must be recalled, too, that the love he felt for Isa when they met was reflected, and shone back upon him: "Dans une détente délicieuse, je m'épanouissais. Je me rappelle ce dégel de tout mon être sous [ton] regard, ces émotions jaillissantes, ces sources délivrées" (p. 35).

Love, an unfamiliar and unwieldy instrument in Louis' inexperienced hands, becomes complicated. He was betrayed by the trust he had placed in the sheer novelty of Isa's early caresses. Once Isa has inflicted her irreparable damage in speaking of Rodolphe, Louis "étouffait avec rage son jeune amour."

In his life of extramarital relationships, he pursues, not love or any affection, but physical pleasure alone: "Les désirs du cœur, je n'imaginais plus qu'ils pussent être jamais comblés; je les étouffais à peine nés. J'étais passé maître dans l'art de détruire tout sentiment" (p. 77).

Brief resurgences of possible affection appear, as when in their old age, Louis and Isa walk briefly together in the garden. She gives a rare indication of her hopes that Louis' affection for her would have returned. Louis is deeply touched and wonders if he has been, perhaps, mistaken. Even this hesitant hope is to be crushed at once, as the old couple comes upon a circle of chairs in the garden. Like the *nœud de vipères,* round and involuted, the circle stands as silent evidence of plots formulated nightly against Louis, and which he has overheard. Hatred quickly regains its sovereignty over love.

The light in which Louis sees himself, which is after all a subjective illumination, reveals a discrepancy from what could be determined of his motivations in an objective analysis. Some clues of language appear from time to time which suggest that the motivations, behavior and purposes are not what they seem, especially when Louis reviews them in the context of his newly-sanctified state. Louis writes at the beginning of his journal, in close textual proximity to his expression of revenge on Isa:

> *J'ai cru* longtemps que ma haine était ce qu'il avait en moi de plus vivant. (p. 10)

Similarly, when he has almost let a spark of affection be kindled toward his wife, he says:

> *Je crus* discerner une lueur dans ses yeux, lors qu'elle croyait "m'avoir eu." (p. 158)

Following his disappointment in his son, Robert, the same phrasing is noted, suggesting again that his analysis of his responses to that situation were erroneous:

> ... *j'avais cru* consentir à la haine, à celle que j'inspirais, à celle que je ressentais. (p. 183)

A similar implication that his emotions were misled prevails regarding his relationship with Isa as they share "la complicité de la vieillesse":

> *En paraissant nous haïr* nous étions arrivés au même point. (p. 154)

The possibility that the mutual hatred might be only one of camouflage is a correlative theme to the one hinted at: that this life is only the shadow-life of a larger reality. This world is not the only life we will know, Louis perceives in a flash of insight. He has glimpses occasionally, in the early peace of loving Isa, of an eternal life more real than the present. "J'eus soudain la sensation aiguë, la certitude presque physique qu'il existait un autre monde, une réalité dont nous ne connaissons que l'ombre..." (p. 39).

The hatred which has sustained Isa in battle on behalf of her children is seen by Louis as a "néant." He asks himself if Isa really can see her God in the void which lies beyond death. Will she be compensated for the nothingness in which she has lived, as the instrument of others less worthy than herself? He has found, himself, little reward in life and expects nothing from death: "Qu'il n'y ait rien au-delà du monde, qu'il n'existe pas d'explication, que le mot de l'énigme ne nous soit jamais donné..." (p. 67). Life will not even have prepared him for death by arming him to meet its contingencies. He fears that death may be "ce qui ne peut se traduire que par le signe...."

Louis would welcome a God who would love and be loved, if he were given some reason to believe in the possibility. He knows that the temptation to hate is strong and satisfying, but comes to realize that gratification of another kind exists: "Je ne puis plus nier qu'une route existe en moi qui pourrait mener à ton Dieu... il existe en moi une touche secrète... celle qu'éveillait Marie... et aussi le petit Luc..." (p. 128). But he knows, too, in the final days, that to keep his destructive emotions at their fullest expression, he has had to make a damning decision: "Inlassablement, j'ai cherché à perdre cette clef qu'une main mystérieuse m'a toujours rendue, à chaque tournant de ma vie" (p. 233).

The key to salvation has been spurned by what, on one level, was a deliberate, and on another level unconscious, effort to avoid a total surrender to God's love. Unaware that its ecstasy would provide a greater joy than the guilt-ridden pleasure of inflicting pain, Louis realizes at the end of the novel that he has chosen to recognize only the meanest qualities of faith, and of human beings, including himself, because he had not suspected the happiness to be found in loving and believing.

While Isa implies that she had been waiting during decades of married life for some gesture of affection on Louis' part, he asks himself if he has seen only one side of her nature. "Se pourrait-il que nous fassions par habitude, le tri de ses paroles et de ses gestes, ne retenant que ce qui nourrit nos griefs et entretien nos rancunes?" (p. 157).

The same question can be raised to measure the validity and objectivity of responses toward institutions like the Church. Louis inquires whether, in rejecting Christianity and its God because of the ineptness, or vulgarity of its worship, such factors are not merely excuses to evade God's accessibility. Having often been repelled by Isa's droning rituals, by her observation usually of the letter, and never the spirit of God's law, Louis made an idol of irreligion. Again, employing the motif of caricature, Louis asserts: "Ce que j'avais tant exécré, toute ma vie, c'était cela ... cette caricature grossière ... de la vie chrétienne, j'avais feint d'y voir une représentation authentique pour avoir le droit de la haïr" (p. 233). Similarly, the same exaggeration of superficial faults within himself creates a parody of himself which can be hated. He later questions the virtue in his refusal to accept the seminarian's utterance, "Vous êtes très bon," which would have destroyed his reputation for malignancy and weakened his power over those near him. He realizes that a refusal of a spiritual gift lay in his rejection of Marie's dying words, as she offered her suffering to God, "pour Papa! pour Papa!" This revelation of the ultimate distortion of self to evade the reflected glory of divine grace comes to Louis only shortly before his death.

He has denied recognition of his true self, offering only a sketch, drawn from one facet of his make-up, to a world too indifferent to seek beyond the proffered characteristics: "... j'en avais usé de même à l'égard des autres. ... Jamais l'aspect des autres ne s'offrit à moi comme ce qu'il faut crever, comme ce qu'il faut traverser pour les atteindre" (p. 213).

Louis' self-application to a lifetime of hatred, he assures us, is no novelty to him. It is easy not to resist the desire to engage in recrimination and abuse. "Le goût de la brouille est un héritage de famille." He is heir to parents and grandparents who have been estranged from their children and relations.

That he has a ruinous effect on the atmosphere of any group he joins, family or social, he attributes to inherited characteristics. But it is the vice of "trop aimer l'argent ... cette passion dans le sang" which is most seriously at odds with spiritual progress toward perfection, and with the lucidity he prizes in himself, which might have opened doors to alternative modes of living.

The emphasis on immediate, short-term gain has distracted Louis from expansion of his talents beyond the quick profit. His desire to retain control of Isa's fortune is offered as the motivating force against a separation or divorce. The loss of her name, an important business asset, as well as of her dowry, is unacceptable.

Louis will not even seek relief from the strains he feels in his home life with Isa and the children by taking a vacation abroad or in other company: "Au vrai, il s'agissait pour moi de ne pas faire double dépense. ... Tel était l'esprit d'économie que ma mère m'avait légué et dont je faisais une vertu" (p. 86). The purpose is seen to be the consolidation of his wealth with that of his wife, and his motivation is the irresistible, inherited attraction to money.

Yet his life is revealed in his journal in involuntary evidence of his longing for Isa's love and attention. He begins writing in anticipation of her reading his remarks after his death, whereby he will hold, uninterrupted, her complete concentration. "... Je reprendrai pour quelques semaines une place dans ta vie" (p. 18). It has been noted that his discovery of letters, written by Isa before death overtook her, fills him with youthful joy, when he realizes that even as destructive an emotion as jealousy, from which Isa had suffered is, after all, at least evidence of interest. That he had held some value or merit in her eyes worthy of such torment, is a dumbfounding revelation. "... j'avais eu ce pouvoir de la torturer. ... je jouissais de n'avoir pas été indifférent à une femme, d'avoir soulevé en elle ces remous" (p. 212).

Louis interprets, in an effort at self-justification of his lonely old age, his unlovable personality as a demonstration of honesty. He finds himself nearly seventy years old and the possessor of the depressing insight: "J'avais été un homme si horrible que je n'avais pas eu un seul ami" (p. 218). He attributes these circumstances to his refusal to put on the mask of nobility or greatness. He makes an analogy with holy men who are hated and scorned because they are not seen for what they are. The world and society require that masks be worn. Only conformity to accepted ideals or standards is approved. The few occasions when Louis found himself in the presence of holiness and purity, as with Luc, Marie and the Abbé Ardouin, he was aware of his "difformité." Yet the magnanimity of these Christ-like souls accepts Louis as he is, and asks no change. Louis cannot disguise his distress at Marinette's recklessness with money, or his support of his granddaughter, Janine, against her family's intentions regarding her marriage and its annulment. Nor could he have feigned a sudden friendliness with boyhood comrades, to assure a full complement of ushers at his wedding. His qualities of "indépendance, inflexibilité" are part of the make-up which can proclaim: "Je ne m'abaisse devant personne, je garde fidélité à mes idées" (p. 48). He notes, on more than one occasion, that even his own family spend their lifetimes, "à déguiser, sous de beaux noms, les sentiments les plus vils" (p. 207).

Mysterious hints, suggesting transcendental visions beyond the material and physical worlds, have been perceived by Louis. The devastating experience of Isa's confession concerning Rodolphe leaves Louis a broken creature; yet he draws some spiritual sustenance, curiously, from the event. "...il est possible que cette défaite renferme une signification, que les événements, surtout dans l'ordre du cœur, sont peut-être des messages dont il faut interpréter le secret..." (p. 58). From his transitory attraction to Marinette comes the satisfaction of virtue, if not of desire: "Pour croire à la resurrection de la chair peut-être faut-il avoir vaincu la chair. La punition de ceux qui en ont abusé est de ne pouvoir plus même imaginer qu'elle ressuscitera" (p. 105).

It is on the occasion of a severe hailstorm which threatens the priceless vineyards, that Louis is freed from bondage to his earthly properties: "Je ne sais quoi, je ne sais qui m'a détaché. ... Quelle force m'entraine? Une force aveugle? Un amour? Peut-être un amour?" (p. 131).

Unsuccessful efforts to dispose of his fortune make it a burden ever more cumbersome to carry. While he still has lingering visions of having his fortune, perhaps, buried with him, some other impulse is gradually separating the direction of his material and spiritual interests. We cannot judge the complete motivation behind the dramatic personality change Louis undergoes. Hubert implies on reading the journal that Louis made his children his heirs when he could find no conclusive way to deprive them of his property. It must be acknowledged that sufficient motifs are present to support the idea of resignation to failure in that quest.

Louis concedes that he is doomed to die the possessor of all he would like to give away, since his first choice as heir, Luc's father, refused in the name of honor, and his second choice, Robert, declined in the exercise of treachery. "Hélas, je ne saurais pas me ruiner! Je n'arriverais jamais à perdre mon argent" (p. 184).

He admits privately in his diary, that his children needed to struggle no longer once their mother had died. Deprived of the principal object of his hatred, those in close association with her are exempted from reprisal. He concedes that even if he were granted an extension of life in which time he could dispose of all his wealth, "... comment apprendre, à mon âge, les gestes des prodigues?" (p. 183). "Je voyais en esprit cette fortune, qui avait été, semble-t-il, le tout de ma vie, que j'avais cherché à donner, à perdre, dont je n'avais même pas été libre de disposer à mon gré..." (p. 200). He suddenly sees himself, not as master, but as "... prisonnier pendant toute ma vie d'une passion que ne me possédait pas." Applying the words of Abbé Ardouin that we may judge only our own behavior in relation to God, Louis is sympathetic to his children's agonized obsession with the acquisition of his wealth: "Qui sait s'ils ne sont pas prisonniers, comme je l'ai été moi-même, d'une passion qui ne tient pas à cette part de leur être la plus profonde" (p. 208).

The harvest of grapes and francs that had been the focal points of Louis' existence have given way to the reaping of richer crops: "Que m'importent à présent les récoltes? Je ne puis plus rien récolter au monde. Je puis seulement me connaître un peu mieux moi-même" (p. 127).

Louis had felt since his youth a repulsion at the demanding nature of love. "C'est ainsi que j'ai compris 'l'amour': donnant, donnant.... Quel dégoût" (p. 78). A sense of obligation, of commitment to the service of his fellow-man is the *caritàs* to be learned from the lessons of Jesus. In this sense of commitment, however, the amelioration of man's physical conditions plays only a small part. Louis says that he had always sensed (perhaps in justification, too, for the brief ignition and extinction of his social conscience in young manhood) that the human *malaise* is spiritual, not material. His convictions are shaped by, "... une certitude que cela ne sert à rien de révolutionner la face du monde: il faut atteindre le monde au cœur" (p. 218).

More specifically, he realizes the need for reciprocity of love in his own life: "Même les meilleurs n'apprennent pas seuls à aimer" (p. 217).

The answer, at once so secret and so obvious, is to be found in "le cœur des cœurs, le centre brûlant de tout amour." God, who is essentially love, is eternally acting to bring about man's reconciliation, with both Himself and with man.

Victory for Louis is not assured by the disposition of worldly power and possessions, or by the assigning of responsibility for his doleful circumstances to his environment, heredity, or the demands of others. He now knows that the same force which alone can unite all men, will assure his spiritual triumph in relieving him of false, mundane afflictions, freeing him to reach toward others: "Quelle force? Quelqu'un ... quelqu'un ... qui serait le garant de ma victoire intérieure" (p. 217). The opportunity is offered him in Janine's request for help. She asks his comfort and direction in seeking release from the intolerable pain of her life. This time, Louis does not lose the key presented to him. "Quelqu'un m'avait entendu, compris. Nous nous étions rejoints: c'était une victoire.... Bien heureux si je réussissais à pénétrer jusqu'à un seul être, avant de mourir" (p. 226). When Louis' life ends, he is a different man from the one said by his son to be able only to love "contre quelqu'un." He is no longer one of the multitudes driven by cruelty, "comme tous ceux qui ne sont du parti de l'Agneau." He dies in the midst of his private account of Revelation, in the supreme religious experience of finding within himself, in a heart throbbing "comme s'il allait se rompre," the Presence of the saviour of all men.

Yet his responses, in spite of their motivating causes, were stimulated by those around him, most particularly by Isa, who remains to her death, the goad which prompts much of Louis' reactive behavior. Her character was an independent one, which also drew on its heredity, and on the environment of her upbringing as did Louis'. Perhaps the difference may be generalized in the observation that Louis, even with the distractions of money, is interested in the substance of things and relationships, while Isa, like other Fondaudèges before and after her, is confident that the appearance of a relationship or object endows it with the characteristics it outwardly possesses.

Isa adapts her behavior to conformity with accepted public standards, whether they are those of religion, family, or society. It must be recalled that her family was present-oriented, dissipating its capital in the extravagant pursuit of pleasure and appearances. The sordid, perhaps immoral aspects of such a display were concealed and endured to maintain the desired effect. The sale of Marinette to the aged Philpot, or indeed that of Isa of the first likely candidate with a suitable financial qualification (Louis), reveals the absence of profound personal involvement beyond the meeting of what might be called public obligations of a great family.

The bequest of such attitudes is readily seen in Geneviève's remarkably similar plans for a brilliant marriage of Janine to a suitable candidate. The strategy seems straightforward: "...avec sa fortune, Janine fera un mariage superbe." No hint of a lesson learned from Isa's identical plans for Marinette, or even from Janine's own absorption in her passion, impedes Geneviève's social ambition.

Some motifs which support such a theme are seen in Isa's representation of "les idées de ton milieu et de ton époque." Isa keeps a considerable domestic staff, but in a near-feudal state of dependence. They must rely on her for all their essentials which she distributes with a harsh "justice," although Louis protests her management as an exercise in injustice which God would deplore. Louis is forced to admit that she retains the esteem of those servants of yesteryear, "qui méprisent les maîtres faibles" (p. 88).

It is known that it was alluring aspect of the Fondaudège family which, before it filled him with horror and contempt, had attracted Louis' gace. He rejected on early acquaintance Isa's mother, a seductive woman, but of whom he must say that "...elle m'ennuyait... sa conversation était plate... elle habitait un univers si borné... qu'au bout de trois minutes je désespérais de soutenir la conversation" (p. 33). He was instead deeply moved by what he saw as Isa's "spirituality," as she knelt to pray in her dress of white. Once he has been initiated into the secretly deplorable family rites of the *haute bourgeoisie,* Isa's motions of devotion are revealed as ritual. In the expectation of raising children who will, too, accept existing moral and social standards, Isa inculcates her values in the pious children. Although they lived "dans un monde merveilleux, jalonné de fêtes pieusement célébrées" (p. 84), Isa is hard-headed in the application of religious teachings regarding her fellow-beings. Dreyfus, because of his differences of background, must remain "un misérable juif," while the man Isa's own sister loves, since he violates the social code by being poor, will always be "un aigrefin," "une espèce de rat d'hôtel."

Pretentions of a saintly mastery of feelings are implied as Isa explains how she can retain righteous feelings of detachment on Marinette's pitiful death in childbirth: "...il y a des occasions où il faut savoir se marcher sur le cœur" (p. 212). Isa may be seen in these pious gestures as legator of similar qualities to her children. Hubert, particularly, is given to the obviating of "vile sentiments" by some appearance of devotion or rectitude.

After he has overheard his betrayal by Hubert in Saint Germain des Près, Louis is further astonished to see Hubert standing at the rear of the church before leaving. "...Hubert plongea sa main dans le bénitier, puis, tourné, vers le maître-autel, il fit un grand signe de croix" (p. 173). Hubert will also disguise his critical personal interest in Louis' testamentary provisions by discussing it pompously as, "...une question de justice, une question de moralité... Nous défendons le patrimoine, les droits sacrés de la famille" (p. 148). Hubert also exploits the face-saving teachings of Christianity as a way of concealing the detrimental remarks about him and Geneviève found in the diary. "Jetons sur ces scènes honteuses le manteau de Noé" (p. 236). Once he has become master of the great fortune, Hubert can find somewhere a cloak of respectability to cover the overt maneuvers of greed. He maintains that it was not the money (the principal) but the principle of the issue which constrained him to confront Louis: "Si je n'avais été chef de famille, responsable de l'honneur du nom et du patrimoine de nos enfants, j'eusse préféré renoncer à la lutte..." (p. 236).

Isa's admission to Louis in her last years that she had always slept alone in her room in the expectation that he might come to be with her, is, like her charge that Louis' infidelity drove her to center her life in her children, in contrast with Louis' analysis of the dismal domestic situation.

Louis sees, perhaps shrewdly, that Isa's principal interest (as was Marinette's) lay in motherhood. Her inability to sustain intimate contact, assigning to Louis the role of procreator, is repeatedly emphasized. He questions her genuine enjoyment of sexual pleasure for its own sake: "Rien ne vous paraissait plus naturel que le célibat" (p. 96). Louis bitterly believes that this girl "vouée au blanc," had encouraged his husbandly love-making only as a means of resolving suspicions or doubts on his part: "... il est toujours aisé d'avoir recours au trouble charnel pour faire croire à l'autre qu'on le chérit" (p. 60). Louis' diary will not give details for Isa to read, of his extramarital love affairs: "Non, ne crains pas que je te raconte, mes amours de ce temps-là. Je sais que tu as horreur de ces choses..." (p. 23).

Yet the indifference, or positive neglect, charged by each of the marriage partners began in sensual revelation on "la nuit désastreuse." It can also be asked why Isa chose the time or the place to torment Louis with images of the rich, handsome and "moins respectueux" Rodolphe. It may be splendid evidence of sexual indifference, which would preclude the possibility of response to her confession. It may also be part of a cluster of related motifs which underscore Isa's own retaliatory capacity.

Louis' deep attachment to Luc is hard for Isa to bear. She strikes at her husband by casually speaking of Luc's possible death in the war. So deep is the thrust of her cruelty that Louis asserts her remarks: "... éveillaient en moi l'instinct du meurtre."

She wounds Louis again in this sensitive area by mocking him for trying to give to Luc a money belt, filled with gold. Luc himself had despised the gift, but had not scorned the giver. Isa debases an honest offering, however inept: " 'Avoue que tu savais qu'il n'accepterait pas ton or. C'était un geste de tout repos' " (p. 125).

Her close alliance with her children seems more secure to Louis than to his adversaries, the children themselves. Hubert and his sister believe they see in Isa an accomplice to Louis' intentions to disinherit them. They are convinced that since their mother's dowry is legally protected for her, her activities on their behalf are lacking in conviction: " 'il ne nous déshérite qu'avec votre permission. Votre silence l'approuve' " (p. 142).

The tragic irony is that Louis condemns the same silence but from yet another perspective. It must be credited to Isa that in spite of her own marital and emotional disappointments, she does not undermine Louis openly. Partly to preserve the myth of the unified family, and to exert the pressures of organized religion, the children are encouraged to think of him as "pauvre papa," whose soul is in imminent danger of perdition.

Isa, always a model of rectitude, and in spite of her indulged childhood, is scrupulously careful in the administration of accounts. It is also a further weapon against Louis' excursions into debauchery. She has further arms in her arsenal, presumably against Louis, in the form of letters so damaging to him that they would assure her a separation if presented in evidence. She can dictate calmly: "Je suis restée avec toi à cause des enfants. Mais si ta présence doit être une menace pour leur âme, je n'hésiterai pas" (p. 82). Louis does not protest his wife's claim as her special domain the assurance of her children's souls' salvation. He reserves for himself the right, "... de défendre l'esprit de mes enfantes..." (p. 81).

So, in different yet similar ways, Louis and Isa contrive to live together for forty years in latent love and open hate. He whose death is expected from day to day lives on to write his intimate journal to be read by his children. Isa, the tower of immutability and strength to her children, dies rather suddenly after a final gesture of self-effacement. Louis wants everyone to know both what he was and what he has become. As noted earlier, man does not learn to love *in vacuo*. Some one person, divine or human, must pass along the secret: "... un secret d'amour que le monde ne connaît plus" (p. 217). Isa, on the other hand, must remain a mystery forever, except for hints provided in the fragmented sources which are outside Louis' discretion. She is elusive as ever, as Louis searches among the ashes of her fireplace — "dans ce néant" — for clues to the many unanswered questions. She chooses, however, that her silence persist beyond the grave: "Elle avait voule disparaître tout entière; elle avait effacé ses moindres traces" (p. 210).

RELATIONSHIP BETWEEN THEMES OF THE STORY AND THEMES OF THE PLOT

It is as though, in Le Nœud de vipères, the themes of the plot and story represent parallel lines, leading in perspective to the infinity of the soul's salvation. The spiritual enervation observed in the principal character is alleviated by an experience, undefined and indescribable, which turns his lack of assurance and security into a burning confidence in divine love. The events of the story in their linear progression reveal his passage from a closely moulded product of his environment and education to a caricature of qualities valued by his background. He finally abandons it for final days of peace.

Louis' description of his volatile and febrile search for self-definition in the journal touches the heart of the matter. He is a man, "dont la route a toujours été fausse." It is in his effort to fulfill his own destiny, on the wrong road to be sure, that the supreme contingent incident intervenes. A man's destiny which is directed toward perpetually deeper corruption, as in Louis' case is reoriented by "Quelqu'un," by "une force inconnue," toward a different goal. Louis' rejection of the insights offered to him by a trinity of innocence (in Marie, Luc and Marinette) is forgiven, by virtue of his conversion, and the quest for spiritual development and personal commitment is given a seemingly anonymous impetus.

The conflict between the impositions of society, family and other secular influences (which are emphasized in the themes of the story) and the impulses of the spirit (which are revealed in the plot as fundamentally unconscious motivations) create the tension of the novel. The strength of the temporal forces is indicated in the story motifs which show the main character focusing, almost against his will, on worldly objectives of possession or domination. The themes of the plot are, in effect, mirror images since they are often reversals, we are told, of the motivations originally attributed to actions and attitudes.

For example, Louis' fixation in taking revenge on others emerges ultimately as revenge on himself for having evaded the spirit of Christ. His obsession with money is found to be a cloak, covering a profound desire for spiritual reward. The obverse side of his hatred for his family is a longing for a more perfect love than that limited relationship can provide. The mirror qualities, then, of themes of the story and plot, may be seen in their parallel progression toward a conclusion of gratification.

In the story, Louis succeeds in amassing a fortune worthy of his unbringing and ambition, and successfully passes it on, after much suffering, to his heirs in a manner which, without knowing why, brings him satisfaction. The plot shows Louis moving steadily from his role as an enraged young man, bent on exacting compensation for his "injuries," to a mature Christian who uses his capacity for passion, and his free will, to move beyond world-oriented objectives.

The quotation in the novel's preface, "we do not know what we want," emphasizes the helplessness of the individual in the quest for his identity and a spiritual ideal. He must flounder from error to error, as did Louis, until he can exercise his free will sufficiently to acknowledge the touch of divine grace.

GENERIC COHERENCE

It is difficult to overlook the prefatory quotation from the writings of Saint Theresa of Avila which Mauriac uses at the beginning of his novel, *Le Nœud de vipères*.

> "Dieu, considérez que nous ne nous entendons pas nous-mêmes et que nous ne savons pas ce que nous voulons, et que nous nous éloignons infiniment de ce que nous désirons."
>
> SAINTE THÉRÈSE D'AVILA

It, combined with the title, goes directly to the central themes whose motif clusters can be found quite apart from themes of either the story or plot. Such central thematic groupings form the nuclei around which correlative and lesser themes are grouped. We see in Mauriac's interpretation of the mystical quest, an explanation, in effect, of the perversities of human behavior. Analyses of the psychical origins of purposes in noting their motivational bases fail to include the kind of spiritual awareness which the diarist's contemplation alone can provide.

Some indication of the aimlessness and futility of much human effort is revealed in this theme, underscoring the waste of energy which often represents a lifetime. The fusion and confusion of temporal objectives, whereby material and spiritual values become indistinguishable, produce a distortion in the lens through which the focus on infinity should be directed. Louis is one of the chosen few, it seems, to whom the opportunity is given to appreciate the proportions of his error.

He saw clearly in Isa the most surface aspects of such misdirection as he chides her for praying to God for temporal goods. Louis was feared as a man who seeks control over others, who is aggressive in the pursuit of his career, and who makes the increase of his personal fortune the center of his "constructive" objectives. Themes of the story and plot revealed that "negative" goals were also determining factors in his behavior. It is to Louis' spiritual benefit that he is made aware of the essential frivolity of such goals. Specific motifs reveal, for example, his unwillingness to accept further administrative promotion in his profession, without actually knowing why: "Au fond, en ai-je jamais eu envie?" (p. 79).

But it is Louis' realization, when he cannot give away or lose his fortune, as he wishes, that the acquisitions of a lifetime were meaningless, which brings into relief the error in emphasis. The concomitance of his efforts to make, and to lose, his wealth are indications of the uncertainties of his desires: "Je me suis toujours trompé sur l'objet de mes désirs. Nous ne savons pas ce que nous désirons, nous n'aimons pas ce que nous croyons aimer" (p. 205).

The consciousness of reaching old age as a prisoner of his obsessions is also an instrument of his deliverance. He is aware, when it is almost too late, that this submission to sin was evidenced in the poisonous stifling of the *nœud de vipères* which breeds within himself and which he has generated in others. Yet somewhere in his being, another and more persistent life rhythm asserted itself and resisted suffocation: "Je connais mon cœur... il continue de battre au-dessous de ce grouillement" (p. 228). His distraction from the true light by its mere reflection, as though mistaking the moon for the sun, is indicated: "Comme un chien aboie à la lune, j'ai été fasciné par un reflet" (p. 207).

It is inexplicable how the sense of error suddenly is apparent to Louis. There seems no doubt, however, that his values have crystallized. He can bring assurance and conviction to his guidance of Janine in her distress and abandonment. Louis would like her to be as lucid as he is concerning man's true object in love. He helps her to examine, not entirely successfully, what her compulsive search for love, in truth, represents: "...elle court et s'affole après cet être, sans rien qui la renseigne sur ce qu'est réellement l'objet de sa poursuite" (p. 230).

In believing, as he had for so long, to seek fulfillment in hate (noted in numerous motifs indicating his desire for revenge), Louis was actually awaiting fulfillment in love. The disproportionate richness he saw in his worldly acquisitions becomes a matter of indifference. Louis asks Janine to re-appraise the depth and intensity of emotion she expends on her husband, Phili: " 'Penses-tu... que Phili soit à la mesure de ce que tu lui donnes?' " (p. 232). He makes the inquiry as he tries to bring into perspective the possibility of applying this "incendie," "cette frénésie," in Janine to an object more worthy of desire.

We do not know if his efforts succeed with his granddaughter, but she is touched sufficiently to have no doubt of Louis' own conversion: "Me comprendrez-vous si je vous affirme que là où était son trésor, là n'était pas son cœur" (p. 245).

Louis' identification with his money was subtly reinforced when he tried to give the most personal gift he can imagine to his beloved young Luc, who was about to leave for the war. Louis, inarticulate with the young, takes from the bust of Demosthenes (the spokesman he might wish to be) handfuls of gold *louis*. The choice of motif reveals that he is, in effect, giving the lad what is most important to him, a part of himself. But the boy, in innocent honesty, rejects the gift as a valueless one.

A second indication of Louis' mistaken association with material possessions involves another source of purity in his life. Louis keeps his liquid assets in a kind of safe which is opened only by a combination. The access word is MARIE, the name of his angelic, tender daughter whose characteristic is unworldliness and generosity, and of whom it is said: "Elle donnerait tout ce qu'elle a; l'argent ne lui tient pas aux doigts." Marie, like Luc, is later perceived by Louis to have been a key to his salvation, a key to riches beyond this world. She was indeed guarding his treasure, but on another and unrecognized plane.

The linking image of the *nœud de vipères* has been previously touched upon as the leitmotif which supports the compound theme of human revenge, hatred and avarice. It can be recalled that Louis, in moments of self-excoriation, found this writhing, venomous tangle within himself. It was closer observation of his family, and its motivations and goals, which gave Louis the insight that the transversions had extended beyond himself. Assuming some responsibility for the breeding of potentially poisonous monsters around him, the narrator sees himself as both their generator and victim. His mistake, as has been indicated, lay in not overcoming the malignancies suggested by the *nid de vipères,* wherever the origins of the evils lay.

A series of repetitious labels involving motifs of a circle sustains the theme. The ugly picture of his family as it intrigues to obtain Louis' money is invariably described in a circular setting:

> La famille, assise en rond, nous regardait venir.... (p. 67)

> ...et lorsque j'ai revu, au complet, cette meute familiale assise en rond... je suis obsédé par la vision des partages. (p. 74)

When Louis' illness appears to worsen, he feels himself disarmed and helpless:

> ...le cercle de famille se resserre autour de mon lit (p. 116)

Geneviève, desperately anxious to secure some financial aid from her father, insists:

> Il fallait tâcher de l'entourer, de faire sa conquête. (p. 139)

Robert has petty, greedy interests which never go beyond "le cercle le plus petit de ses convenances" (p. 172). He is suborned by the "vipères emmêlées," Alfred and Hubert, who, in reinforcing their figurative reptilian convolutions, "encadraient" their victim.

The universal nature of this *nœud de vipères* is denoted in a contingent incident. Louis had almost allowed his heart to be touched by Isa's deference and concern as they walk in the garden in their old age. She is unaware of his mental association of the circle of chairs and the spasms of hate and avarice he knows among his children. The sight of the abandoned circle drives Louis into a fury, and smothers nascent emotions of tenderness.

> Les fauteuils vides formaient encore un cercle étroit.... La terre était creusée par les talons.... L'ennemie avait campé là cette nuit.... [Les vipères] formaient ce cercle hideux au bas du perron et la terre porte encore leurs traces. (p. 158)

No peace can be assured to man until his soul is freed from the toxic embrace of the *nœud de vipères*. The interlacing of the component emotions (or sins) it comprises, is so intricate that gradual unentanglement is impossible. Quoting Matthew 10:34, "Je ne suis pas venu apporter la paix mais le glaive," Mauriac suggests the direct, dramatic divine intervention which will be necessary to cut the knot. Louis finally knows that moment when, for the first time, he longs in genuine love to be with his children: "Le nœud de vispères était enfin tranché..." (p. 214). The bonds have been severed which had held him prisoner for a lifetime, and chained by crimes he had not wanted to commit.

Mauriac's thematic emphasis reveals that in the absence of some focus on the eternal, or of a goal which extends beyond the acquisition of a possession, or the domination of another being, earthly standards become arbitrary and objectives are short-range. Without permanent values by which to find a haven in the spiritual world, the measurement of human efforts and achievements suffers from a myopic distortion. The most concrete example is seen, of course, in Louis' preoccupation with money. The satisfaction is so short-lived that even Louis himself deplores the lack of deeper purpose, that he has lived only in order to "gagner gros, comme l'épicier du coin." He describes his failure as never having sacrificed "une passion basse à une passion plus haute" (p. 73). Indeed he sees himself as "un vieux Faust" (p. 63).

The sacrifices have instead been those made to the false idol of money. He has refused the pleas of colleagues to pursue a judicial career, because the loss of earning power was intolerable to him. He later sees as a misinterpretation the criticism leveled at political figures who accept some small financial profits from their positions. They should instead be congratulated for having "...préféré la gloire aux affaires les plus fructueuses" (p. 73). He himself has been unable to resist the immediate appeal of instant profit, even at the sacrifice of larger, more intangible rewards. He knows himself to be "...incapable de lâcher la petite et médiocre proie des honoraires pour l'ombre de la puissance, car il n'y a pas d'ombre sans réalité; l'ombre est une réalité." Perhaps more importantly, he let escape an occasion for loving Marinette, when he was frustrated by "ce goût maniaque de l'argent" (p. 99).

In a similar vein, Louis has overlooked the presence of spiritual love in his household in the person of Abbé Ardouin, who was engaged by Louis because of his low salary requirements, but who, "à notre insu," was there as "l'esprit du Christ."

That Louis is not alone in neglecting advantages beyond his immediate vision is noted in other motifs. Isa misses the opportunities which are part of acts of charity and which would sanctify and enlighten her life. She instead reduces these corporal works of mercy to the abrasive execution of temporal duties. In the same way, her exercise of the Catholic faith, "avec cet instinct bourgeois du confort," has the quality of satisfying some personal need for participation in a ritual without thinking what purpose, if any, it may serve.

Robert is so paralyzed by fear that he cannot face, with freedom or imagination, the enormous gift of Louis' wealth. He cannot endure the strains of risk, or of waiting to see what results chance might bring: "Sans doute aurait-il préféré recevoir cent mille francs à la main, que d'avoir à dissimuler cette énorme fortune" (p. 163).

Similarly, Louis cannot interest Robert in the science of horseflesh and breeding. We are told of Robert: "Ce qui l'intéressait, c'était de gagner. Les chevaux l'ennuyaient" (p. 161).

His mother is as much brutalized by her difficult and degrading life into dreading the unknown, and settling for what is quickly obtainable:

> C'était elle, sans aucune doute, qui avait poussé Robert à s'entendre avec mes enfants. . . . (p. 177)

> . . . hantée par des souvenirs judiciaires, sa mère lui conseillerait de composer avec la famille et de vendre son secret le plus cher. (p. 172)

It may well be that this same fear of the unknown, of unwillingness to take a risk, is evidenced in Louis' preoccupation with material possessions, which serve as a diversion from his possible route to salvation. Concentration on secular matters causes a resistance to insights which may hint at greater but remote rewards beyond the material. As is implied in "the gamble" proposed by Pascal, the road to salvation does require either complete faith or a willingness to risk disappointment. Louis recognizes that he had had occasional intuitive perceptions of "un autre monde": "...ce ne fut qu'un instant qui, au long de ma triste vie, se renouvela à de très rares intervalles" (p. 39). He senses at one moment that this other life is within reach, yet his attraction to objectives closer at hand deny him access to it: "Je sentais à la fois tout proche, à portée de ma main, et pourtant à une distance infinie, un monde inconnu de bonté" (p. 174). A correlative theme might be suggested in the sense of power enjoyed in dominating others. It is perhaps too obvious to imply that lacking a positive spiritual goal, the human spirit is debilitated and lured into the immense and immediate pleasure afforded by evil. A primary source of gratification for Louis lies in the abuse of his power over his family, keeping them in a state of continual uncertainty and near-terror. Such exploitation of the helpless, in any sense, suggests a cowardice based on self-loathing and pusillanimity.

The principal pleasure of Louis' lifetime lies not in making a definitive announcement that he has disowned his family, but in denying to them specific knowledge of both his, and their circumstances. Threats of changed testamentary provisions, of outright disinheritance, are only part of the general torment. Louis keeps his family off-balance by pendulum-like swings between health and near-death. His insistence on eating meat on Friday is a religious affront to them, but it is a warning as well not to take his immediate expiration for granted: "...je tiens à manger une côtellette en ce jour de pénitence, non par bravade, mais pour vous signifier que j'ai gardé ma volonté intacte..." (p. 44). He suffers repeated cardiac crises which seem to signal the end, yet can rejoice in the resiliency of his constitution: "...qui me croyait mort, me voit, de nouveau surgir; et j'ai la force, pendant des heures, dans les caves des établissements de crédit, de détacher moi-même des coupons" (p. 16). He enjoyed disrupting his family by announcing his intention to dine with them: "Ma présence au milieu de vous, hier soir, dérangeait vos plans" (p. 45). While he has complete control over the destinies of those near him, Louis savours the exercise of that power and the reaffirmation of their dependence. Isa keenly differentiates between Louis' motivation and stated purpose in keeping the Abbé Ardouin in their home:

" 'Mon mari joue avec lui comme le chat avec la souris... voilà pourquoi il le supporte malgré son horreur des soutanes' " (p. 90).

A similar motif is used to indicate his anticipation of torturing the helpless Robert, who is unaware that Louis knows of his treachery: "Je n'osais m'avouer le plaisir que je me promettais, à jouer, comme un chat, avec ce triste mulot" (p. 175). Louis' satisfaction is surely complete since the two other conspirators are discovered *en flagrant délit*. The motif related to the above is obvious as Louis watches his children betray him, and he becomes intoxicated with the new power this knowledge gives him. "Un policier, qui voit le voleur entrer dans la souricière, n'éprouve pas une plus délicieuse émotion..." (p. 171). The spiritual immaturity which is so noticeable in such present-oriented gratification is Mauriac's best evidence that his character, Louis, is not ready to receive the gift of divine love.

Yet another correlative theme is offered in the motif clusters which reveal that spiritual uncertainty deprives the individual of his assumption of responsibility for his own development. Without a target of self-improvement, the very concept of man's perfectability is denied. Louis has come to the end of his life, a point where he sees with "une lucidité affreuse," that old age "...c'est d'être le total d'une vie, un total dans lequel nous ne saurions changer aucun chiffre" (p. 184).

Louis clumsily evades that total responsibility for the creation of himself. He insists that the characters of individuals are formed by responding automatically to the expectations others have of them, and by their ascribing to others only those qualities which fill their own immediate needs. In both of these exercises, the emphasis is on the short-range and the immediate. In fear of displeasing those whose love, or hatred, we seek, we grant prompt acquiescence to what they ask of us. In seeking easy satisfaction, one accepts the most surface qualities observed in others as definitive characterizations, although this is obviously not the case on further study.

Louis easily fulfills the role of the figure of hate expected of him in youthful company and in his family. He had never learned how to "se détendre et se divertir..." (p. 160). He was so immersed in plodding school routines, where he wrote "...ce qu'il faut écrire pour les examinateurs..." (p. 20) that his childhood, instead of representing a lost paradise, is only "une steppe dès le début de ma vie" (p. 21), where initiative and originality withered.

His behavior is determined by the man he has only somewhat willingly become:

> ... je suis tellement accoutumé à être haï et à faire peur, que mes prunelles, mes sourcils, ma voix, mon rire se font complices ... et préviennent ma volonté. (p. 179)

Even if he wanted to change his approach to others, he is seriously impaired from doing so by the further complicity of old age:

> A cet âge, l'expression des traits ne changera plus. Et l'âme se décourage quand elle ne peut s'exprimer au-dehors ... (p. 64)

> Si j'étais plus jeune, les plis seraient moins marqués, les habitudes moins enracinées, mais je doute que, même dans ma jeunesse, j'eusse pu rompre cet enchantement. (p. 217)

The notion of human beings as the creation of the needs of others, denying the freedom of will toward perfection, is summarized in Louis' self-exculpating outburst.

> Tous, femme, enfants, maîtres et serviteurs, ils s'étaient ligués contre mon âme, ils m'avaient dicté ce rôle odieux. Je m'étais figé atrocement dans l'attitude qu'ils exigaient de moi. Je m'étais conformé au modèle que me proposait leur haine. (p. 217)

Yet a repetitious label, that of "monster" is employed throughout the novel, in which is emphasized Louis' denial of such "type-casting." "Comment y fus-je amené, moi qui n'étais pas un monstre?" (p. 10). He protests, "Je n'étais pas un monstre" (p. 60). His children, insist, however, that his feelings for them are un-natural, "C'est un monstre" (p. 140). He gradually learns of the ugliness of their own motivations, seeing that they, too, are monsters and he is their victim.

The final days of his life bring Louis to a state of atonement. His wife died without knowing that his ugly exterior concealed

a virtuous man: "...je n'étais pas seulement ce monstre, ce bourreau, ... il existait un autre homme en moi" (p. 191). He must
accept the consequences of a life-pattern, regardless of its genesis:
"Il n'est rien en moi, jusqu'à ma voix, à mes gestes, à mon rire,
qui n'appartienne au monstre que j'ai dressé contre le monde et
à qui j'ai donné mon nom" (p. 213).

Mauriac gives particular emphasis, by repetitious phrasing in
singling out a particular characteristic, to the theme of involuntary
repulsion of others. The effect is indeed nearly one of caricature
since a being, almost grotesque, results in the portrait. He knows
all too well that his is a figure of revulsion: "Tout le monde te
redoute et te fuit, Louis," Isa had warned. His innocent children
stop speaking and singing at the sound of his footsteps (p. 84) and
he must spring upon his family to force a conversation: "...vous
ne saviez pas que je me cachais derrière un massif d'arbres, et
tout à coup, j'intervenais avant que vous ayez pu battre en re-
traite" (p. 90). His wife and children conspire to conceal social
activities undertaken in his absence, and he returns often to find,
"les signes d'une fête interrompue." The terror his family and as-
sociates experience is put into extraordinary contrast with the
most prominent single trait cited about Louis. It is, ironically, his
laughter, which is the means by which Louis is often cut off from
his present company, and by which he creates "autour de soi le
désert." He reminds his wife: "Tu connais mon rire, ce rire qui...
avait le pouvoir de tuer autour de moi toute gaieté" (p. 93). He
cannot resist reacting to Janine's spurious concern for him when
he knows she is among those plotting against him: "Alors, je me
mis à rire, de ce rire dangereux qui... les terrifiait" (p. 151). He
genuinely tries to suppress his awesomeness before Robert, and
is bitterly amused that it is his modified glance which freezes his
son: "Mais plus je riais et plus l'éclat de cette gaieté lui apparais-
sait d'un présage sinistre" (p. 179). His children are shocked into
silence at Louis' knowledge of their agreement to pay Robert a
niggardly sum in exchange for a fortune. Louis is mocking as he
discusses their "generosity," and enjoys his triumph: "Je riais
de ce rire qui me fait tousser. Les enfants ne trouvaient pas de
paroles" (p. 192).

An explanation is suggested in a final reference. In a dreadful
faux-pas, inquiring after the health of his servants' daughter, Louis

is told that the girl has been dead for ten years. "... comme quand j'étais gêné et intimidé, je ricanais un peu, je ne pouvais pas me retenir de ricaner" (p. 216). Hubert is seen to have on his face, "un rictus," as he readies himself to confront Louis in requesting funds. The same stimulus of fear and hesitancy causes Robert to smile at his father, as he would "to an angry employer."

The laugh, in speaking generally of Louis' case, is symptomatic of, perhaps, spiritual unease and discomfiture. Reinforcing the thesis that the man who presents his grossly repugnant façade to the world differs from the secret heart within him, the laugh represents a temporary release from the strain of conflicting motivations.

The complaint registered by Louis, which was mentioned earlier, that all those he was connected with, created a role for him which he felt obliged to fulfill, is supported by his grand-daughter, Janine. In a spirit of reparation for her un-Christian attitudes and those of her family, she accepts the burden of guilt which he has assigned to them. By presenting to Louis a consistent view of Christianity as a doctrine of expediency, the family had nourished his scorn for Catholic teachings. They had shown him lives lived without principle, and he accepted them as typical of conventional ambition and religiosity, worthy only of contempt. Janine tries to explain the family's part in Louis' unhappy develop-ment: "Ne croyez-vous pas que votre père eût été un autre homme si nous-mêmes avions été différents.... ce fut notre malheur à tous qu'il nous ait pris pour des Chrétiens exemplaires" (p. 245).

The responsibility of one man for another is only indirectly suggested in the novel, although Louis, in his tentative approaches throughout, was groping blindly toward such commitment. Reject-ing surface impressions of Janine, Louis answers her call for help in her marital estrangement. He forces a direct encounter between his newly-enlightened spirit and hers, and she reports the success of his efforts: "... une admirable lumière l'a touché dans ses der-niers jours et... c'est lui, lui seul, à ce moment-là, qui m'a pris la tête à deux mains, qui a détourné de force mon regard" (p. 244).

There is not a principal character in the novel, except for the three graces, Marie, Luc and Marinette, who does not live under some kind of fictive, or even fictional, pressure. They are driven by inner needs of varying complexions and wear a veneer of response drawn from conventional romantic sources. "Comme on se laisse influencer par les pontifs du roman et du théâtre!" Louis' estimation of his own character suffers from a myopic bias which makes objective commentary impossible. He believes that he is free from the need to wear a cloak of hypocrisy in the world. He justifies his reputation as hateful by his refusal to adopt false, although admirable, public postures. He, in effect, makes a choice and decides on honesty rather than nobility. There is a sense of righteousness as he combats Marinette's plans to jettison her inherited fortune by remarrying: "J'aurais eu tout intérêt à parler comme elle, et à jouer les nobles cœurs; mais il m'était impossible de feindre..." (p. 99). When, however, his own resources are threatened, as by requests from Olympe for money for her husband, Hubert, Louis adopts the same chameleon tactics as the others, protecting himself: "...je feignais d'être à mille lieues de comprendre ce qu'elle voulait" (p. 101). Marinette's suggestion of Louis' hypocrisy regarding money is supported further in their moonlit walk in the woods. It is the contingent incident of an unidentified sound in the trees that prevents an imminent seduction of the willing Marinette. Not acknowledging his fear at being caught, "Je feignais de ne m'être pas aperçu de ce qu'il pouvait y avoir eu d'un peu trouble dans son abandon et dans ses larmes." Louis had thought in those instants of wounding his wife by making love to her sister. He desisted only on thinking he heard the step of Abbé Ardouin. He conceals beneath paternal condescension the profound shame these two emotions provoke.

The lack of depth which is implicit in human behavior is indicated by a motif, in which Louis' children deplore his exceptional parental hostility. Geneviève, especially given to the ready-made phrase, reports of her father's latest activities: "Quelle chose inimaginable! On ne voit pas ça, même dans les livres."

The adoption of masks is a related, and assumed, part of such behavior, providing a kind of social leaven, and facilitating superficial, undemanding relationships. It is in moments of profound emotion that the disguises fall away and some vestiges of original personality emerge, sometimes so unfamiliar as to be unrecognizable. Grief on the death of Isa, for example, has shocked her children into unfamiliar roles:

Leurs visages me semblaient différents, rouges, altérés,
quelqu'uns verdâtres. (p. 190)

Le chagrin nous avait tous démasqués et nous ne nous
reconnaissons pas. (p. 195)

For Louis, the sight of his family exposed in unexpected emotion is not displeasing, since it has always been the pretentious
adoption of social and moral mannerisms which had repelled him.
His granddaughter is denuded of vanities and affectations when
she finds herself alone with a passion for a man who has fled her.
"... le désespoir avait tout détruit de ce que je haïssais: ce pauvre
être si façonné, si maniéré, était devenu terriblement dépouillé et
simple" (p. 221).

In contrast with Louis' usual unwillingness to accommodate
himself to social amenities, in the name of honesty, an example
is given of the lesson to be learned from simulated courtesy. Having
arrived ill at Calèse after Isa's death, Louis is surprised to hear
coming from his own lips conventional expressions of grief as they
normally are publicly phrased:

> Je répétais, comme un acteur qui cherche le ton juste:
> "Puisque je n'ai pas pu lui dire adieu..." et ces mots
> banals qui ne tendaient qu'à sauver les apparences, et qui
> m'étaient venus parce qu'ils faisaient partie de mon rôle
> dans la pompe funèbre, éveillèrent en moi... le sentiment
> dont ils étaient l'expression. (p. 190)

There is a kind of reverse example, in Louis' case, which suggests that the mask of hatred and hostility which he has always
worn conceals sentiments of a sentimental, affectionate nature. His
family is stupefied at the spectacle. Subsequent reversions to
hypocrisy among the children restore the mask to Louis, too, and
he continues his relentless pursuit.

The universal expression of counterfeit feelings under various
guises leads to a debasement of the genuine emotional currency.
Louis had rejected as self-seeking adventuresses, a number of
women whose appeal he acknowledged and who might have
brought some compassion into his life.

> ... je revois avec une lucidité qui... me ferait hurler, tout
> ce que j'ai repoussé, non par vertu mais par méfiance et

ladrerie... soit que mon esprit soupçonneux interprétât
mal la plus innocente demande... soit que je me rendisse
odieux par [des] manies.... (p. 77)

His mistrust is not always wrong, however. As Robert's mother
visits Louis' sickbed in Paris, in guilty knowledge of her son's
betrayal, Louis correctly appraises her kindness.

... je vis d'abord son sourire. Son attitude obséquieuse
aurait suffi à me mettre en défiance... et à m'avertir que
j'étais trahi. Une certaine qualité de gentillesse est toujours signe de trahison. (p. 176)

The general theme of human pretentiousness which is manifest-
ed in concealments of vile sentiments or of attitudes of a corrupt
nature, is stressed in the linking image cited below:

Même avec la fenêtre ouverte, l'odeur de la pompeuse
table de nuit, au-dessus de marbre rouge, emplissait le
pièce. Un tapis à fond moutarde recouvrait la table. Cet
ensemble me plaisait comme un raccourci de la laideur
et me la prétention humaine. (p. 176)

The faith that prevails without prompting in the human spirit
against the obstacles of sin and corruption is also that of overcoming defeat in death. A connection is established by Mauriac
between human expectations of spiritual rebirth and the natural
cycles observed in the cultivation of vineyards such as Louis owns.
"... l'espérance est indéracinable et qu'il reste toujours en nous
de ce chiendent."

Louis' identification with his vineyards is clarified in mid-diary
in his realization that the love he has for them is not, as he had
always assumed, based on their return of profit. "Ce que j'ai pris
pour un signe d'attachement à la propriété n'est que l'instinct
charnel du paysan, fils de paysan, né de ceux qui depuis des siècles
interrogent l'horizon avec angoisse" (p. 207).

The near-personification of the vines was emphasized by Louis'
reaction when they were threatened by hail: "Un profond instinct
paysan me jetait en avant, comme si j'eusse voulu m'étendre et
recouvrir de mon corps la vigne lapidée" (p. 130). The feeling of
kinship with his vines is made explicit in Louis' fear of approach-

ing death. "En ce qui me concerne, la mort ne sera pas venue en voleuse. Elle rôde autour de moi depuis des années; je l'entends; je sens son haleine..." (p. 15).

He must take precautions to evade these vital threats, and to outwit death. "A mon âge, le sommeil attire l'attention de la mort, il ne faut pas faire semblant d'être mort. Tant que je resterai debout, il me semble qu'elle ne peut pas venir" (p. 75). His own fears are mirrored in Marie's sensitive observation before a storm reaches the vines: "La vigne a peur..." (p. 167). It is at the moment when Louis realizes that the important harvests are not to be of grapes but of self-knowledge, that he also sees the vines offered as sacrificial bait:

> A peine la vigne a-t-elle "passé fleur,"... mais il semble qu'elle soit là comme des jeunes bêtes que le chasseur attache et abandonne dans les ténèbres pour attirer les fauves: des nuées grondantes tournent autour des vignes offertes. (p. 127)

The sense of expiation, in the offering up of an innocent victim, leads to Louis' awareness that both in the natural and supernatural worlds, organisms die only to be reborn. Physical and spiritual regeneration represent life itself. The vines in autumn are laden with fruit, and can no longer hope for conditions of heat and sunlight. The fruits have reached their maximum perfectability and their span on earth ends. But since the vines die, only to live again in the spring, the hope is eternal. Louis who saw himself as "le tronc" of his family tree, will pass on spiritual vitality to Janine. Louis recognizes that he is about to be reborn at the moment of death: "Mais pour nous, peut-être n'est-il jamais trop tard. J'ai besoin de me répéter, qu'il n'est jamais trop tard."

He leans against the same vines, stripped of their grapes, and watches the setting sun, as he "... regarde le dernier automne de ma vie endormir la vigne, l'engourdir de fumées et de rayons" (p. 213). The hillsides covered with vineyards are touched by the mantle of night. All implications suggest a profound sleep in Nature with a reawakening ahead: "... au loin les côtes perdues ressemblaient à des épaules courbées; elles attendaient le brouillard de la nuit pour s'allonger peut-être, pour s'étendre, pour s'endormir d'un sommeil humain" (p. 214).

The belligerent nature of Louis' relations within his family is revealed repeatedly in terms of military terminology. His early years of marriage signal the beginnings of a misunderstanding with Isa which became "une guerre ouverte." The alignment, as adversaries, of Louis and the rest of his family, is invariably presented as "cette guerre," while open battles, in which Louis is sometimes defeated, drive him into "une guerre souterraine." The omnipresence of the struggle to assert individual values is revealed in Marinette's resistance to the pressures of others in agreeing to behave as they wish her to. The forces of family opposition erode her determination, and in the same military motif, Mauriac underscores her surrender. "De guerre lasse, elle me demanda de l'escorter" (p. 98). Even Louis' brief contacts with Robert have placed the two men on opposing sides. He must adjust his attitudes and plan his strategy to defeat his son: "...il fallait changer mes batteries" (p. 175). Louis' final confrontation with Geneviève and Hubert regarding the disposition of his wealth is well described as he arms himself: "Je ne voulais pas engager cette bataille, en malade que l'adversaire ménage et protège. ... J'avais pris les drogues nécessaires... je me sentais moins oppressé..." (p. 197). This last-mentioned scene is a turning point of the novel, where Louis has at last relieved himself of the debilitating burden of his treasures. The theme and motifs change dramatically from the joy of the skirmish to the bliss of peace. Louis' hopes for deliverance from his oppression are simple: "Qu'ils me laissent mourir en paix!" (p. 203). That the same goal might have been part of Isa's search is suggested in a priestly letter, which gave guidance to her tormented spirit. The letter is headed simply, *Pax*.

Louis watches autumn and darkness fall upon nature, dulling them in the sleep already discussed. Confident now of his own resuscitation, "...je revenais vers la maison, pénétré jusqu'au cœur par la paix qui remplissait la terre..." (p. 214). The spell of his enchantment is completed in his last hours, as he awaits departure from this life with a newly-found composure which comes close to the miraculous. "...j'éprouvais une profonde paix. Démuni de tout, isolé, sous le coup d'une mort affreuse, je demeurais calme, attentif, l'esprit en éveil" (p. 228). There is no doubt that "cette paix qui me possédait" was in truth the presence within Louis of the Creator of the new existence he is confident lies before him.

A theme correlative by contrast, in particular to the spiritual suffocation by the sins represented in the *nœud de vipères,* to that of crippling cruelty revealed in the image of cat and mouse, and to the solitude revealed by self-depiction as a monster is that which presents the growing state of grace as an improved physical state of well-being. This state of well-being is represented by an expansiveness, not only noted in connection with bodily symptoms, but by charity and generosity as well. As he begins his diary, Louis is feeling his way toward discovery of his state of spiritual health. He also for the first time is seen to make tentative efforts to know his physical condition. It is appropriate that such an assessment take place before the amelioration of his moral and physical maladies. "Je pose ma main sur ma poitrine, je tâte mon cœur" (p. 15).

It is in the early years of hate, as Louis learns that his wife's interest in him is severely limited, that the first signs of *malaise* commence. His initial courtroom success in the Villenave case, which made his name famous in much of France, has embittered him in its failure to bring him recognition in his own home. "Cette fameuse affaire Villenave, si elle consacra mon triomphe, resserra l'étau qui m'étouffait" (p. 68).

Subsequent experiences which draw upon his desire for revenge are invariably accompanied by incapacitating pain around the heart. His efforts to convince Robert result in "le resserrement de ma poitrine, cette contraction atroce" (p. 162). After another visit with his son which is even more frustrating, "...un poids énorme m'é-touffait" (p. 186).

Again, there is a distinct change from his spiritual oppression when he feels a sense of absolution on learning of his children's ugly plans to commit him: "J'éprouvais un état de bien-être..." (p. 194). A continued improvement, in the gradual diminution of his physical and spiritual discomfort, is observed as the bonds of hatred and revenge gradually loosen: "...Or je n'éprouvais rien que du soulagement, un allègement physique: je respirais mieux" (p. 205). Once he has left his secular objectives behind, and has directed his energies toward helping another, his whole being benefits: "Jamais mon cœur ne m'avait laissé un si long répit" (p. 227). The guilt and anger of fifty years are dissipated as he writes that he no longer was feeling "le poids de ces années tristes"

(p. 228). Love, the powerful counter-force to the paralysis of hatred, invaded Louis' heart in his final days. His final experience with its overwhelming presence is one of glorious surrender.

> Ce qui m'étouffe, ce soir... ce qui fait mal à mon cœur comme s'il allait se rompre, cet amour dont je connais le nom ador.... (p. 234)

CHAPTER V

THE DEVELOPMENT OF THEMES

THE NOVELS which have been discussed are three major represen-
tations of Mauriac's literary production in the ten-year period,
1923-1932. *Génitrix,* while not his first novel, is an early example
of what constitutes Mauriac's "mature" novel output. *Le Désert
de l'amour* and *Le Nœud de vipères* are milestones on the path of
his career as a novelist.

The decade from *Génitrix* to *Le Nœud de vipères* is one in
which Mauriac, and his works as well, were seen to undergo
dramatic modifications. Fundamental alterations in outlook and
content are reflected not only in important thematic changes but
in a shift from undercurrents of pessimism to those of optimism.
It was in the repeated offerings to his reading public of characters
and situations corroded by evil that Mauriac found himself
vulnerable to attack by both supporters and critics.

His creation, as suggested earlier, of a personage like Félicité
in *Génitrix* comes close to caricature in its one-dimensional emphasis on a particular negative characteristic or trait. His implication that such singularly repellent qualities may be found universal-
ly, and that they were not the exception, but rather the rule, was
unacceptable. To the woman who asked Mauriac, "Où allez-vous
chercher toutes ces horreurs?" his reply "En moi, madame," [1] can
have given little incentive to read the works of the renowned
Catholic intellectual. His exposition of moral malignancy as being

---

[1] François Mauriac, "Le romancier et ses personnages," in *Œuvres
Complètes,* VIII, 299.

of pandemic proportions caused sincere questioning of his motives and objectives.

An especially painful goad to the author's reconsideration of his work, in its substance, intention and direction, was felt in a letter dated April 7, 1927, addressed to him in the *Nouvelle revue française*. In this brief communication, which purportedly pertains to *La vie de Racine* published by Mauriac, André Gide challenges what he sees as his friend's desire to enjoy the best of two worlds. Racine, Gide points out, had thanked God for welcoming him to a state of Grace, "... malgré les tragédies qu'il voulait n'avoir pas écrites."

Mauriac is accused, however, of wanting a similar dispensation, to "be a Christian without having his books burned." Gide's letter taunts slightly what he calls a reassuring compromise which allows Mauriac to love God, "sans perdre de vue Mammon." Gide makes jibes at Mauriac for having enlisted his readers as "ses complices." The concentration on unconscious patterns of evil was pleasing to tastes which concealed the pleasure found therein under a cloak of devout interest. This is the part of the reading public which, "... en abhorrant le péché, seraient bien désolés de n'avoir plus à s'occuper du péché." [2] While deploring the dire consequences of sinful lives, Mauriac's "conscience angoissée" attracted a large and voracious following for his works.

It is in response to such public, and probably private, pressures that Mauriac sought to defend himself and to justify the character and quality of his novels. The most visible indication of such a reevaluation of his philosophy was in the virtual repudiation of his article, "Souffrances du chrétien," which had appeared in the *NRF* in October 1928. [3] Its blatantly pessimistic stress on Christianity's failure as a workable guide to life, particularly in its denial of human appetites, revealed the severe conflict to be found in love, which is both essential and inaccessible, and which is reflected in his *Génitrix* and *Le Désert de l'amour*. The incapacity to find love in human relationships is shown to be a consequence of man's failure to find love in God, although in these two novels,

---

2 André Gide, "A François Mauriac," *Nouvelle revue française*, No. 30 (1928), p. 726.
3 François Mauriac, "Souffrances du chrétien," *Nouvelle revue française*, No. 31 (1928), pp. 460-487.

there are only hints of the One Love which might be the basis
for all love. "Voilà le drame: une concupiscence qui lie l'âme au
corps. C'est l'âme qui aime, c'est l'âme qui est aimée." [4]
Particularly noted by Catholic critics was the paucity of expectation of redemption or salvation. Mauriac seemed to suggest
a sense of terrible election overhanging man's relationship with his
God, with an implied and awesome predestination to human folly
and loss of the soul.

> Dieu est ce chasseur qui relève les pistes et qui guette sa
> proie.... Il observe les foulées du gibier humain que ses
> instincts guident aux mêmes heures, par les mêmes dé-
> tours, vers les mêmes plaisirs. Dieu est patient: il sait où
> tendre le collet qui étranglera la bête. [5]

The revelation, too, of Mauriac's view of Christian marriage as
a condemnation to, at best, chastity and at worst, sterility, was a
shocking one. "...le mariage chrétien, en condamnant la femme
à la fécondité perpétuelle, condamne l'homme à la perpétuelle
chasteté." [6] The very pursuit of physical love implied a rejection
of the spiritual: "...une chair qui s'assouvit accompagne toujours
un esprit incapable d'adhérer au surnaturel." [7] A couple in marriage
are victims of "un mirage," and are subject to "une folie manifeste
et de toutes les folies, la plus folle." [8]

These few references drawn from *Souffrances du chrétien* give
some indication of the painful futility of man's aspiration toward
community with others and with God. It is in the three-year period
from 1928-1931, that a transition to a moderately hopeful view of
the human situation is expressed. In 1931, Mauriac published *Bonheur du chrétien,* as a sequel of clarification to *Souffrances.* To
emphasize, perhaps, the rectification of his views, the first title
was changed to *Souffrances du pécheur,* to stress the likelihood
of unhappiness of those not a part of Christ. The combined essays,
which amount virtually to a handbook of themes, mirror the
thematic development in the three novels under discussion here.

---

[4] François Mauriac, *Souffrances et bonheur du chrétien* (Paris: Grasset, 1931), p. 25.
[5] *Ibid.,* p. 38.
[6] *Ibid.,* p. 23.
[7] *Ibid.,* p. 56.
[8] *Ibid.,* p. 31.

What is often described as the Manichean overtone of much
of the morality in the writings of François Mauriac is symbolized
in a phrase which he particularly admired: "Maurice de Guérin
compare sa pensée à un feu du ciel qui brûle à l'horizon entre
deux mondes. ... J'y admirais l'expression parfaite de mon destin...." [9] This ambivalence cannot be acceptable to Catholics as
the basis of a Christian morality, oriented as is church teaching
to the presumption of the superiority of the Good. A more positive
affirmation is essential to insure sincerity of motivation in emotional and spiritual undertakings. Mauriac appreciates the error
of such dual attraction, in admitting to a kind of blindness which
allowed him to be duped by an image. He concludes that there
can exist no such fire, "... qui brûle à égale distance de Dieu et
du monde." [10] There is an admission, not that Mauriac denied God
as a refuge and nourishment in the Grace he provides, but rather
that the author had disclaimed His accessibility.

Mauriac shifts his emphasis subtly, from the body as an object
of sensuality to the importance which will be accorded to the flesh
henceforth as "Cathédrale de chair où repose la chair du Seigneur."
All his good intentions notwithstanding, even in his "confessions"
the lingering doubt which is present in Mauriac's thinking is seen
in the recurrence of references to the two equally powerful forces
of good and evil struggling for the conquest of the soul, "... les
deux forces puissantes qui chacune tirant une âme à soi, la dé-
chirent. Deux forces toutes puissantes." [11]

These forces remain always the same: attractions toward sins
of the flesh, and toward the protective haven of divine Grace.

It is in *Bonheur* that we see an emphasis on the role of Grace
in the happiness of being a Christian. The enigma (of predestination and the use of free will to accept Grace) does persist which
was described in the author's earlier statement. That the heavenly
father intends the salvation of all, but without allowing humans
to take their reward for granted, is Mauriac's explanation:

> L'éternelle contradiction, sans cesse rappelée, entre la
> liberté de l'homme et la prescience divine, nous apparaît

[9] *Ibid.*, p. 96.
[10] *Ibid.*, p. 98.
[11] *Ibid.*, p. 102.

sinon moins mystérieuse, du moins plus rassurante ... une
partie qui n'est pas gagnée d'avance et qui pourtant doit
l'être finalement. [12]

Mauriac's declaration of personal belief in 1931 celebrates the
Christian who is inundated by Grace: "... il découvre cette joie
de naître. Il est un nouveau né, conscient de sa venue au monde. ...
Joie de la naissance à la Grace." [13]

Sin, though, remains the lot of most of mankind in spite of
spiritual reservoirs of intercession and prayer which await tapping.
The concept of an elect few who pass successfully beyond the
recognition and acceptance of Grace to final salvation seems un-
avoidable in Mauriac's theological view: "... cette ascension n'est
achevée que par le petit nombre, mais il est donné à tous de la
tenter." [14]

The solitude which was formerly seen in *Souffrances* as the
natural, unloved state of man, becomes in the fulfilled, Christ-
loving soul "... une solitude peuplée ... une solitude comblée." [15]
Mauriac reserves to the end of *Bonheur du chrétien* the privilege
of correcting his definition of what constitutes the essential suffering of humanity: "La vraie souffrance du Chrétien ne consiste
pas, comme je l'insinuais, à ne pouvoir suivre en paix sa convoi-
tise ... c'est de ne pas être un saint." [16]

The authenticity of an individual's religious experience can be
determined only by his own evaluation of it. One cannot dispute
a man's claim to spiritual insight. What is referred frequently to
in critical writings as Mauriac's 1929 "conversion" is an over-
statement of the case. His worthiness as a privately-practicing
Catholic had not come under attack. It was his virtue as a Catholic
figure of public stature which was, however, seriously challenged.
The directness of the attack did produce instead a specific reply
to Gide's charge of serving two masters, God and man, in Mauriac's
publication of *Dieu et Mammon* in 1929.

As striking as his confessions of error or misdirection may have
been, it is the examination of his novels themselves which

---

[12] *Ibid.*, p. 62.
[13] *Ibid.*, p. 109.
[14] *Ibid.*, p. 111.
[15] *Ibid.*, p. 127.
[16] *Ibid.*, p. 135.

translates the ideas and attitudes of Mauriac. With a change of tone so abrupt as to have been considered "miraculous," the "converted" Catholic author produced in 1932, as though on command, a work which retains to this day a description as his "most Catholic novel." Whether it is due to the contingent incident, so to speak, of the intervention of Grace, or to that of his reading public, the fact remains that a reoriented religious and literary direction followed in the works of François Mauriac.

Speaking in the most general terms, it can be said that the three novels reviewed herein represent a comparable "moral ascent" in their conclusions as was observed in the personal expressions of their author cited earlier. There can be seen in *Génitrix,* for example, an outcome as brutally negative as the consequences of godlessness can create. The character, Fernand, pays the penalty for his apathetic submission to domination in the amorous possession of him by his mother, Félicité. He is barely living physically at the end of the novel. His life is stripped, with one exception, of human contact. He is immobile, resigned to a living death, with no explicit promise of rebirth either in this world or the next. The themes of fear and resignation, and an infinite solitude, which Mauriac saw as premises of human existence in *Souffrances du pécheur,* are revealed in the final experiences of both mother and son.

Perhaps it can be called a step upward to discuss briefly the conclusion of the second novel, *Le Désert de l'amour.* The ending lacks the downward, sinking sense of passive desperation of the first work. There is instead a kind of plateau at the novel's end. Raymond Courrèges has been condemned, probably, to a life without love. The difference, however, is seen in his condemnation, as well, to hope. He does have a love-object, in Maria Cross, around whom he will circulate in orbiting pattern as long as he lives. Although the orbit is a fixed one, he is sustained by the anticipation that the woman he loves will become, by some miracle, accessible to him. He will even have a kind of negative pleasure in this continual expectation of a future joy, a joy he is destined never to taste. Mindless, passive resignation to fear in *Génitrix* has given way in *Le Désert de l'amour* to hopeful expectancy, even though doomed to failure.

A complete vindication of Mauriac's past omission in his work of some promise of salvation is observed in the resolution of *Le Nœud de vipères*. The essentially similar thematic basis as in previous novels provides a springboard, however, to an ecstatically confident ending. The maximum "bonheur du Chrétien" is assured in Louis' ultimate joyful recognition that God has claimed him as one of his own. Louis, in effect, undergoes a reformation not unlike that of Mauriac himself, or the Christian sinner in *Souffrances et bonheur du chrétien*. From darkest pessimism, to indifference, to glorious awareness, the path is increasingly illumined by the knowledge of Divine Grace.

The fame, or notoriety, of many Mauriac novels rests on the publicity values which attach to some of their more sensational aspects. It is not surprising that his expositions of what are deviations from accepted conventional behavior are among the best-recalled of his works. It may be relevant that the three novels under consideration are novels of parental, not juvenile, delinquency. The latent incest of Félicité in *Génitrix,* as well as the exceptional circumstances of father and son loving the same woman in *Le Désert de l'amour,* are strikingly bold ideas, especially in the writings of a religious author. The cruelties wished for, and practiced by, Louis on his own family reach the point of being bizarre, and are at least as remarkable as the transgressions of the first two novels.

The themes which became apparent in the depiction of all these extraordinary accounts are repeated, in various guises, from one novel to the next. They are not merely repetitive, however, in the light of Mauriac's skill in presenting them so differently that their relativity and importance change with each novel. A diagrammatic view of the themes of these three novels, drawn from the specifically identified motifs, gives an interesting tabulation. The six major thematic groups, under which themes of story, plot, and generic coherence, may be classified are those of (1) Free Will; (2) Love; (3) Sexuality; (4) Evasion; (5) Solitude; and (6) Rebirth, Resurrection and Redemption.

Critical comment abounds on the themes two through five, while the first theme and the last are treated rather more diffusely and infrequently. Yet the question of human freedom is revealed in the numerical distribution, to be the most prevalent of all six basic thematic groupings, appearing rather evenly through the three works. The most important fundamental question, whether man is free to work out his temporal and spiritual destiny, underlies the actions of the story, the motivations and purposes of the plot, and many unifying threads of generic coherence. It can be said that the general groupings of love, expressions of sexuality, evasion, and solitude are either instruments of consequences of the presence, or absence, of free will. If we think of *Génitrix* in these terms, we see a struggle for freedom — a contest between the jailer, Félicité, and her prisoner, Fernand. Several important thematic units were derived from analyzing this relationship, and these concern principally the limitations which are imposed on human freedom.

The sources of such limitations are manifold. It will be recalled that Mauriac wrote in *Souffrances et bonheur*, "Le pécheur en soi est un mythe. Ce qui existe c'est une accumulation de tendances héritées." [17] Thus inherited characteristics of both a negative and positive nature can shape the man. Both Fernand and Félicité would have been modeled quite differently had they been free from the "inherited" attitudes toward love and marriage, and their legacy of passion. Mathilde, it is to be remembered, responded to yet another pressure, that of social and emotional deprivation. She was "façonnée" by her miserable circumstances.

Other kinds of specific restrictions limit the exercise of will, such as the apathy induced in Fernand by Félicité's perennial domination, thereby depriving him of even the desire to taste freedom and anticipating his failures at attempts toward independence.

Least Christian, and presented in generic coherence, is the theme of the role of destiny. Nothing obviates the need for freedom of action more than the belief that the choices have already been made and are to be imposed on the individual. Motifs revealed that "destiny" (1) brought Mathilde and Fernand together; (2) ended Mathilde's life; (3) routed Fernand from his comfortable niche in his home, and (4) eventually tricked him into an awareness of love when it was too late to implement it. Fernand is disoriented in the anarchy which follows removal of restrictions which, how-

---

17 *Ibid.*, p. 58.

ever negative in nature, formed the guideliness of his existence. He is free, but to do what?

It is in illustration of the futility of human aspirations toward freedom that man's servitude to dominating pressures is given thematic importance. Father and son in *Le Désert de l'amour* are victims of their legacy of a capacity for passion. They are prey too, to the paradox of love whereby they lose their independence to respond fully and creatively to the revelation of love in another. They instead are molded by the wishes or ideals of their beloveds. They become, not the dynamic figure in love as they had intended, but the compliant product of another's imaginings. Obstacles of other kinds constrict development as the individual might wish. The reputation for sanctity enjoyed by Paul Courrèges, for example, was assigned to him by others, and prevented exploitation of his desires regarding Maria Cross. Such restraints imposed by other people can serve thereby to protect the individual from himself.

Like class- and social-distinctions, the closed-ranks of a family are a notable impediment to liberated action. In the short-run, this proves in *Le Désert de l'amour* to be a distinct irritation. The burdensome Courrèges family becomes Paul Courrèges' greatest safeguard against himself. By this means, fundamentally, the responsibility for the doctor's actions is invariably shifted to someone other than himself. Dr. Courrèges, in his conviction that he is "destined to solitude," abdicates finally his claim to autonomy and surrenders in resignation to his failure to love.

The powerlessness to resist forces greater than those of the individual self is made especially clear in its generic coherence. The images of Raymond and others are proposed as satellites in mindless orbit around Maria Cross. He is without will to leave the attracting force of the woman, and can never achieve the moral energy to strive beyond such an ephemeral relationship. He is granted his freedom to live within a fixed pattern, finding no way to live except by creating false, short-term goals. A rendezvous or even a changed appointment, for example, can provide the incentive to endure to the next day.

Given the emphasis in *Le Nœud de vipères* on material possessions, it is not surprising that a similar stress will be placed on the confinement of the individual by secular institutions. The denial to Louis of the right to decide his career; the acquired importance attached to money; and the vice inherited from his mother of "trop aimer l'argent ... cette passion dans le sang," are some of the forces which shape his life. Children "sold" into repugnant marriages for economic gain are deprived their birthright of free choice. A man such as Louis is constrained by the complicity of old age, which accepts at "face" value the human product created over the years. Having thus fixed forever the individual traits on the face and demeanor of the man, he can do no more than live up to the portrait, however grotesque, which is presented to the world. Like Raymond Courrèges, Louis has never succeeded in imposing his true personality on another. He too has been basically reactive in his formation, responding to what he believes (mistakenly in his case) to be love, and hatred.

The idea of the exercise of free will, in its more orthodox sense, to reach for and find the love of God, is fully touched upon in *Le Nœud de vipères*. It is the principal motivating force of a positive nature in the book. It can be said that a complete picture of the pursuit of Grace is presented, since there is also seen Louis' use of will to reject the early, tentative touches of grace. This is what Mauriac describes in *Souffrances et bonheur du chrétien* as, "un très léger avant-goût ... bonheur indicible et fragile." [18] Its touch is so tentative that it cannot at first distract Louis from concentration on revenge.

The manner in which the author depicts Louis' invasion by Grace, as an unrecognized force which engulfs him, never allows Louis to make any assertion of a strong and vigorous will to be saved. What is emphasized rather is the contradiction of terms touched upon earlier, those of human liberty and divine foreknowledge. Louis is described as helpless before the irresistible wave of Divine Love in its final assault. He does not understand the mystery of his experience, but accepts it and in pliancy before the Divine Will, earns everlasting reward.

He is one of the "petit nombre" to be so invited to accept salvation, among the numerous members of his family. "Il est absous ... mais autour de lui et jusque sur ses mains, le sang

---

[18] *Ibid.*, p. 128.

d'Abel fume encore." [19] Louis is to be saved. He has been shown
the lighted way. Did he choose, or was he chosen, to be the
recipient of the eternal reward?

Correlative with the theme of freedom to exercise the human
will is that of love, the principal objective of such an occasion of
choice. Its development can be traced along with the themes concerning free will, and their close affinity might be indicated in a
motif like the following. Is the love of God as cruelly preordained
as is the brutal hazard of chance in human relationships? "La
plupart des êtres humains ne se choisissent guère plus que les
arbres qui ont poussé côte à côte et dont les branches se confondent par leur seule croissance." [20]

Like those people who would never have known what love is
unless they heard it spoken of, Fernand knew nothing of its con-
figuration. The magnanimity, compassion and selflessness of love
had escaped him. When he becomes aware of his capacity to love,
it is too late. His characteristic, such as he analyzed it, of "aimer
contre quelqu'un," missed the point of love's kindness. Love is an
imprecise instrument in the hands of Fernand and Félicité. The
instinct is there, but without insights of its use beyond exploitation.
Love in its negative aspects is an important thematic consideration
in Génitrix. The appreciation of its value is seen as though in a
photo-negative. All the grotesque variations of what might have
been are present, if only accessibility to a loving guidance had been
possible.

Some hints that there is but One Love are offered, but they are
never brought to broader purpose. The capacity to find and give
love remains unfilled. It is in the expression of the correlative
theme, by contrast, of self-hatred, that the conventional expressions of love are distorted. Marriage is a retaliation; seduction
is an escape; and pleasure is taken in reprisal — all thematic
evidence of the sterility of the effort to love.

Love, as a major thematic nucleus, receives more concentrated
attention in Le Désert de l'amour. It is the pursuit of love which
is the raison d'être of the novel, expressed principally in the form
of a vain search. The connection is established between images of

---

[19] Ibid., p. 113.
[20] Nœud de vipères, p. 106.

burning thirst and longed-for refreshment at oases, first suggested in the title. Although the theme, and its correlatives, are almost inextricably mingled with that of sexuality — love's supreme human expression — nevertheless the novel treats as an abstraction the nature of the emotion itself. The change observed in Dr. Courrèges from compassion toward Maria Cross to passion is only one of the distinctions proposed in the novel. Is the abiding affection of a family a legitimate substitute for carnal passion? Is love so ephemeral that it cannot withstand its erosion by life, which forces priorities of greater immediacy to take precedence, dissipating the primacy of love?

A theme is offered, that love is a falsely creative force in its urgings to the lovers to create a desirable image capable of being loved. Maria Cross, for instance, created a Raymond who did not exist, making of a salacious youth a model of purity and innocence. Paul Courrèges wants to worship a beautiful, grieving mother, misunderstood in her wretched social circumstances. He has projected an ideal from the shabby existence of an indolent, kept woman. The weak foundations of these fantasies dooms the possibility of love to failure. The futility of each kind of approach is revealed in repeated and generally related themes, which present the sorrowful route of love, whose ill-defined termination lies invariably over the horizon.

Love, as an interior bleeding wound, incurable to be sure, is further evidence of its unwholesome and painful nature. The theme, presented in generic coherence, recalls paintings of the heart of Christ, bleeding in redemptive love. The lack of such a salutary dimension, however, in the love of the Courrèges men and of Maria Cross, points up the tragic frivolity of their quest.

It is only in Le Nœud de vipères that a transition is made completely. Physical love is touched upon just briefly between Louis and Isa, but the greater emphasis is given to love in trust and to its generosity. It is the imperative to love and to be loved which is developed thematically, especially in Louis' early acquaintance with Isa. Her later mistreatment of him twists Louis' ability to discriminate, and he becomes as mistaken in his judgments about love as he is about hate.

It is the physical experience of a state of grace, in which love is revealed as the breath of life (or as Mauriac's Journal suggests, the breath of God), which corrects his spiritual vision.[21] The legacy of lovelessness which he believed to be his fate is countermanded by another divine destiny. The perpetual conundrum of the nature of love is resolved in a gift of faith, which, by removing doubt, reveals its source to be in receiving, and transmitting to others, the love of God Himself.

For Mauriac the development of this critical theme to its majestic conclusion must confirm indications, revealed in the section entitled Decade of Decision, of new spiritual objectives in his writing. The theme of love triumphant, in all its aspects, is a direct link, as Le Nœud de vipères comes to a close, with another most important group of themes under the general classification, Rebirth, Resurrection, and Redemption.

All six of the major thematic groupings, whether by contrast or affinity, are correlative with each other; and in this way are linked affinitively the themes of love and rebirth. A culmination is reached in Le Nœud de vipères where it becomes apparent that the author had actually been aiming in previous novels toward the surrender of the human soul to divine grace. Each of the works which has been reviewed approaches the matter in its characteristic way, and to its characteristic extent.

In numerous motif clusters which constituted a generic coherence of death and resurrection themes, images of crucifixion were indirectly proposed in Génitrix, while the specific suggestions of new beginnings, of rebirth, were related only to this world. It is true that Fernand hopes to begin a new life in fantasy love, but destiny intervenes with the event of Félicité's death. The resurrection of the flesh, described in rote-learning by a chanting child, reaches Fernand and Félicité only as a reminder of the dead Mathilde, and it provides no solace.

So strong is the emphasis on the search for love among mankind in Le Désert de l'amour that themes relative to rebirth or resurrection are limited to the death of innocence in boyhood and rebirth as a man, infused with sin. It is in a similar context that Raymond becomes "un être neuf" as he becomes aware of Maria Cross' interest. Implications of a search for immortality are suggested in the pursuit of youth by Paul and Raymond Courrèges. Le Désert

---

[21] Journal, II, 13.

de l'amour remains on the level of a hopeless wasteland peopled by *mirages.* The transition to a higher plane of loving existence is not proposed.

It remains for *Le Nœud de vipères* to present the climactic vision of the man singled out, visibly, for rebirth in eternal salvation. The unsatisfying accommodation to life which was made by Paul Courrèges in *Le Désert de l'amour* in accepting the affection of his wife as a substitute for his passion for Maria Cross, cannot be compared with the blessed tranquility achieved by Louis. Even acknowledging that Louis himself could not understand whence came his sudden indifference to previous goals of his life, his willingness to submit to the new spirit is amply illustrated. The transition from passive virtue, in his gradual disinterest in inflicting or enjoying pain, toward active virtue and the glorification of human commitment, represent the visible effects of his invasion by divine enlightenment.

The mystery of the movements of divine will is as obscure but as certain as what was noted in the image of sleeping vines as a promise of renewal. A sense of universal order is proclaimed in Louis' confident expectation of resurrection in blessedness, as it is in the dead-seeming vines which will be revived in their summer splendour. The vast cycle of nature includes the material and the spiritual, and the cyclical pattern of all is reinforced in the Biblical analogy of Christ's words: "I am the vine and you are the branches.... If a man abide not in mine he is cast forth as a branch and is withered; and men gather them and cast them into the fire and they are burned." [22]

Mauriac's interest in the elaborations of man's activities to avoid undesirable or unknown experiences is indicated in his citation of another author interested in authenticity of behavior. "One never really knows anyone. What is actually left of you when the last mask that Nietzsche mentions is tossed aside?" [23]

It will be noted that in *Génitrix*, the easy reflex of role-playing was characteristic. In Félicité's case, it signalled a controlled disguise of her aggressive domination, while for Mathilde, the

---

[22] St. John, 15:6.
[23] François Mauriac, *Letters on Art and Literature* (New York, 1953), p. 110.

adoption of a mocking façade served as a protective device in a lifetime of exposure to brutalizing circumstances. Role-playing is only one evidence of man's inability to endure stressful situations. Fernand's retreat into his world of loving a phantom, as he learns to love the dead Mathilde, is his solution to the intolerable strain of recognizing that he has been duped over a lifetime.

Quite different forms of escape are presented in *Le Désert de l'amour* although they serve essentially to meet the same objectives in reducing the level of pain. This is so explicitly the case that references to work as an anesthetic are offered literally, as Paul Courrèges tries to obscure the agony of his failure to possess Maria Cross. Withdrawal in the form of deliberate detachment, to avoid the responsibility of commitment, is the form of evasion preferred by Raymond. The fantasy world exists as a refuge in this novel as well, but here it is the private realm of Maria Cross as she enriches the meager adventures of her daily life with colorful romanticization. It is the passive pain of boredom and a vague sexual longing that is filled by her imaginings. The active world of frightful pain is minimized by Paul Courrèges as he creates a world of self-delusion, where he can postpone recognition of his anguished inability to conquer his love. Motifs and themes which repeat a longing to sink into a void, into nothingness, carry the extremes of evasion suggested in the novel.

When the themes of *Le Nœud de vipères* are examined for their classification, the strong contrast is at once apparent between the numerous devices for escaping one reality or another, and most important, the greatest reality of all — the presence of God among men. It might be proposed that the search for love on earth is itself a benevolent mask concealing a longing for redemption.

The various "retreats" described in the analysis of the work serve as Louis' and Isa's format of life. Even the quarrels over religion are, in effect, staged to provide some active form of communication, avoiding public acknowledgment of the lack of a common bond. The social requirements of the pretentious are more commonly accepted means of creating false public images. Pretentiousness to cover the meanness of the individual within is portrayed with particular scorn in the leitmotif offered in the linking image of the elaborately concealed, malodorous commode.

Generic coherence was found in motif clusters, supporting important themes which must finally be classified as ones of evasion. Louis' fascination with only the reflection of the essential, as he devotes his years to material acquisition, is a first representation. His attraction to those activities, in business or personal affairs, which provide an immediate return, points up the avoidance of the long-range goals which are the rightful domain of the Christian man. *Le Nœud de vipères* is a vivid illustration that evasion is believed by Mauriac to be a widespread component of everyday life. It is revealed in the relative abundance of themes pertaining to this general idea in two of the three novels under review. From novel to novel, the deception of self and others is the movement of a frightened man fumbling without divine guidance. It is, in *Le Nœud de vipères,* somewhat more degrading since the search is not for human contact and communion, but merely for the increase of material possessions.

As indicated previously, Mauriac's treatment of the relationship of love and sexuality creates motifs and their themes which are often inseparable. Yet by creating links with the divine, even if only in brief references, some direction is determinable in themes regarding the various aspects of love.

It will be noted that Mauriac opens *Souffrances du pécheur* with words which are indicative of a significant ambivalence regarding not love, but sexuality. In affirming the appetites of the flesh, the author condemns Christianity's role, "... il la supprime." He offers to his readers Bossuet's view that as men, all are: " '... souillés dès notre naissance et conçus dans l'iniquité... nous devons combattre jusqu'à la mort le mal que nous avons contracté en naissant.' " [24]

It is part of the Christian's plight that his religion allows small tolerance for the instinctive sexual drive. And in his revised viewpoint, depicting *le bonheur du chrétien,* Mauriac makes every effort to decry the pleasure of love. In a phrase which makes of it a parody of love's main purpose — the expression of love for God — he writes, "La volupté devient la recherche des abords immédiats du Néant. Il s'agit d'en approcher le plus possible sans mourir: la drogue." [25]

---

[24] Mauriac, *Souffrances et bonheur,* p. 23.
[25] *Ibid.,* p. 101.

The presentation of love in its sensual elements is most concretely detailed in *Le Désert de l'amour*. Sexuality as a source of pleasure and disgust is characterized by Maria Cross, who experiences both of these reactions at nearly the same moment, much like "l'éclair et la foudre...." [26]

But there is also emphasized the animality of sexual interest. Instinctive, indiscriminate, irresistible attraction (as suggested in the phrase "danse des moustiques") [27] is proposed as the driving force. The generically coherent theme, described as "the Beast in man," is derived from motif clusters which show the universality of this bestiality.

The less acceptable aspects of sexual attraction, as were seen in Félicité's amorous longing to possess her son, are hinted at as well in *Le Désert de l'amour*. The curious intermingling of Maria's image of Raymond with that of her dead son is one example, while Paul's jealousy regarding his daughter is indicative of an unusual paternal affection. The sensuality described in Maria's eventual adoration of her stepson, Bertrand, opens yet another possibility in sexual expression as Maria sublimates her responses into a mystical, non-physical worship. Passion in a pure and idealistic man like the doctor becomes explicit physical longing, while the guilty allurements of Maria Cross toward Raymond become innocent in their unfulfillment.

A series of motifs common to the three novels, with some differences in emphasis, are those describing sex as unquenchable thirst, the slaking of which provides no satisfaction. The contrasting component motifs of fire and water, of barren aridity and the oasis, are repeated elements in *Génitrix* and *Le Désert de l'amour*. There is a translation of passion to that of desire to possess money and property rather than a person in *Le Nœud de vipères*. The few references to the quenching of Louis' thirst, in the context of sensuality as indicated, are limited to his brief excursion into what he believed to be love when he initially knew Isa. A warning is prophetic of his tortured years to come: "Etanche ta soif, une fois pour toutes: tu ne boiras plus." [28]

---

[26] Mauriac, *Le Désert de l'amour*, p. 200.
[27] Mauriac, *Souffrances et bonheur*, p. 87.
[28] Mauriac, *Le Nœud de vipères*, p. 37.

Isa's abuse of their sexual union is an expression of her indifference. She accepts his love-making to hide the fact that no love exists in their relationship. Critics are fond of speaking of the degraded role women play in Mauriac's work. The principal female characters do subvert the gift of sensual energy to fill varying needs. Félicité, Mathilde, Maria Cross, Isa and even Marinette, victimize their love-objects through sexual means. By the time of the appearance of *Le Nœud de vipères,* however, the emphasis is less on the sin than on its absolution. The road to love, as seen in *Le Désert de l'amour,* has given way to finding the route to Divine Love. A more indirect sexual question is raised in the possible jealousy of Fernand, Paul Courrèges, and Louis toward the desire of their women, not to be wives, but to be mothers.

Solitude is, *a priori,* the natural state of man. He exists in a one-to-one relationship with God. No human can substitute for him in repaying the redemptive price of divine love, and no one can accept on his behalf the gift of Grace. The same essential isolation is immensely more sinister and profound when the possibilities of communication with the Redeemer are nonexistent. No human contact of a loving nature is possible without the energizing force of love through Grace, Mauriac suggests.

The godless, nearly pagan, wellsprings on which Félicité draws, offer no remedy to cure the isolation of one cut off by an obsession. At the same time, the prey she covets in her son is in a kind of solitary confinement as well. Their joint condemnation is irreversible since death takes Félicité and Mathilde, deepening the aloneness in which Fernand must survive, with only the faintest implications of spiritual comfort to console him.

Mathilde's deliberate self-withdrawal, in addition to being an evasion, is the consequence of her inability to call for love from a divine protector. So, too, is Raymond's detachment self-imposed, in the absence of a commitment toward his fellow-men. The major thematic unit, in generic coherence, entitled, "Hands through the grill," is another facet of man's inept grasping at the unattainable. Only Paul Courrèges had the ability to recognize in himself a destiny to solitude: yet without some godly assistance, all those with whom he is connected are doomed to the same fate.

Perhaps the most interesting form of solitude, thematically, is that of Louis in *Le Nœud de vipères.* In creating an image of

himself so hateful as to be unapproachable, Louis has been successful in condemning himself to life imprisonment. Although its origins lay in motifs of social and class isolation in his youht, the
onset of adolescent anxieties added a further protective reaction.
He learned to displease intentionally, with control, before doing so
unintentionally, and at the caprice of circumstance, What serves
as a weapon to control the behavior of others, also is useful in
controlling their effect on him. His solitude is offered as evidence
of integrity, as one who refuser to adopt the masks, roles and
other subterfuges which are the means by which human communal
existence is facilitated.

Although Louis resents the isolated state in which he feels his
wife's indifference has sequestered him, he is touched by self-pity,
knowing that he has reached old age without a single friend. He
is no less alone after his fortune is gone, except for the solace of
assisting his granddaughter in her troubles. Yet the solitude he now
inhabits is radiant with joy. He has made the one movement of
magnanimity which allows Divine Grace to enter, and his solitary
existence is filled with the presence of God.

* * *

The major themes discussed here can be seen to represent a
carefully-dovetailed literary mechanism whose elements provide
complements and contrasts which make a unified whole. It is the
very repetition of themes from novel to novel which produces an
overall effect of tapestry. The same motif or theme — now seen
as dark, now as light — interwoven in textural, and textual, variations, emerges as a different image from one part of the tapestry
to another. Yet the sense of continuity is binding, and it is only
from the vantage point of distanciation that the relative values of
the contrasting and similar components can be identified and appreciated in their varying contexts.

Free Will, for example, is correlative by contrast with themes
of Domination. Solitude is correlative with the theme of Evasion
in man's intended or unintentional isolation. Sexuality and Love
are correlative themes which contain the potential of Rebirth.
Love in its sublimated thematic form is correlative with Spiritual

Rebirth, which is the final correlative theme to that of Redemption and Salvation.

Thus a complete thematic cycle in the three works may be said to exist, beginning with distorted love and its negative consequences in *Génitrix,* and concluding in *Le Nœud de vipères* in the glorification of man in conversion, wherein the fullest exercise of his free will is permitted to accept the gift of eternal love.